BERKELEY'S DOCTRINE OF NOTIONS

Berkeley's Doctrine of Notions:
A Reconstruction based on his Theory of Meaning

DANIEL E. FLAGE

ST. MARTIN'S PRESS
New York

© 1987 Daniel E. Flage
All rights reserved. For information, write:
Scholarly & Reference Division,
St. Martin's Press, Inc., 175 Fifth Avenue, New York, NY 10010
First published in the United States of America in 1987
Printed in Great Britain

Library of Congress Cataloging-in-Publication Data
Flage, Daniel E., 1951-
  Berkeley's doctrine of notions.

  Bibliography: p.
  Includes index.
  1. Berkeley, George. 1685-1753. 2. Notions
(Philosophy) — History — 18th century. 3. Meaning
(Philosophy) — History — 18th century. I. Title.
B1348.F59 1987   121'.4'0924   86-20328
ISBN 0-312-00208-4

CONTENTS

Acknowledgements
A Note on Abbreviations
Introduction   1

1. Abstraction   13
    The Abstractionists   14
    Berkeley and the Abstractionists   23
    Introduction, Section 10   30
    Introduction, Sections 11-12   36
    Introduction, Section 13   41
    An Argument in the Third Edition of the *Alciphron*   44
    Berkeley, Abstract Ideas, and Mental Images   46
    Notes   47

2. Possibility and Impossibility   54
    Criteria of Possibility and Impossibility   55
    Berkeley's Distinction between Ideas and 'Real Objects'   69
    Berkeley's Metaphysical Criteria   74
    Berkeley's Epistemological Criteria   78
    Possibility and Impossibility in the *Principles*   82
    Notes   89
    Appendix   91

3. Berkeley's Theory of Meaning   94
    Extensions and Paradigms   94
    Berkeley and Categorematic Terms   98
    Berkeley and Syncategorematic Terms   111
    Conventional Meaning   115
    Analogical and Metaphorical Meaning   123
    Conclusions   130
    Notes   130

4. The Epistemic Intent of Berkeleian Notions   133
    Positive and Relative Notions   134
    The Describing Model of Relative Notions   137
    Notions of Substance   142
    Notions of Actions and Relations   154
    Conclusions   167
    Notes   168

5.	**The Nature of Notions**	173
	Notions and Meanings: The Sergeant Connection	174
	Notions as Intentional Acts	180
	Notions and Ordinary Objects	192
	Conclusions	208
	Notes	208
6.	**Conclusions and Historical Speculations**	212
	Notes	220
Bibliography		221
Index		225

It is a riddle wrapped in a mystery inside an enigma.
                                        Winston Churchill

ACKNOWLEDGEMENTS

In working on this study, I have benefited greatly from discussions with or comments from a number of friends and colleagues. I particularly wish to thank Edwin Allaire, Herbert Hochbert, A.P. Martinich, and Nicholas Asher of the University of Texas at Austin; Ronald J. Glass of the University of Wisconsin-La Crosse; Phillip Cummins and Richard Fumerton of the University of Iowa; Kenneth Winkler of Wellesley College; David Raynor of the University of Ottawa; Don Gotterbarn of Allegheny College; and Barry Brown of Virginia Commonwealth University.

The research for this book was supported by grants from the University of Wisconsin-LaCrosse and the University of Texas at Austin. I wish to thank both institutions for their encouragement and support.

Some of the early research for *Berkeley's Doctrine of Notions* was presented in two articles: 'Berkeley's Notions', *Philosophy and Phenomenological Research*, 45 [1985], pp. 407-25; and 'Berkeley on Abstraction', *Journal of the History of Philosophy*, forthcoming. I wish to thank the editors of these two journals for permission to reprint an expanded version of these articles in this book. An early version of Chapter 2 was presented at the Berkeley Tercentenary Conference in Newport, Rhode Island in March 1985, and part of Chapter 1 was presented at the Western Division meeting of the American Philosophical Association in April 1985.

I wish to thank Don Gotterbarn for granting permission to comment upon his unpublished manuscript, 'Berkeley's Mistaken Notion About Relations'.

I also wish to thank Earl Roy for his careful proofreading of the manuscript.

Finally, I wish to thank my wife, Dana, for her encouragement and patience throughout the research and writing of this book.

D.E.F.
Austin, Texas

A NOTE ON ABBREVIATIONS

All passages quoted from Berkeley's writings will be from *The Works of George Berkeley, Bishop of Cloyne*, edited by A.A. Luce and T.E. Jessop (9 vols., Thomas Nelson and Sons, Ltd., London, 1948-1957). References to Berkeley's writings will be made parenthetically within the text of the book on the basis of the following set of abbreviations:

PHK, x   *A Treatise concerning the Principles of Human Knowledge*, Part I, section x
Intro., x   Introduction to the *Principles*, section x
DHP, x,y   *Three Dialogues between Hylas and Philonous*, dialogue x, page y in volume 2 of the *Works*
PC, x   *Philosophical Commentaries*, entry x
NTV, x   *An Essay Towards a New Theory of Vision*, section x
TVV, x   *The Theory of Vision, or Visual Language Vindicated and Explained*, section x
A, x,y   *Alciphron, or the Minute Philosopher*, dialogue x, section y
DeM, x   *De Motu*, section x
S, x   *Siris*, section x
FTM, x   *Free-Thinking in Mathematics*, section x
Cor., x,y   Correspondence with Samuel Johnson, letter x, section y
Works x:y   *The Works of George Berkeley*, volume, page
HR x:y   *The Philosophical Works of Descartes*, 2 vols. (trans. Elizabeth S. Haldane and G.R.T. Ross) (Cambridge University Press, London, 1911), volume x: page y

INTRODUCTION

The primary objective of this study is to develop a philosophical reconstruction of Berkeley's doctrine of notions. I shall be concerned with the nature of notional knowledge, the ontological analysis of notions, and the relationship between notions and ideas in Berkeley's metaphysics. I shall defend three theses. First, notional knowledge is of two distinct kinds, and the distinction between these two kinds of notional knowledge is analogous to Bertrand Russell's distinction between knowledge by acquaintance and knowledge by description.[1] One's knowledge of the relations of causality and perception involves positive notions (is analogous to knowledge by acquaintance), while one's knowledge of one's own mind, God, other finite minds, actions of one's own mind, and relations among ideas involves relative notions (is analogous to knowledge by description).

Second, notions are to be analyzed as intentional acts, that is, acts by which the mind directs itself at objects or states of affairs. I shall argue that Berkeley analyzed intentionality in terms of an intentional object, a certain cognitive content, and an act that relates the cognitive content to the intentional object. If my account is correct, one finds both descriptive (acts in which the cognitive content is propositional) and nondescriptive intentional acts in Berkeley's philosophy.

Finally, I shall examine the relationship between notions, ideas, and ordinary objects. First, I shall argue that in so far as Berkeley construed notions as intentional acts, ideas are the intentional objects of some of these acts. Then I shall argue that even though intentional objects are subjective and vary among persons with the variations in the propositional content of the acts, there is a clear sense in which 'ordinary objects' are identical with intentional objects, or, in so far as a distinction can be drawn between intentional objects and ordinary objects, Berkeley considered that distinction neither ontologically nor epistemologically significant.

While a significant amount of literature has been devoted to Berkeley's discussions of notions, the doctrine continues to be covered with a shroud of mystery. There is a sense in which this is not surprising. Although Berkeley held that the world is composed solely of minds, operations of minds, and ideas, he wrote relatively little regarding one's knowledge of minds and their operations and virtually nothing regarding the ontological analysis of notions. Furthermore, it is only in some brief passages added to the 1734 editions of the *Principles of Human Knowledge* and the *Three Dialogues Between Hylas and Philonous*, and to the 1752 edition of the *Alciphron*, that Berkeley appears to use the term 'notion' technically; in the earlier editions of these works he used the term 'notion' as ambiguously as most other writers of the time.[2] Because the technical sense of 'notion' apparently was introduced only in the 1734 editions of the *Principles* and *Dialogues*,[3] one issue upon which scholars have focused is whether the introduction of a technical sense of the term marks a doctrinal change,[4] and if it does, whether it is anything more than an *ad hoc* addition to his philosophy.[5] Indeed, some commentators have questioned whether these additions provide sufficient evidence that Berkeley had developed a doctrine of notions by 1734. Woozley recently has argued that there is nothing so austere as a *doctrine* of notions prior to the 1752 edition of the *Alciphron*,[6] and Winkler has questioned whether Berkeley ever believed it was necessary to explain something so obvious as one's ability to think of one's self, and, therefore, whether he considered it necessary to develop a doctrine of notions.[7]

It is clear that at one time Berkeley had intended to provide a discussion of one's knowledge of mind. The *Principles* was originally intended to be a work in four parts,[8] and in the second part of the *Principles* Berkeley planned to consider such issues as the nature of the distinction between mind and body (*PC*, 878). In his letter to Samuel Johnson of 25 November, 1729, Berkeley claimed that he had 'made a considerable progress in it [the second part], but the manuscript was lost about fourteen years ago during my travels in Italy; and I never had leisure since to do so disagreeable a thing as writing twice on the same subject' (Cor., 2,6). Berkeley's contention that he had made 'considerable progress' on the manuscript provides some evidence that by 1716 he had developed (or was developing) a discussion of the doctrine of notions.

But even if Berkeley had developed his doctrine of notions by 1716, this alone would not show that such a doctrine was implicit in the first editions of the *Principles* and *Dialogues*. Nor is it clear that, apart from the discovery of a pre-1710 manuscript in which Berkeley provided an extensive discussion of notions, one could have *conclusive* evidence that a doctrine of notions is implicit in the first editions of the *Principles* and *Dialogues*. From the fact that already in the first edition of the *Principles* Berkeley distinguished between ideas and spirits and claimed one can have knowledge of spirits (*PHK*, 1-2),[9] it does not follow that he had developed an account of one's knowledge of spirits. Nor does it follow Berkeley had developed an account of notions from the fact that he considered adding the phrase 'or notion' to Section 140 of the first edition of the *Principles*.[10] At most, the latter shows that he did not believe the mind is known on the basis of ideas properly so called, and this is conveyed by his claim in both editions that '*In a large sense indeed* [my emphasis], we may be said to have an idea of *spirit*' (*PHK*, 140). If the question of whether or not Berkeley changed his philosophical position in the 1734 editions of the *Principles* and the *Dialogues* — whether the doctrine of notions is a late addition to his philosophy, and if so, whether it is an *ad hoc* addition — is ever to be answered, it is only reasonable to begin with an examination of his *later* works. If one can provide a systematic account of a doctrine of notions in his later works, one will know what kinds of issues are germane to the doctrine of notions, and one can then profitably ask whether there is any evidence that the same doctrine is implicit in the earlier editions of his works.

I shall take it as a working assumption that there is a doctrine of notions implicit in Berkeley's works, but I shall consider this assumption warranted only if by the end of this work I have found sufficient evidence to provide plausible answers to: (1) the question of the nature and extent of one's knowledge of minds, operations of minds, and relations; (2) the question of the ontological analysis of notions; and (3) the question of the relationship between notions and ideas. But given that none of Berkeley's extant writings contains a systematic discussion of the doctrine of notions, and given that there are few clues to the content of that doctrine, the reader might ask how I propose to reconstruct Berkeley's doctrine of notions.

Although Berkeley provided no systematic account of notions, there is a common theme sounded in many of the passages germane to the topic, especially those added in the last editions of the *Principles*, the *Dialogues* and the *Alciphron*. Berkeley claimed that although one has no ideas of minds, the operations of minds, and relations, one has notions of them in so far as one knows the meaning of such words as 'mind', 'loving' and 'hating'. Notice what he wrote. After denying that one has *ideas* of minds and their operations, he added the following to Section 27 of the *Principles*:

> Though it must be owned at the same time, that we have some notion of soul, spirit, the operations of the mind, such as willing, loving, hating, in as much as we know or understand the meaning of those words. (*PHK*, 27)

In Section 89 Berkeley argued that, fundamentally, all existents are either spirits or ideas, and in the second edition he added some comments on one's knowledge of spirits and relations. He wrote:

> We comprehend our own existence by inward feeling or reflexion, and that of other spirits by reason. We may be said to have some knowledge or notion of our own minds, of spirits and active beings, whereof in a strict sense we have not ideas. In like manner we know and have a notion of relations among things or ideas, which relations are distinct from the ideas or things related, in as much as the latter may be perceived by us without our perceiving the former. To me it seems that ideas, spirits and relations are all in their respective kinds, the object of human knowledge and *subject of discourse* [emphasis added]: and that the term *idea* would be improperly extended to signify every thing we know or have any notion of. (*PHK*, 89).

In Section 140 he added the phrase, 'or rather a notion', so in the second edition of the *Principles* one finds this: 'In a large sense indeed, we may be said to have an idea, or rather a notion of *spirit*, that is, we understand the meaning of the word, otherwise we could not affirm or deny anything of it' (*PHK*, 140).

In Section 142 of the *Principles* he added: 'I have some knowledge or notion of my mind, and its acts about ideas, inasmuch as I know or understand what is meant by those words' (*PHK*, 142).

In the 1734 edition of the *Third Dialogue* Berkeley added this: 'Farther, I know what I mean, when I affirm that there is a spiritual substance or support of ideas, that is, that a spirit knows or perceives ideas' (*DHP*, III, 234; cf. *DHP*, III, 231).

Finally, in the 1752 edition of the *Alciphron* Berkeley added: 'Certainly it must be allowed that we have some notion that we understand, or know what is meant by, the terms *myself, will, memory, love, hate,* and so forth; although, to speak exactly, these words do not suggest so many distinct ideas' (*A*, 7,5).

Berkeley's repeated claim that one has notions of minds and actions of minds in so far as one knows the meanings of terms such as 'mind' and 'will' suggests that there is an intimate relationship between his theory of linguistic meaning and his doctrine of notions. I hope to show that by closely examining Berkeley's account of linguistic meaning, it will be possible to provide a plausible reconstruction of Berkeley's doctrine of notions that will answer the three questions I have proposed. Although Berkeley's contention that there is a relationship between semantics and his theory of notions has not been overlooked by Berkeley scholars,[11] none has plumbed the depths of Berkeley's own semantic theory as a propaedeutic to an examination of the doctrine of notions. As I shall show, a careful examination of Berkeley's semantic theory will suggest various conceptual analogies that will tie together many of the scattered remarks on the doctrine of notions.

Berkeley's discussion of linguistic meaning consists of two parts: First, he proposed a series of arguments against semantic theories holding that 'abstract ideas' provide the meanings of sortal or categorematic terms. Second, he proposed an alternative account of the meaning of sortal terms. Similarly, my discussion of Berkeley's semantic theory will consist of two parts. In Chapter 1, I shall examine Berkeley's criticisms of theories of abstract ideas. Since many commentators believe that Berkeley's critique of abstraction was directed solely against Locke's theory, I shall begin by showing that theories of abstraction were common at least since the time of Aristotle, that Berkeley was familiar with many of these theories of abstraction, and that it is reasonable to believe that he intended his attack on that doctrine to be relevant to the entire tradition.

Turning to his arguments, I shall show that no fewer than four distinct arguments against the doctrine of abstraction are contained in Sections 10 through 13 of the Introduction to the *Principles*. I shall argue that the argument from introspection in Section 10 is, and was recognized by Berkeley to be, a very weak criticism of the theory of abstraction. Through an examination of Section 10 in conjunction with both Section 7 of the Introduction and the *First Draft* of the Introduction, I shall show that Section 10 contains a second and much stronger argument against abstraction. This second argument, though enthymematic, is intended to show that, given the principles the abstractionists themselves accepted, it is inconsistent to maintain that the mind is capable of abstracting.

Among other things, Berkeley's enthymematic argument shows that it is inconsistent to accept both a traditional theory of substance and to hold that the mind can abstract. The third argument, found in Sections 11 and 12, is intended to show that theories of abstract ideas must be rejected on grounds of parsimony. It is within the context of this argument that Berkeley provides the first clues to his own semantic theory. Finally, in Section 13 Berkeley presents his 'killing blow' (*PC*, 687) against the theory of abstraction, that is, the argument that since abstract ideas are inconsistent, they can neither be existents nor can they be conceived. As we shall see, here, as in the case of the enthymematic argument in Section 10, Berkeley's argument rests upon principles endorsed by the abstractionists themselves.

Chapter 2 can be construed as a lemma for Chapter 3. Since my objective in Chapter 3 is to show that Berkeley proposed an extensional theory of meaning that included possible objects in the extension of a term, it is essential to provide an account of Berkeley's criteria of possibility and impossibility and an account of his distinction between possible and actual ('real') objects if one is to make his positive theory of meaning intelligible. These are my objectives in Chapter 2.

It is commonly claimed that Berkeley accepted a conceivability criterion of possibility and an inconceivability criterion of impossibility, although little attention typically is paid to either what this entails or to the distinction between metaphysical and epistemological criteria of possibility and impossibility. Further, in the 1734 edition of the *Dialogues* he seems to champion a formal or describability criterion of possibility and impossibility, that is, a criterion based upon the consistency of a description or definition (*DHP*, III, 232-3). Did Berkeley, then, have several extensionally equivalent criteria of possibility and impossibility? Or did his conceivability criteria play a philosophically different role from his describability criteria? My discussion of these issues will consist of five parts.

First, employing the machinery of quantified modal logic, I shall attempt to provide a clear explication of the several things one might mean in claiming that if it is conceivable (or describable) that x is Φ, then it is possible that x is Φ, and I shall ask which of these several principles would be plausible metaphysical or epistemological criteria of possibility and impossibility. Since 'conceivability' and 'describability' are themselves modal notions, it will be shown that one must concern oneself with the distinction between *de dicto* and *de re* conceivability (describability) in the antecedent, as well as the distinction between *de dicto* and *de re* possibility in the consequent, of any propositional function expressing a conceivability (describability) criterion.[12]

Second, I shall examine Berkeley's distinction between ideas and 'real objects'. I shall show that real sensible objects are lawfully describable collections of ideas and that ideas are possible components of real objects. This provides the basis for understanding the *de dicto/de re* distinction in Berkeley: ideas are *de re* possible objects, and any object God could create is a *de dicto* possible object.

Third, I shall examine Berkeley's metaphysical criteria of possibility and impossibility, that is, the principles that express the distinction between those things that are possible and impossible (whether or not they are known to be possible or impossible). Regarding *de re* possibility and impossibility, I shall show that Berkeley accepted the principle that there is a y that conceives that there is an x that is Φ if and only if there is an x that is possibly Φ. Regarding *de dicto* possibility and impossibility, I shall show that Berkeley accepted the principle that it is possible that God conceives that there is an x that is Φ if and only if it is possible that there is an x that is Φ.

Fourth, I shall examine Berkeley's epistemic criteria of possibility and impossibility. Regarding one's knowledge of *de re* possibility, I shall show that Berkeley accepted the principle that if there is a y that conceives that there is an x that is Φ, then there is an x that is possibly Φ. Regarding one's knowledge of *de re* impossibility, I shall show that Berkeley accepted the principle that if there is not a y such that y is a consistent description of an x as Φ, then it is impossible that there is an x that is possibly Φ. Finally, regarding one's knowledge of *de dicto* possibility and impossibility, I shall show that Berkeley accepted the principle that there is a y such that y is a consistent description of an x as Φ if and only if it is possible that there is an x that is Φ.

Finally, since most of the evidence I shall consider to support my account of Berkeley's criteria of possibility and impossibility is drawn from works he wrote after 1712, I shall conclude the chapter by examining the evidence supporting Willis Doney's recent claim that an inconceivability criterion of impossibility 'is clearly implied in Part I of the *Principles*, Sections 5, 6, 10, 22, and

23'.[13] It will be shown that the grounds Berkeley sets forth for claiming impossibility in those sections are consistent with the criteria I attribute to him.

In Chapter 3 I shall examine Berkeley's positive theory of the meaning of sortal terms. I shall show that Berkeley proposed an extensional theory of meaning that ranges over both actual and possible objects. First, I shall provide a general discussion of the distinction between extensional and intensional theories of meaning and the distinction between the several kinds of extensions and intensions that are germane to the explication of an extensional theory of meaning. Second, I shall show that the textual evidence supports my contention that Berkeley proposed an extensional theory of the meaning of categorematic terms. Third, I shall show that the available evidence strongly suggests that Berkeley accepted Locke's view that syncategorematic terms (particles) 'signify the *connexion* that the Mind gives to *Ideas, or Propositions, one with another*',[14] and that he recognized that he could consistently accommodate such a position in his extensional theory of meaning. Fourth, after considering an objection to my contention that Berkeley's theory of meaning is extensional, I shall examine Berkeley's account of conventional meaning and one's knowledge of linguistic conventions. Finally, I shall briefly discuss Berkeley's theories of analogical and metaphorical meaning.

In Chapter 4 I shall begin my discussion of Berkeleian notions as such. My objectives are to discuss the epistemic issues relevant to Berkeley's doctrine of notions in light of both his theory of meaning and the historical context in which he wrote. Several scholars have recently acknowledged that Berkeley's notions of substance are 'relative notions',[15] and at least one commentator has acknowledged that he drew a distinction between positive and relative notions.[16] None the less, little progress has been made in attempting to elucidate these distinctions. In the first section of the chapter, I shall examine Berkeley's positive/relative notions distinction in light of both his theory of meaning and the historical context in which it was developed. I shall argue that Berkeley's distinction between positive and relative notions is analogous to Thomas Reid's distinction between direct and relative conceptions: a positive notion is a conception of a thing as it is in itself, while a relative notion is a conception of a thing on the basis of the relations it bears to some other object of which one has a positive conception. Second, through an examination of Berkeley's discussions of relative notions in light of the logical theories that were current at the time he wrote, I shall argue that a relative notion is analogous to what Russell called knowledge by description. I call this 'the describing model of relative notions'. Third, I shall show that the describing model of relative notions is consistent with both Berkeley's criticisms of material substance and his brief accounts of one's notions of immaterial substance. Finally, I shall discuss notions of operations of the mind and relations. I shall argue that so long as it is granted that one has *positive* notions of causality and perception, one can have relative notions of operations of the mind and relations among ideas. For this claim to be plausible, one must understand the nature of Berkeleian relations among ideas. For this reason, my discussion of one's notions of relations among ideas will be preceded by a discussion of the nature of such relations. I shall argue that Berkeleian relations among ideas are reducible without remainder to certain kinds of actions of the mind, that is to say, judgments.

Chapter 5 focuses on metaphysical issues, that is, it is concerned with the nature, rather than the epistemic intent, of Berkeleian notions. My thesis is that a notion is an intentional act.[17] In defending this thesis, I shall first consider the *prima facie* plausible claim that notions are the meanings of terms, that is, notions are concepts. Such an interpretation has been supported on the basis of analogies to other doctrines of notions with which Berkeley was familiar, notably those of John Sergeant and several of the Cartesians.[18] Examining first the analogy between Sergeant's doctrine and Berkeley's, I shall show that it is consistent with Berkeley's theory of meaning to suggest that notions *qua* meanings are 'the things themselves', but this is not Sergeant's contention. Sergeant claimed that notions are the things themselves *as they exist in the mind*, that is, they are intelligible forms, and such a position is inconsistent with Berkeley's critique of abstraction. Turning to the Cartesian doctrine of notions, I shall argue that one does not find the relevant ideas/notions distinction in the Cartesian tradition, and, consequently, it is implausible to construe a notion *qua* meaning as a Cartesian innate idea. Nor is it consistent with Berkeley's general theory of meaning to identify notions with something like a Malebranchean 'idea in the mind of God',[19] since, at best, it is only the meanings of terms denoting *de dicto* possible objects that obtain their meanings on such a basis.

Second, I shall develop my positive case for construing notions as intentional acts. First, I shall examine the analogy between Berkeley's account of meaning and recent theories of intentionality. In this way we shall see that the same issues are germane to consideration of an extensional theory of meaning that are germane to considerations of intentionality and, consequently, it is possible to provide an account of the nature of notions as intentional acts. Second, I shall examine the textual evidence. I shall show that both in the *Third Dialogue* and in Section 308 of *Siris* there is evidence that notions are to be construed as intentional acts. I shall show that Berkeley's account of notions differs from those of his predecessors, in so far as earlier doctrines identified notions with intentional *objects*, while Berkeley identified notions with intentional *acts*. This will explain why Berkeley apparently was hesitant to use the term 'notion'.[20]

Finally, I shall examine the relationship between notions and ideas. I shall begin by considering a distinct, but related issue, that is to say, the sense in which Berkeley held that the mind is active in perception. While at various points Berkeley claimed that the mind is passive in perception, several scholars have indicated that he either changed his views or he was inconsistent.[21] I shall argue that while Berkeley held that the mind is passive in what might be called 'simple perception', that is, simple awareness of ideas, it is active in perceiving 'ordinary objects'. I hope to show that the several ideas that are united in a complex object are united by an intentional act, that is, it is individual minds that 'collect' ideas into objects, and with respect to complex sensible objects, Berkeley held that ultimately there is no distinction between an intentional object and an 'ordinary object'.[22]

In Chapter 6 I shall provide a summary of my conclusions and examine the historical questions of whether the doctrines of notions is implicit in the first editions of the *Principles* and the *Dialogues*. I shall argue that if my account of Berkeleian notions is correct, then one can reasonably conclude that such a doctrine is implicit in the first editions of the *Principles* and the *Dialogues*.

Notes

1. On the distinction between knowledge by acquaintance and knowledge by description, see Bertrand Russell, *The Problems of Philosophy* (Oxford University Press, New York, 1912), pp. 46-59.
2. Park has noted that Berkeley used the term 'notion' in at least five distinct

senses in the two editions of the *Principles* alone. See Desiree Park, *Complementary Notions: A Critical Study of Berkeley's Theory of Concepts* (Martinus Nijhoff, The Hague, 1972), pp. 54-7.

3. As we shall see later, there is some evidence that Berkeley occasionally used the term 'notion' in this technical sense even in the earlier editions of the *Principles* and *Dialogues* — for example, in his discussion of one's knowledge of oneself and God in the *Third Dialogue* (cf. *DHP*, III, 231-2) — although this use of the term became more pronounced in those works he published in 1734 and later.

4. See A.A. Luce, *Berkeley's Immaterialism* (Thomas Nelson and Sons Ltd., London, 1950), p. 99, cf. pp. 146-8; A.A. Luce, *Berkeley and Malebranche: A Study of the Origins of Berkeley's Thought* (Clarendon Press, Oxford, 1967), pp. 104-5; T.E. Jessop, 'Editor's Introduction' to the *Principles*, in *Works* 2:13; Park, *Complementary Notions*, pp. 55-6; John W. Davis, 'Berkeley Doctrine of the Notion', *Review of Metaphysics*, 12 (1959), pp. 379-80; Brand Blanshard, 'Foreword' in Warren E. Steinkraus (ed.), *New Studies in Berkeley's Philosophy*, (Holt, Rinehart, Winston, New York, 1966), p. vii.

5. Cf. James W. Cornman, 'Theoretical Terms, Berkeleian Notions, and Minds', in Colin Murray Turbayne (ed.), *George Berkeley, Principles of Human Knowledge: Text and Critical Essays*, (Bobbs-Merrill, Indianapolis, Indiana, 1970), pp. 166-7; James W. Cornman, 'A Reconstruction of Berkeley: Minds and Physical Objects as Theoretical Entities', *Ratio*, 13 (1971), p. 76.

6. See A.D. Woozley, 'Berkeley's Doctrine of Notions and Theory of Meaning', *Journal of the History of Philosophy*, 14 (1976), pp. 427-34.

7. Kenneth Winkler, 'Editor's Introduction' to *George Berkeley, A Treatise Concerning the Principles of Human Knowledge* (Indianapolis: Hackett Publishing Company, 1982), pp. xxxiv-xxxv.

8. Cf. Jessop, 'Editor's Introduction', *Works* 2, 3-4; and E.J. Furlong, 'Berkeley on Relations, Spirits, and Notions', *Hermathena*, 106 (1968), p. 61.

9. Cf. Furlong, 'Berkeley on Relations, Spirits, and Notions', pp. 62-3.

10. See Jessop's note in *Works* 2:53n; Davis, 'Berkeley's Doctrine of the Notion', pp. 380-1; Park, *Complementary Notions*, pp. 55-6; Woozley, 'Berkeley's Doctrine of Notions and Theory of Meaning', p. 428.

11. Woozley, 'Berkeley's Doctrine of Notions and Theory of Meaning'; Robert Merrihew Adams, 'Berkeley's "Notion" of Spiritual Substance', *Archiv für Geschichte der Philosophie*, 55 (1973), pp. 47-69; M.W. Beal, 'Berkeley's Linguistic Criterion', *Personalist*, 52 (1971), pp. 499-514; Harry M. Bracken, *Berkeley*, Philosophers in Perspective (St Martin's Press, New York, 1974), pp. 82-4 and 135-48; Harry M. Bracken, 'Berkeley and Mental Acts', *Theoria*, 26 (1960), pp. 140-6; cf. I.C. Tipton, *Berkeley: The Philosophy of Immaterialism* (Methuen & Co. Ltd., London, 1974), p. 270.

12. In this section a significant number of propositional functions will be presented, and the issues discussed in the third and fourth sections of the chapter will refer back to them. For the benefit of those readers who, like me, have trouble keeping track of numbered propositions, a complete list of the propositional functions in Chapter 2 is provided in an appendix to the chapter.

13. Willis Doney, 'Berkeley's Argument Against Abstract Ideas', in Peter A. French, Theodore E. Uehling, Jr, and Howard K. Wettstein (eds), *Midwest Studies in Philosophy VIII, 1983: Contemporary Perspectives on the History of Philosophy* (University of Minnesota Press, Minneapolis, 1983), p. 306, note 3.

14. John Locke, *An Essay concerning Human Understanding*, P.H. Nidditch (ed.) (Clarendon Press, Oxford, 1975), Book 3, Chapter 7, Section 1, p. 471. Further references to Locke's *Essay* will be by Book, Chapter, and Section.

15. See S.C. Brown, 'Berkeley on the Unity of the Self', *Royal Institute of Philosophy, Lectures V* (Macmillan, London, 1972), pp. 69-72; George Pitcher,

Berkeley, Arguments of the Philosophers (Routledge & Kegan Paul, London 1977), p. 120.

16. Phillips Cummins, 'Hylas' Parity Argument', in Colin Turbayne (ed.), *Berkeley: Critical and Interpretive Essays* (University of Minnesota Press, Minneapolis, 1982), pp. 288-9 and 293, note 9.

17. Cf. Davis, 'Berkeley's Doctrine of the Notion'; Sidney C. Rome, 'Berkeley's Conceptualism', *Philosophical Review*, 55 (1946), pp. 680-6; and Sami M. Najm, 'Knowledge of the Self in Berkeley's Philosophy', *International Philosophical Quarterly*, 6 (1966), pp. 248-69.

18. Cf. Bracken, *Berkeley*, pp. 82-5 and 135-48.

19. Cf. Bracken, 'Berkeley and Mental Acts', pp. 145-6.

20. Remember, in an early manuscript for Section 140 of the *Principles* Berkeley had added the terms 'or notion', only to drop it from the published first edition and to add 'or rather a notion' in the second edition.

21. Cf. Reinhardt Grossman, 'Digby and Berkeley on Notions', *Theoria*, 26 (1960), pp. 17-30; Bracken, 'Berkeley and Mental Acts', pp. 140-6; Tipton, *Berkeley*, pp. 268-9; and E.J. Furlong, 'Berkeley on Relations, Spirits, and Notions', p. 65.

22. Both Bracken and Stack have developed similar cases. See Harry M. Bracken, 'Substance in Berkeley', in *New Studies in Berkeley's Philosophy*, pp. 85-97; and George J. Stack, *Berkeley's Analysis of Perception*, 2nd printing, (Mouton, The Hague, 1972), p. 155.

1 ABSTRACTION

In this chapter I shall examine Berkeley's critique of the doctrine of abstract ideas. By understanding both the principal tenets of that doctrine and Berkeley's grounds for rejecting it, we shall be in a position more fully to understand Berkeley's own semantic theory. There are several issues that are germane to Berkeley's critique of abstraction. First, given his close attention to Locke's discussion of that doctrine, was Berkeley's objective solely to refute Locke's doctrine of abstract ideas, or was his critique more general in scope?[1] Second, what are the grounds upon which Berkeley believed himself to have refuted that doctrine? Finally, given that Locke's doctrine of abstract ideas is closely related to his semantic theory, does Berkeley's rejection of the doctrine of abstract ideas constitute a rejection of a particular kind of semantic theory?

In this chapter I shall show, first, that the doctrine of abstraction was quite generally entertained by philosophers from several traditions, and that both Berkeley's rhetoric and the tenets he ascribed to the abstractionists suggest that he intended his refutation to be general in scope. Second, I shall show that Berkeley's critique in the Introduction to the *Principles* proceeds along four distinct lines, and that there is a fifth line, peculiar to some of Berkeley's philosophical tenets, that is developed in the *Alciphron*. In the *Principles* he argued (1) that as a matter of introspective fact, it is impossible to form an abstract idea; (2) that given the tenets commonly accepted by the abstractionists, it is impossible to form an abstract idea; (3) that the doctrine of abstract ideas is theoretically superfluous; and (4) that abstract ideas are inconsistent, and therefore cannot claim 'existence in the mind' (Intro., 6). To these he added an additional argument in the *Alciphron*, that given the passive nature of ideas, it is impossible to have an abstract idea of a mind.[2] Finally, I shall argue that in so far as the doctrine of abstract ideas is an intensional or connotative theory of meaning, Berkeley's refutation of that doctrine constitutes a general refutation of intensional theories of meaning.

14 *Abstraction*

The Abstractionists

While Locke's is the most celebrated discussion of abstraction, it was certainly not the only discussion Berkeley could have had before him while writing the *Principles*. To see that the doctrine of abstraction was, in one form or another, common throughout the medieval and early modern period, we shall start by examining some of the features and ambiguities in Locke's account of abstraction and then briefly compare this account with those of some of the earlier abstractionists. As we shall see, there are certain strains of thought that are common to these several accounts, and many of the differences in the terminology employed are due to the differences in the philosophical traditions from which they hail.[3]

Locke's first and most general statement of the doctrine of abstract ideas is stated in Book II, Chapter II, Section 9 of his *Essay concerning Human Understanding*. There he wrote:

> The use of words then being to stand as outward Marks of our internal *Ideas*, and those *Ideas* being taken from particular things, if every particular *Idea* that we take in, should have a distinct Name, Names must be endless. To prevent this, the Mind makes the particular *Ideas*, received from particular Objects, to become general; which is done by considering them as they are in the Mind such Appearances, separate from all other Existences, and the circumstances of real Existence, a Time, Place, or any other concomitant *Ideas*. This is called ABSTRACTION, whereby *Ideas* taken from particular Beings, become general Representatives of all of the same kind; and their Names general Names, applicable to whatever exist conformable to such abstract *Ideas*. Such precise, naked Appearances in the Mind, without considering, how, whence, or with what others they came there, the Understanding lays up (with Names commonly annexed to them) as the Standards to rank real Existences into sorts, as they agree with these Patterns, and to *denominate* them accordingly. Thus the same Colour being observed to day in Chalk or Snow, which the Mind yesterday received from Milk, it considers that Appearance alone, makes it a representative of all of that kind; and having given it the name *Whiteness*, it by that sound signifies the same quality wheresoever to be imagin'd or met with; and thus Universals, whether *Ideas* or Terms, are made.[4]

Although there are some ambiguities in this passage, this much is clear: Locke took abstraction to be the ability of the mind to single out simple and, as we shall see later, complex qualities that are common to several particular ideas of objects, and it is on the basis of this abstraction that one is able to employ general terms. In abstraction one considers the quality in question apart from any of the circumstances of time, place, or the concomitant ideas of other qualities which allow one to distinguish one particular complex idea from others. Abstraction is, at least, the ability of the mind to attend to certain qualities of sensible objects to the exclusion of others and to recognize that this same quality is common to several complex ideas.

The issue arises, however, whether Locke's commitment to the claim that the mind is capable of engaging in abstraction commits him to the claim that the mind forms abstract ideas of those qualities in separation from all other qualities in a complex idea, or whether, as J.L. Mackie and J.O. Urmson have suggested, the term 'abstract idea' marks nothing more than selective attention to specific qualities in a complex idea.[5] In one sense, this is nothing more than a pseudoquestion. Locke's notion of an idea as 'whatsoever is the Object of the Understanding when a Man thinks'[6] indicates that in attending to a particular component of a complex idea, the distinct component that is the object of one's attention is an idea, and in so far as one obtains this idea through the process of abstraction, it is an abstract idea. Further, in so far as one is concerned with an *appearance* of a particular quality, one's abstract idea might reasonably be understood as a mental image.[7] On the other hand, as Jonathan Bennett has acknowledged,[8] Locke's own commitment to the thesis that all existents are particulars[9] indicates that even abstract ideas are particulars, and therefore there is nothing numerically identical in the idea of a piece of chalk of which I was aware today and the idea of the glass of milk of which I was aware yesterday. In claiming one can form an abstract idea of the whiteness of several objects, Locke holds one can attend to the whiteness of each and recognize their resemblance in color. Nonetheless, since one's idea of the whiteness of a piece of chalk is distinguished from all the other qualities including its 'circumstances in time and place', the abstract idea is general and could be based upon an idea of anything that is white. According to Locke, it is this kind of idea that sets the reference of the term 'white' or 'whiteness'.

Before considering Locke's further discussions of abstraction and abstract ideas, one should notice the distinction between abstraction as a mental process and the abstact idea one obtains by engaging in that process. Abstraction is nothing more than the mental process of selective attention. Locke maintains that the mind can attend to one quality in an idea of a complex, spatially and temporally located object to the exclusion of all others. It is this object of one's selective attention that is an abstract idea. Further, his contention that abstract ideas provide the meaning of general terms commits him to the claim that there are several levels of abstraction. By attending to the whiteness of a particular complex idea, for example, the whiteness of an idea of a particular piece of chalk, one can form an abstract idea of the whiteness of that particular piece of chalk. Let us call this first-order abstraction. By attending to the resemblances among one's several particular abstract ideas of whiteness, for example, the whiteness of this piece of chalk and the whiteness of this glass of milk, one can form an abstract idea of whiteness in general. Let us call this second-order abstraction. Finally, by attending to the resemblances among one's general abstract ideas of whiteness, redness, blueness, greenness, and so on, one can notice the resemblances among these several general abstract ideas and can form an abstract idea of color in general.[10] Although a first-order abstract idea, that is, a particular abstract idea of the particular shade of color of a particular object, might be a mental image, it is less than clear that those at a higher level are images,[11] and, as I hope to show later, Berkeley's criticisms stand or fall independently of construing abstract ideas as images.

Locke's account of abstraction, however, is not limited to abstract ideas of particular simple qualities or kinds of simple qualities. He also held that one has abstract ideas of qualitatively complex kinds of things. Although this is suggested in the passage we have been examining, it becomes much more clear in his discussion 'Of the Names of Substances'. There Locke wrote:

> The measure and boundary of each Sort, or *Species*, whereby it is constituted that particular Sort, and distinguished from others, is that we call its *Essence*, which *is* nothing but that *abstract* Idea *to which the Name is annexed*: So that every thing contained in that *Idea*, is essential to that Sort. This, though it be all the *Essence* of natural Substances, that we know, or by

which we distinguish them into Sorts; yet I call it by a peculiar name, the *nominal Essence*, to distinguish it from that real Constitution of Substances, upon which depends this *nominal Essence*, and all the Properties of that Sort; which therefore, as has been said, may be called the *real Essence: v.g.* the *nominal Essence* of *Gold*, is that complex *Idea* the word *Gold* stands for, let it be, for instance, a Body yellow, of a certain weight, malleable, fusible, and fixed. But the *real Essence* is the constitution of the insensible parts of that Body, on which those Qualities, and all the other Properties of *Gold* depend. How far these two are different, though they are both called *Essence*, is obvious, at first sight, to discover.[12]

Ideas of substance are qualitatively complex, and the construction of an abstract idea that is the nominal essence of a substance presupposes second- and third-order qualitative abstraction. A nominal essence is simply an abstract idea of the several kinds of qualities that are considered essential for a thing to be a substance of a certain kind.[13] Locke's description of the abstract idea (nominal essence) of gold is sufficient to show that abstract ideas of substances of certain kinds presuppose such qualitative abstraction. Gold is conceived to be a body (third-order abstraction, and itself a complex idea),[14] yellow (second-order), of a certain weight (second-order), fusible (second-order), and fixed (second-order). The sole function of an abstract idea as a nominal essence is to fix the meaning of a substance-term, and, as Locke indicates in his later discussions of nominal essences, such abstract ideas can change as one's knowledge of an object of a certain kind increases.[15] Locke held that all abstraction with respect to kinds of thing rests upon one's ability to recognize and attend solely to the aspects in which particular ideas resemble one another, and abstract ideas of more general kinds are developed by deleting those ideas of kinds of qualities that distinguish a species from its genus. Thus, it is 'by leaving out the shape, and some other Properties signified by the name *Man*, and retaining only a Body, with Life, Sense, and spontaneous Motion, [one constructs the abstract idea] comprehended under the name *Animal*'.[16]

Although Locke differs from earlier essentialists in so far as he explicitly drew a real essence/nominal essence distinction, the association in Locke between abstractionism and essentialism is part of a long tradition. Many philosophers who held that things have essential properties accepted some form of abstractionism, although few referred to the product of abstraction as an 'abstract idea'. Further, as we shall see, in attempting to effect a break with scholasticism, some of the Cartesians rejected the term 'abstraction' while remaining abstractionists in spirit.

The abstractionist tradition can be traced back at least as far as Aristotle. At several places in the *Metaphysics* he alludes to the process of abstraction. In Book A one finds this: 'And these things, the most universal, are on the whole the hardest for men to know; for they are the farthest from the senses.'[17] In Book K, one finds this:

> As the mathematician investigates abstractions (for before beginning his investigation he strips off all the sensible qualities, e.g. weight and lightness, hardness and its contrary, and also heat and cold and the other sensible contrarieties, and leaves only the qualitative and continuous, sometimes in one, sometimes in two, sometimes in three dimensions, and the attributes of these *qua* quantitative and continuous, and does not consider them in any other respect, and examines the relative positions of some and the attributes of these, and the commensurabilities and incommensurabilities of others, and the ratios of others, but yet we posit one and the same science of all these things — geometry) — the same is true with regard to being.[18]

According to Aristotle, the mind abstracts by stripping an object of its sensible qualities. It is on this basis of this 'stripping away of sensible qualities' that a mathematician abstracts the notions of pure quantity and dimension from the sensibly given and that a philosopher abstracts the notion of being from the sensibly given. Like Locke, Aristotle maintained that all knowledge is based upon sense. Although Aristotle did not use the term 'abstract idea' to mark the psychological state that results from the process of abstraction, his suggestion that abstraction proceeds by 'stripping the sensible qualities' from things indicates that, like Locke, Aristotle held that the mind is capable of focusing in upon one of the sensible qualities of an object to the exclusion of others, and more general qualities to the exclusion of more particular qualities.

Although there are strains of abstractionism in Aristotle, the doctrine reached its height in the writings of the scholastics. Those 'great masters of abstraction' accepted the general dictum *Nihil est in intellectu quod prius non fuerit in sensu,*[19] maintaining that all knowledge is based upon abstraction from what is given in the senses.[20] As Aquinas wrote:

> The things which belong to the specific nature of a material thing, such as a stone, or a man, or a horse, can be thought of without the individual principles which do not belong to the understanding of the species. This is what we mean by abstracting the universal from the particular, of the intelligible species from the phantasm. In other words, this is to consider the specific nature apart from its individual principles represented by the phantasm.[21]

According to Aquinas, it is by the process of abstraction that the mind grasps the nature or intelligible species (intelligible form) of an object on the basis of the phantasm. As in Aristotle and Locke, the mind (active intellect) strips the individuating characteristics of matter from the phantasm and grasps the nature that is common to many individuals. Also like Aristotle and Locke, Aquinas held that all existents are particulars[22] and that universality is introduced into the world only due to the ability of the mind to abstract.[23] The intelligible form that is grasped by the mind is numerically distinct from the material form of the object; it is the form of the object as it exists in the mind.[24] The intelligible form is also known as a 'formal concept' or a 'notion', and this use of 'notion' was common throughout the scholastic tradition. One finds it, for example, in the works of the late seventeenth-century scholastic, John Sergeant.[25] Finally, as in Locke, one finds several orders or levels of abstraction in Aquinas and the scholastic tradition in general: one can grasp the intelligible species of a particular object as well as the forms of the higher genera.[26]

With the rise of Cartesianism in the seventeenth century, there was an attempt to effect a conscious break with the scholastic tradition. For this reason the term 'abstraction' fell into disrepute with several — but not all — of the Cartesians. One reason for this is fairly clear. The scholastics maintained that all change can be explained on the basis of a form-matter ontology, claiming that all change is simply change of form. In explaining a change in color, for example, the scholastics claimed that the form in the matter changed from redness to blueness. Such an explanation is less than illuminating, and it was subject to the following kind of criticism. Malebranche wrote:

> ... I have no hesitation in saying that we make such ill use of the best of the mind's disordered abstractions, and consquently, [it is one of the main causes] of that abstract and chimerical philosophy that explains all natural effects with the general terms act, potency, causes, effect, substantial forms, faculties, occult qualities, and so on. For it is certain that all these terms and several others arouse in the mind only vague and general ideas, i.e., those ideas that present themselves to the mind with no difficulty or effort on our part, those ideas that are contained in the ineradicable idea of being.[27]

Although the Cartesians rejected abstraction in the scholastic sense of an abstraction of form from matter, and therefore some of them rejected the term 'abstraction' due to its scholastic connotations, it is clear that they were abstractionists in a more general and nonscholastic sense of that term. This fact is illustrated by Descartes' letter to Clerselier of 12 January 1646. There Descartes drew a distinction between distinguishing and abstracting a substance from its accidents, a distinction which, as we shall see, will still leave Descartes in the camp of the abstractionists. As he wrote:

> ... in distinguishing a substance from its accidents, we must consider both one and the other, and this helps greatly in becoming acquainted with substance; whereas if instead one only separates by abstraction this substance from these accidents, i.e. if one considers it quite alone without thinking of them, that prevents one from knowing it well, because it is by its accidents that substance is manifested.[28]

This passage indicates that Descartes held it is impossible to conceive of a substance apart from its essential attribute, and, consequently, if the abstractionist were to require that a substance be conceived apart from all its attributes, such abstraction would be futile. But although Descartes rejected such extreme abstractionism, his doctrine of essential attributes and his notion of 'distinguishing' indicate that he allowed that the mind is capable of conceiving the principal attribute of a substance apart from the substance of which it is an attribute and apart from its modes. As he wrote in the *Principles of Philosophy*:

> But although any one attribute is sufficient to give us a knowledge of substance, there is always one principal property of substance which constitutes its nature and essence, and on which all the others depend. Thus extension in length, breadth and depth, constitutes the nature of corporeal substance; and thought constitutes the nature of thinking substance. For all else that may be attached to body presupposes extension, and is but a mode of this extended thing; as everything that we find in mind is but so many diverse forms of thinking. Thus, for example, we cannot conceive figure but as an extended thing, nor movement but as in an extended space; so imagination, feeling, and will, only exist in a thinking thing. But, on the other hand, we can conceive extension without figures or action, and thinking without imagination or sensation, and so on with the rest; as is quite clear to anyone who attends to the matter.[29]

Notice that in allowing that one can conceive of extension or thought apart from both a substance and any of the modes of either attribute, Descartes accepts a theory of abstraction that is similar to that of both Locke and the scholastics.[30] One finds the same kind of move in Malebranche.[31] Thus, although some of the Cartesians denied that the mind can abstract due to the scholastic overtones of the term 'abstraction', like other abstractionists they allowed that the mind is capable of conceiving one property of an object apart from all others and of conceiving general properties apart from any of their particular manifestations.

Although some of the Cartesians were hesitant to use the word 'abstraction', others were not. In his *Art of Thinking*, for example, Arnauld wrote that '... we can consider a mode without reflecting explicitly on the substance of which this mode is a mode. Such consideration of a mode is an instance of knowledge by *abstraction*.'[32] Arnauld distinguished among three types of abstract knowledge. First, there is the knowledge of the integral parts of things, that is, of 'parts that are actually distinct'.[33] He subdivided such abstract knowledge into two kinds. There is (1) knowledge of the integral parts of such things as human bodies, that is the consideration of arms and legs in separation from or in comparison to other parts of the human body. There is also (2) consideration of the integral parts of numbers (numerals) in arithmetic computation, since 'It would be impossible no matter how agile the mind, to multiply two numbers of eight or nine digits, were each number merely considered as a whole.'[34] Arnauld notes, however, that although this is an important kind of knowledge, 'knowing a thing by a consideration of its integral parts is not what is commonly meant by abstraction'.[35] Second, there is abstract knowledge of the 'parts' of things which 'occurs when we consider a mode without paying attention to its substance or consider two modes which are joined together in a single substance, regarding each mode separately'.[36] His example is a geometer's knowledge of extension based upon consideration of, first, extension in one dimension, second, extension in two dimensions, and, finally, extension in three dimensions.[37] Finally, there is the abstraction which 'occurs when we think exclusively of one characteristic of a thing that possesses several characteristics separable only in thought'.[38] His examples here are knowledge of thought as a principal attribute of oneself and knowledge of triangularity apart from any of the accidental characteristics of a particular triangle.[39] It should be clear that, at least with respect to these latter two kinds of abstraction, Arnauld's theory of abstraction bears a strong resemblance to the theories of Aristotle, the scholastics, the other Cartesians, and Locke.

As we have seen, the claim that the human mind is capable of engaging in abstraction and forming what might be called abstract ideas has a long and venerable history. If Berkeley had any acquaintance with the philosophical traditions prior to Locke, one should find it surprising if he intended to direct criticisms solely at Locke's version of the doctrine of abstraction rather than at the tradition as a whole. In turning now to Berkeley's own discussions of abstraction, I shall first show that Berkeley was acquainted with the works of abstractionists other than Locke. Next I shall show that the rhetoric he employs at various points in his writings suggests that his objective was to provide a general refutation of abstraction. Finally, I shall turn to his summary of the claims made by the abstractionists and shall show that virtually all the figures we have considered held the views he attributes to the abstractionists.

Berkeley and the Abstractionists

It is beyond doubt that Berkeley was acquainted with several works on abstraction other than the discussion of John Locke. Not only does he refer to the scholastics as 'those great masters of abstraction' (Intro. 17), in the First Draft of the Introduction he quoted the passage we cited above from Book A of Aristotle's *Metaphysics* in which Aristotle noted the difficulty of forming a universal notion since such a notion is farthest removed from sense (*Works* 2:130). Similarly, some of the entries in the *Philosophical Commentaries* that were marked as relevant to the Introduction show that he was familiar with some of the abstractionists we have noted above. He made the following general allusions to the scholastics:

- I. I abstain from all flourish & pomp of words & figures using a great plainness & simplicity of stile having oft found it difficult to understand those that use the Lofty & Platonic or Subtil & Scholastique strain. (*PC*, 300)
- I Even to speak somwhat favourably of the Schoolmen & shew that they who blame them for jargon are not free from it themselves. Introd: (*PC*, 716)
- I.M. I approve of this axiom of the Schoolmen nihil est in intellectu quod non prius fuit in sensu. I wish they had stuck to it. It had never taught them the Doctrine of Abstract Ideas. (*PC*, 779).

Given the intellectual environment in which Berkeley wrote, that is, that the works that marked the first serious break with scholasticism had been written within less than a century prior to the publication of the *Principles*, it would be quite surprising if Berkeley had not been fairly well-versed in the works of the scholastics.[40] At the very least, it is clear that Berkeley had at least a passing acquaintance with the work of the late seventeenth-century scholastic, John Sergeant (*PC*, 840). Further, since it is characteristic of the early moderns to consciously distinguish themselves from the scholastics, and given that he described them as the 'great masters of abstraction' (Intro. 17), one would expect the scholastics to be among the objects of Berkeley's criticisms.

The scholastics are not the only philosophers whose views were cited as relevant to the Introduction. In entry 784 of the *Philo-*

sophical Commentaries, he took Descartes to task. In Berkeley's words:

> I   Descartes in Med: 2. says the Notion of this particular wax is less clear than that of Wax in General. & in the same Med: a little before he forbears to Consider Bodies in general because (he says) these General Conceptions are usually confused. (*PC*, 784).

In suggesting that this entry is relevant to the Introduction, Berkeley seems to have been concerned with the contention that the idea of wax *in general* is clearer than that of a particular piece of wax, a contention that presupposes the possibility of engaging in abstraction. Since Descartes's clear and distinct ideas are general ideas of the essences of things,[41] it is reasonable to claim that knowledge in the Cartesian tradition presupposes the ability to form abstract ideas. Further, since Malebranche accepted Descartes's view on the relationship between clear and distinct ideas and one's knowledge of the truth,[42] and Berkeley's acquaintance with the work of Malebranche is indisputable,[43] Berkeley's questions regarding the adequacy of Descartes's views on abstraction apply to Malebranche as well.[44]

So far we have seen that Berkeley was acquainted with the writings of abstractionists other than Locke. While this alone will not show that he intended his critique of abstraction to be general in scope, it at least shows that the question of the scope of Berkeley's criticisms can reasonably be asked. In turning now to a brief examination of the rhetoric with which Berkeley prefaced his critique, we shall find that this also tends to support the suggestion that his intended object was the entire abstractionist tradition.

In Section 6 of the Introduction to the *Principles* Berkeley announces his intent to 'premise somewhat, by way of introduction, concerning the nature and abuse of language' (Intro., 6). He indicates that this initial inquiry is of great significance, because it points to the source of great perplexity and error in philosophy. As Berkeley wrote:

> But the unravelling this matter leads me in some measure to anticipate my design, by taking notice of what seems to have had a chief part in rendering speculation intricate and per-

plexed, and to have occasioned innumerable errors and difficulties in almost all parts of knowledge. And that is the opinion that the mind hath a power of framing *abstract ideas* or notions of things. He who is not a perfect stranger to the writings and disputes of philosophers, must needs acknowledge that no small part of them are spent about abstract ideas. There are in a more especial manner, thought to be the object of those sciences which go by the name of Logic and Metaphysics, and of all that which passes under the notion of the most abstracted and sublime learning, in all which one shall scarce find any question handled in such a manner, as does not suppose their existence in the mind, and that it is well acquainted with them. (Intro., 6)[45]

Notice that Berkeley's claims here are quite general. He asserts that 'the writings and disputes of philosophers' are concerned primarily with abstract ideas, that is, that the objects of their discussions are things of which it is claimed one has abstract ideas. His claim is very general and suggests that *some* doctrine of abstract ideas is presupposed by virtually all of his philosophical predecessors. Their disputes assume the 'existence [of abstract ideas] in the mind and that it is well acquainted with them'. Now, as we have seen, the doctrine of abstraction was common to the Aristotelian-scholastic tradition, the Cartesian tradition and Locke, and Berkeley had at least some acquaintance with each of these traditions. Hence, it seems reasonable to take the object of Berkeley's criticism to be the doctrine of abstraction in general.

In the First Draft of the Introduction there is further evidence that Berkeley intended his critique of the doctrine of abstract ideas to apply to the abstractionists from many traditions. Notice what he wrote:

By abstract ideas, genera, species, universal notions all which amount to the same thing, as I find those terms explain'd by the best and clearest writers, we are to understand ideas which equally represent the particulars of any sort, & are made by the mind which observing that the individuals of each kind agree in some things, and differ in others, takes out & singles from the rest, that which is common to all, making therefore one abstract, general idea; which general idea contains all those ideas wherein the particulars do agree & partake separated from & exclusive of all those other concomitant ideas, whereby the individuals are distinguish'd from each other. (*Works* 2:123)

There are two things to notice here. First, here again Berkeley uses the plural in referring to 'the best and clearest writers' who have explained the doctrine. This at least suggests that, even though his strongest criticisms were directed toward Locke's theory of abstraction, the intent of his criticism was much broader in scope. Second, he claimed that the terms 'abstract ideas', 'genera', 'species', and 'universal notions' should be understood as synonymous. This also suggests that Berkeley intended his criticisms to apply to the doctrine of abstraction in each of the several traditions in which it is found. In his discussions of abstraction, Locke was fairly consistent in his use of the term 'abstract idea' to mark the product of abstraction, and, at least on those occasions that he claimed to use the term 'notion' technically, he applied the term 'notion' solely to one's abstract ideas of mixed modes.[46] Although the term 'notion' was used quite broadly in the seventeenth and early eighteenth centuries to denote the concept or mental state that provides the meaning of a word,[47] the term tended to have scholastic overtones, since the scholastic tradition tended to use the terms 'notion', 'formal concept' and 'intelligible form' interchangeably.[48] Further, the terms 'genera' and 'species' have scholastic connotations, and one of the advantages Locke claimed for his doctrine of abstact ideas is that it resolves the 'whole *mystery* of *Genera* and *Species*, which make such a noise in the Schools'.[49] Berkeley's suggestion that for his purposes the terms 'abstract idea', 'genera' and 'species' are synonymous, suggests that he intended his critique to be very general.

So far we have seen that Berkeley was acquainted with the writings of abstractionists from several philosophical traditions, and that the rhetoric he employed in introducing his discussion of abstraction in both the First Draft and the published Introduction to the *Principles* suggests that he intended his critique of abstraction to be quite general in scope. A final source of evidence that Berkeley intended his critique to be germane to abstractionists from several philosophical traditions can be gleaned from Sections 7-9 of the Introduction, where Berkeley spells out what he takes to be the tenets advanced by the abstractionists. It is to these sections that we shall now turn.

In Section 7 of the Introduction, Berkeley wrote:

It is agreed on all hands, that the qualities or modes of things do never really exist each of them apart by itself, and separated from all others, but are mixed, as it were, and blended together, several in the same object. But we are told, the mind being able to consider each quality singly, or abstracted from those qualities with which it is united, does by that means frame to itself abstract ideas. For example, there is perceived by sight an object extended, coloured, and moved: this mixed or compound idea the mind resolving into its simple, constituent parts and viewing each by itself, exclusive of the rest, does frame the abstract ideas of extension, colour, and motion. Not that it is possible for colour or motion to exist without extension: but only that the mind can form to itself by *abstraction* the idea of colour exclusive of extension, and of motion exclusive of both colour and extension. (Intro., 7)

In this section Berkeley states the points of general agreement among the abstractionists, that is, what is 'agreed on all hands'.[50] One should notice that there are two explicit claims made in this section: (1) 'that the qualities or modes of things do not really exist each of them apart by itself', indeed, as he indicates in the last sentence, that it is impossible for these qualities or modes to exist in isolation. (2) That in spite of the impossibility of such independent existence of modes or qualities, the mind is capable of conceiving each of these modes or qualities in isolation from all others with which it is found in existents, that is, the mind is able to abstract. Since we have already considered the wide acceptance of the second claim, we shall focus on the first.

One should notice, first, that Berkeley's references to the inseparability of 'qualities *or* modes' (my emphasis) tends to mask a distinction between several philosophical theories. Although some philosophers used the terms 'mode' and 'quality' as virtual synonyms,[51] the term 'mode' is generally related to a substratum theory of substance, while the use of the term 'quality' was generally broader and took on certain special connotations among the proponents of the primary/secondary qualities distinction. As we shall see, regardless of the specific connotation of the term, the abstractionists were agreed that 'the qualities or modes of things do not really exist each of them apart by itself, and separated from all others'. Let us first consider this issue with respect to modes.

The proponents of the substratum theory of substance drew a

distinction between a substance and its modes or modifications, maintaining that while a substance as such is an independent existent, modes depend for their existence upon the substance of which they are modes. Such a view was common to the scholastics and early moderns alike.[52] Those philosophers who were proponents of a substratum theory maintained that, although a mode cannot exist apart from a substance, it is possible to conceive a mode in isolation from a substance.[53]

The notion of a 'quality' is broader than that of a mode, but the abstractionists were no less inclined to assert that qualities neither do nor can exist apart from those things of which they are qualities. For example, Aristotle, who held that mathematicians abstract the notions of quantity and dimension from the sensibly given,[54] held that the properties which a mathematician so conceives do not *exist* apart from objects: 'the mind when it is thinking the objects of Mathematics thinks separate, elements which do not exist separate'.[55] Indeed, Aristotle went a step further and held that it is *impossible* for any qualities of objects to exist apart from objects. As he wrote in the *Physics*:

> The statement that complete separation never will take place is correct enough, though Anaxagoras is not fully aware of what it means. For affections are indeed inseparable. If then colours and states had entered into the mixture, and if separation took place, there would be a 'white' or a 'healthy' which was nothing *but* white or healthy, i.e. was not the predicate of a subject. So his 'Mind' is an absurd person aiming at the impossible, if he is supposed to wish to separate them, and it is impossible to do so, both in respect of quantity and quality — of quantity, because there is no minimum magnitude, and of quality, because affections are inseparable.[56]

Furthermore, one can construe the notion of a 'quality' as broadly as an Aristotelian form, and it is a basic tenet of the Aristotelian-scholastic tradition that it is impossible for forms to exist apart from matter. Indeed, this tenet is common to all philosophers who maintain that while there are universals, they are all *universalia in rebus*. Consequently the tenet that Berkeley claimed to be 'agreed on all hands' was accepted in one form or another throughout the Aristotelian-scholastic tradition, and the vestiges of such a position remain in Locke's discussion of the idea of substance. There Locke argued that one's positive ideas of substances of particular kinds are collective of qualities, each quality being taken to be constitutive of a substance of a particular kind.[57]

Finally, if one narrows the notion of a 'quality' to conform with the sense of that term employed by the proponents of the primary/secondary qualities distinction, one finds the same claims made by these philosophers. The proponents of that distinction maintained that the primary qualities (extension, solidity, figure, texture, number, motion and rest) are constitutive properties of material objects, and consequently they do not exist in separation from one another.[58] Further, since they held that the secondary qualities (as powers to produce the sensations of color, sound, savor, odor, pain, heat and cold in a sentient being) are reducible to the actions of corpuscles possessing only primary qualities,[59] the proponents of the primary/secondary qualities were also committed to claiming that all the qualities of an object are intimately related to one another and that no quality can exist in isolation from all others. Hence, Berkeley's initial claim was generally accepted by the abstractionists, and he could reasonably claim they held that it is impossible 'for color or motion to exist without extension', even though they held that it is possible to conceive of these qualities in isolation from one another. As we shall see, this claim plays a very significant role in Berkeley's criticism of abstraction.

In Sections 8-9 of the Introduction Berkeley discusses third-order qualitative abstraction and abstraction with respect to qualitatively complex kinds of things. Although the position he summarizes is drawn directly from Locke's *Essay*,[60] we saw in the first section of this chapter that the similarities between Locke's account of abstraction and those of his predecessors are sufficient to allow Berkeley to take Locke's discussion as a paradigm of abstractionism and, given Berkeley's great respect for the relative clarity of Locke's philosophy (*PC*, 467), it is reasonable to assume that Berkeley was simply using Locke's account of abstraction as a paradigm.

Thus, we have seen that many of Berkeley's predecessors had held that the mind is capable of engaging in abstraction, that is, of conceiving of a particular mode or quality in separation from the thing of which it is a particular mode or quality, even though they held that it is impossible for these modes or qualities to exist in separation from those particulars. Berkeley was acquainted with the works of abstractionists from several traditions, and the rhetoric he employs in introducing his discussions of abstraction suggests that he intended his critique to apply to the abstractions in each of the several traditions from which they hail. In turning now to his criticisms of the abstractionists, we shall see that although he continued to take Locke's discussions of abstract ideas as paradigmatic, most of his criticisms apply to virtually all of the abstractionists.

Introduction, Section 10

Having completed his summary of the abstractionists' position, Berkeley raises his first criticisms in Section 10. This section includes the well-known argument from introspection in which Berkeley looks into his mind and finds that he *can* abstract in the sense of imagining proper parts of things in isolation from those things of which they are parts, but that he cannot, in fact, conceive of a (putatively) simple quality (for example, extension) or a complex quality (for example, animality) in isolation from all others. It is unlikely that such an argument would persuade a serious abstractionist. I shall show, however, that there is a second and more serious argument embedded in the section, an argument which shows that, given the principles accepted by the abstractionists, it follows that it is impossible to engage in abstraction. So let us begin by examining Berkeley's argument from introspection.

The argument from introspection takes up the bulk of Section 10. It reads as follows:

> Whether others have this wonderful faculty of *abstracting their ideas*, they best can tell: for myself I find indeed I have a faculty of imagining, or representing to myself the ideas of those particular things I have perceived and of variously compounding and dividing them. I can imagine a man with two heads or the upper parts of a man joined to the body of a horse. I can consider the hand, the eye, the nose, each by itself abstracted or separated from the rest of the body. But then whatever hand or eye I imagine, it must have some particular shape and colour. Likewise the idea of man that I frame to myself, must be either of a white, or a black, or a tawny, a straight, or a crooked, a tall or a low, or a middle-sized man. I cannot by any effort of thought conceive the abstract idea above described. And it is

equally impossible for me to form the abstract idea of motion distinct from the body moving, and which is neither swift nor slow, curvilinear nor rectilinear; and the like may be said of all other abstract general ideas whatsoever. To be plain, I own my self able to abstract in one sense, as when I consider some particular parts or qualities separated from others, with which though they are united in some object, yet, it is possible they may really exist without them. (Intro., 10; cf. *NTV*, 123)

In examining his mental states and mental capacities, Berkeley notes that he *is* able to abstract in the sense that he can imagine qualitatively complex parts of objects in isolation from the objects of which they are parts and that he can combine these complex ideas to form ideas of fictitious things, for example, to form ideas of two-headed men and centaurs. This type of 'abstraction' is what Arnauld called abstraction in terms of the integral parts of objects, and he acknowledged, as Berkeley acknowledged later in the Section, that this is commonly not considered a 'proper acceptation of abstraction'.[61] In imagining an integral part of an object, the idea one forms is of a qualitatively complex thing which could exist as one imagines it, that is, the qualitative complexity of the object one imagines is (generally) as great as that of real things.[62]

Although introspection shows Berkeley that he is able to abstract in this very limited sense, he claimed that 'it is impossible for me to form the abstract idea of motion distinct from the body moving, and which is neither swift nor slow, curvilinear nor rectilinear' (Intro., 10). Remembering that this is an introspective report, Berkeley's intention in using the word 'impossible' must have been that he simply finds himself unable to form such an idea and not that the formation of such an idea is impossible in any stronger sense. But relatively little follows from the fact that one person is unable to form such an idea. Even assuming that the abilities of human beings are fairly uniform, the fact that one person cannot form an idea of motion in separation from some object moved provides nothing more than inductive evidence that no one can form such an idea. Further, the (ironic?) language he employs at the end of the section, suggesting that since abstract ideas are allegedly difficult to form, they are perhaps 'confined to the learned' (Intro., 10), suggests that Berkeley was aware of the inconclusiveness of the argument from introspection. Hence, if this were the only argument to be found in Section 10, there would be

32 Abstraction

little reason to claim that Berkeley had provided a serious challenge to the abstractionists.

In continuing his discussion, however, Berkeley shows that the abstractionists themselves cannot consistently hold that it is possible to abstract. He seems to have proposed the following argument: (1) whatever is impossible in existence is inconceivable; (2) it is impossible for qualities or modes to exist independently; and (3) therefore, it is impossible to conceive of modes or qualities independently, that is, it is impossible to abstract.[63] In the published version of the Introduction, his argument is enthymematic and consists of a single statement. He wrote: 'But I deny that I can abstract one from another, or conceive separately, those qualities which it is impossible should exist so separated; or that I can frame a general notion by abstracting from particulars in the manner aforesaid' (Intro., 10).

While the last phrase of this sentence might be construed as a continuation of Berkeley's argument from introspection, the first clause of the statement was almost certainly intended to show that the abstractionists themselves could not consistently claim that abstraction is possible. This is quite clear if one compares part of the corresponding section from the First Draft of the Introduction. There we find this:

> It is, I think, a receiv'd axiom that an impossibility cannot be conceiv'd. For what created intelligence will pretend to conceive, that which God cannot cause to be? Now it is on all hands agreed, that nothing abstract or general can be made really to exist, whence it should seem to follow, that it cannot have so much as an ideal existence in the understanding. (*Works*, 2:125)

Further, although he did not explicitly spell out this argument in the printed introduction to the *Principles*, he provided a similar argument in the first and second editions of the *Alciphron*. There we find this:

> **Euphranor.** Pray, Alciphron, which are those things you would call absolutely impossible?
> **Alciphron.** Such as include a contradiction.
> **Euphranor.** Can you frame an idea of what includes a contradiction?

Alciphron. I cannot.
Euphranor. Consequently, whatever is absolutely impossible you cannot form an idea of.
Alciphron. This I grant.
Euphranor. But can a colour or triangle, such as you describe their abstract general ideas, really exist?
Alciphron. It is absolutely impossible such things should exist in Nature.
Euphranor. Should it not follow, then, that they cannot exist in your mind, or, in other words, that you cannot conceive or frame an idea of them?

(*Works* 3:333-4)

As we have seen, the abstractionists held that it is impossible for the modes or qualities of objects to exist independently from objects. If they also accepted Berkeley's axiom that an impossibility cannot be conceived, then it would follow that one could not form ideas of qualities separated from the object of which they are qualities, that is, it would follow that it is impossible to abstract in the manner prescribed. But did the abstractionists accept this axiom?

One of Aquinas' discussions of omnipotence makes it quite clear that this axiom was accepted within the scholastic tradition. As he wrote:

> ... everything that does not imply a contradiction in terms is numbered among those possibles in respect of which God is called omnipotent; whereas whatever implies a contradiction does not come within the scope of divine omnipotence, because it cannot have the aspect of possibility. Hence, it is more appropriate to say that such things cannot be done, than that God cannot do them. Nor is this contrary to the word of the angel, saying: *No word shall be impossible with God* (*Luke* i. 37). For whatever implies a contradiction cannot be a word, because no intellect can possibly conceive such a thing.[64]

Notice, Aquinas held that what is contradictory is absolutely impossible and that whatever is contradictory is inconceivable (not possible to conceive), and this is a tenet that seems to have persisted throughout the scholastic tradition.[65] It is also clear that it persisted into the early modern period, since Locke held that it is impossible to form an idea of an inconsistency.[66] For our present purposes, however, it is only important to notice *that* these abstractionists held that what is impossible is inconceivable, and we need not concern ourselves with their criteria of impossibility.

Further, many philosophers in the early modern period who might not have explicitly claimed Berkeley's axiom accepted a tenet which entails that axiom. The conceivability criterion of possibility was extremely popular during the early modern period. This principle holds that for any state of affairs x, if x is conceivable, that is, if it is possible to conceive of x, then x is possible, that is, it is (logically) possible for x to exist. Berkeley's axiom is the transposition of that principle. Now such a criterion is to be found in Descartes's *Principles of Philosophy*. As Descartes wrote:

> The *real* is properly speaking found between two or more substances; and we can conclude that two substances are really distinct one from the other from the sole fact that we can conceive the one clearly and distinctly without the other. For in accordance with the knowledge we have of God, we are certain that He can carry into effect all that of which we have a distinct idea.[67]

Arnauld took it as one of the 'axioms which can serve as the basis for greater truths' that '*Existence, at least possible existence, is included in the idea of whatsoever we conceive clearly and distinctly*'.[68] As Thomas Reid indicates in his *Essays on the Intellectual Powers of Man*, the conceivability criterion of possibility retained its popularity throughout most of the eighteenth century.[69] Now, in so far as the conceivability criterion of possibility entails the axiom to which Berkeley appeals, the abstractionists' acceptance of both the conceivability criterion and the inseparability thesis entails that it is impossible to conceive of a mode or quality apart from the object of which it is a mode or quality. Hence, on the basis of the principles the abstractionists themselves accept, it follows that it is impossible to engage in abstraction: abstract ideas are inconceivable.

At this point some commentators will come to the defense of Locke and the other abstractionists, suggesting that while Berkeley held that in abstracting a mode from a substance one must conceive of a mode as existing separately from a substance, the abstractionists themselves understood abstraction as the ability to selectively attend to a characteristic of an object. Pointing out that Berkeley himself allows that selective attention is possible (Intro., 16), they would contend that his objection to the abstractionists in Section 10 fails.[70] In coming to Berkeley's defense, one should notice that such abstractionists as Descartes, Arnauld, and Locke held that 'A mode's relation to a substance is contained — at least obscurely — in the very idea of that mode',[71] while also holding, in Arnauld's words, that 'A mode can be conceived without giving separate and direct attention to its substance; but the mode's relation to its substance cannot be denied without destroying the very idea of the mode.'[72]

Is this selective attention possible? It seems not. Modes are necessarily related to substances. If one attends to a mode, as a mode, one must conceive it as related to a substance. If it were possible to attend to a mode while paying no attention to its relation to a substance, one would not have an idea of a mode *qua* mode. But to abstract requires that one be able to attend to a mode *qua* mode without attending to its relation to a substance, and, given the necessary connection between a mode and its substance, this is impossible. One should notice that the same problem arises if one claims that qualities are necessarily related to objects or to each other: problems with selective attention arise when one claims that the thing to which one would selectively attend is necessarily related to something else. On the other hand, Berkeley's contention in Section 16 of the Introduction that 'a man may consider a figure merely as triangular, without attending to the particular qualities of the angles, or relations of the sides' is not subject to this objection, for there is no necessary connection between being a triangle and the characteristics of the three angles or sides of a particular triangle. Thus, appeals to selective attention cannot save the abstractionist.

The defender of abstraction might still pose another reply to Berkeley's objection. He might suggest that in the idea of a mode, the mode's relation to a substance is (sometimes) obscure, and it is due to the obscurity of one's idea of this relation that one can form an idea of a mode without attending to its relation to a substance. Such an idea of a mode *qua* mode might itself be obscure, but it can still be formed. If he would allow such a move, Berkeley would contend that this would pose a different kind of problem for the abstractionist. Modes and one's corresponding ideas of them are either simple or complex. Further, there is no difference in kind between one's ideas of complex modes and one's ideas of the essences of substances of various kinds: both are no more than ordered collections of qualities. In the Cartesian-Lockean tradition, modes and substances are classified on the basis of abstract ideas. To function as a standard for classifying modes and substances, one's abstract idea must be clear and determinate. But if it is granted that a clear idea of a mode involves a relation to a substance and that an *abstract* idea of a mode or essence, that is an idea in which one does not attend to the relation between a mode or essence and a substance, is an obscure idea, it follows on the abstractionist's own principles that such an idea cannot function as a standard for classification. It is the question of the need for such a standard for classification that Berkeley raises in Sections 11 and 12, and it is to this discussion that we shall not turn.

Introduction, Sections 11-12

In Sections 11 and 12 of the Introduction Berkeley develops a second line of argument against the abstractionists, one that presupposes the principle of parsimony (Ockham's Razor). He argues that one can give an adequate explanation of the phenomenon of linguistic meaning without introducing the category of abstract ideas and, consequently, there is no good theoretical reason to posit that category of entities.

In Section 11 Berkeley explores the rationale that 'inclines men of speculation to embrace an opinion, so remote from common sense as [the doctrine of abstract ideas] seems to be' (Intro., 11). In doing this, he introduces two claims that are common to the abstractionists: (1) abstract ideas or intelligible forms provide the meanings of words;[73] and (2) the ability to form abstract ideas or to use general words is a characteristic that distinguishes human beings from the lower animals.[74] Focusing on passages from Book 2, Chapter 11, Sections 10 and 11 of Locke's *Essay*, Berkeley begins by attacking the contention that the ability to form abstract ideas is what distinguishes human beings from the lower animals. Berkeley wrote:

> I readily agree with this learned author, that the faculties of brutes can by no means attain to *abstraction.* But then if this be made the distinguishing property of that sort of animals, I fear a

great many of those who pass for men must be reckoned into their number. The reason that is here assigned why we have no grounds to think brutes have abstract general ideas, is that we observe in them no use or words or any other general signs; which is built on this assumption, to wit, that the making use of words, implies the having general ideas. From which it follows, that men who use language are able to abstract or generalize their ideas. That this is the sense and arguing of the author will further appear by his answering the question he in another place puts. 'Since all things that exist are only particulars, how come we by general terms?' *His answer is*, 'Words become general by being made the signs of general ideas.' *Essay on Human Understanding B.3. C.3. Sect. 6.* (Intro., 11)

As Berkeley indicates, Locke accepted the general principle that a being uses general words or signs if and only if that being can frame abstract general ideas, and he seems to have accepted this principle uncritically, that is, Locke and the other abstractionists simply assumed that it is possible for the mind to engage in qualitative abstraction.[75] Given this principle together with the fact that the lower animals (apparently) do not use general words, it follows that the lower animals do not frame abstract ideas and Locke suggests, it is this that distinguishes them from human beings. Given the introspective report given in Section 10, Berkeley could claim that *he*, in fact, was unable to conceive of simple or complex qualities in abstraction from the objects of which they are qualities and, given the assumptions that he is a human being and that there is a great deal of similarity in the psychological make-up of human beings, he has good evidence that there are many language-users who cannot frame abstract ideas. Hence, it is implausible to use the ability to frame abstract ideas as a standard for distinguishing humans from the lower animals.

Although Berkeley first attacked the tenet that human beings are to be distinguished from the lower animals on the basis of their ability to engage in abstraction, his attack on the abstractionists' semantic theory is of greater philosophical interest. Contrary to the abstractionists, Berkeley claimed that a general word signifies many particular (determinate) ideas, rather than an abstract general (determinable) idea. As he wrote:

But it seems that a word becomes general by being made a sign, not of an abstract general idea but, of several particular ideas, any one of which it indifferently suggests to the mind. For example, when it is said *the change of motion is proportional to the impressed force*, or that *whatever has extension is divisible*; these propositions are to be understood of motion and extension in general, and nevertheless it will not follow that they suggest to my thoughts an idea of motion without a body moved, or any determinate direction and velocity, or that I must conceive an abstract general idea of extension, which is neither line, surface nor solid, neither great nor small, black, white, nor red, nor of any other determinate colour. It is only implied that whatever motion I consider, whether it be swift or slow, perpendicular, horizontal or oblique, or in whatever object, the axiom concerning it holds equally true. As does the other of every particular extension, it matters not whether line, surface, or solid, whether of this or that magnitude or figure. (Intro., 11; cf. Intro., 12, 15, 18; *Works* 2:127 and 129; *A*, VII, 6, 334-5)

Berkeley held that general words denote each of the several particular objects in the extension of a term, not an abstract general idea which 'contains' all the properties that are common to things of a particular kind. To put it differently, while the abstractionists proposed an intensional theory of meaning, Berkeley proposed a purely extensional theory. What I hope to show is that in proposing an alternative to the intensional theory of the abstractionists, Berkeley's intent was to show that an extensional theory of meaning is theoretically simpler than that of the abstractionists, and, given the principle of parsimony, it should be accepted rather than that of the abstractionists. To understand this, we should compare the abstractionists' semantic theory with Berkeley's.

There are several similarities between Berkeley's semantic theory and that of the abstractionists. Both held that language is a conventional sign system. Words do not *naturally* have meanings. Rather, the meaning of a word in a language is a matter of social convention, and that meaning is introduced into the world on the basis of the mind's mapping of words onto ideas or objects.[76] They argued that mental entities are the primary denotata of words (that which is signified by words), although they disagreed regarding the nature of the mental entities denoted by general terms. The abstractionists maintained that general words denote abstract general ideas (in the case of the scholastics, intelligible forms).

Berkeley held that a general term denotes each of the entities of a particular kind, whether these entities be ideas (sensible entities), minds, actions of minds, or relations.

Consider first the claims of the abstractionists. A general term denotes a general abstract idea. The mind *constructs* an abstract idea by noticing the similarities among (determinate) particular ideas and includes in its abstract idea all and only those qualities that are common to those particulars. Abstract ideas, then, are entities of a kind that is distinct from that of determinate particular ideas. There is a relation of signification between a word and an abstract idea, and it is on the basis of this relation of signification that a word *represents* an abstract idea. There is a relation of resemblance between an abstract idea and all the determinate particulars of a certain kind, and it is on the basis of this relation of resemblance that an abstract idea *represents* all the determinate ideas of a particular kind.[77]

As we have already seen, Berkeley argued that it is impossible to conceive of an abstract idea. In proposing an alternative account of meaning, however, his point seems to be different. If there are abstract ideas as well as determinate particular ideas, then there must be ideas of two fundamentally different kinds. But if one is to posit the existence of abstract ideas, one must have a theoretically sound reason to do so. The reason given by the abstractionists — to provide the meaning of general terms — is inadequate. Since they grant that one must be able to perceive the resemblances among particulars to construct an abstract idea, it is theoretically simpler to suggest that a general word denotes the several things that resemble one another rather than to introduce a distinct kind of idea that is the denotation of a general term, that is, it is theoretically simpler to contend that meaning is extensional rather than intensional. Thus, if an extensional theory of meaning is adequate, the principle of parsimony demands that one accepts an extensional theory rather than an intensional theory of meaning, and there is, therefore, no basis for introducing abstract ideas into one's ontology.[78]

Someone might object that there is a problem with my interpretation of Section 11, that objection being that at no point in his discussion does Berkeley appeal directly to the principle of parsimony. There are, however, two reasons to believe that Berkeley presupposed this principle in his discussion. First, Berkeley's discussion is apparently intended to provide a criticism of the doctrine of abstract ideas. The abstractionists posited the existence of that kind of entity to explain how general terms could be meaningful. In attacking the abstractionists' theory of meaning, Berkeley is attacking the grounds upon which the abstractionists posit the existence of abstract ideas. His contention that it is possible to explain linguistic meaning without positing abstract ideas shows that there is no good reason to believe that there are abstract ideas, and therefore, in accordance with the principle of parsimony, one ought not posit their existence. If this was not his intent in Sections 11 and 12, it is difficult to understand why he placed this discussion where he did, for, as we have seen, in Section 10 he argues that it is impossible to form an abstract idea, and, as we shall see shortly, in Section 13 he argues that abstract ideas cannot exist. Hence, I think it reasonable to take the principle of parsimony to be a tacit premise in Berkeley's argument.

Second, the theory of meaning posed by the abstractionists is analogous to the representative theory of perception. Just as the representative theory holds that one perceives external objects only through the mediation of an idea or sense datum, so the abstractionists' theory of linguistic meaning holds that general words signify determinate particular objects only through the mediation of an abstract idea. Now it is quite clear that one of the grounds upon which Berkeley rejected the representative theory of perception was that positing the existence of external objects does not explain how perception is possible. Notice what he wrote in Section 19 of the *Principles*: 'for though we give the materialists their external bodies, they by their own confession are never the nearer knowing how our ideas are produced: since they own themselves unable to comprehend in what manner body can act upon spirit, or how it is possible it should imprint any idea in the mind' (*PHK*, 19). Since positing the existence of material objects fulfills no explanatory purpose, there is no reason to posit the existence of such objects. Indeed, in Section 20 he invites his reader to consider the possibility that 'an intelligence, without the help of external bodies, [is] affected with the same train of sensations or ideas that you are, imprinted in the same order and with like vividness in his mind' (*PHK*, 20), and he argued that since such a one would have exactly the same grounds for believing in the existence of external objects (material substance) as those philosophers who claim that such objects exist, there is no reason to posit the existence of such objects (cf. *DHP* II, 218). This criticism of the representative theory of perception and the doctrine of material substance clearly presupposes the principle of parsimony.[79] Now, since the representative theory of perception is analogous to the abstractionists' theory of meaning and since this criticism of representationalism is analogous to the criticism of the doctrine of abstraction in Section 11 of the Introduction, the fact that the principle of parsimony is implicit in his critique of representationalism makes it reasonable to assume that it is also implicit in his critique of abstraction.[80]

Introduction, Section 13

In Section 13 Berkeley developed his fourth criticism of the doctrine of abstract ideas, a criticism that is intended to show that in so far as an abstract idea is composed of inconsistent qualities, it is impossible. In his argument, he takes the description of an abstract idea of a triangle that Locke presented in Book 4, Chapter 7, Section 9 of the *Essay* as a paradigmatic description of an abstract idea. Quoting that passage at length, Berkeley added the emphasis to the words 'all and none' and 'inconsistent' in the following two sentences:

> For example, does it not require some pains and skill to form the general idea of a triangle (which is yet none of the most abstract comprehensive and difficult) for it must be neither oblique nor rectangle, neither equilateral, equicrural, nor scalenon, but *all and none* of these at once. In effect, it is something imperfect that cannot exist, an idea wherein some parts of several different and *inconsistent* ideas are put together. (Intro., 13).

He then asked his reader to try to form such an idea:

> If any man has the faculty of framing in his mind such an idea of a triangle as is here described, it is in vain to pretend to dispute him out of it, nor would I go about it. All I desire is, that the reader would fully and certainly inform himself whether he has such an idea or no. And this, methinks, can be no hard task for any one to perform. What more easy than for any one to look a little into his own thoughts, and there try whether he has, or can attain to have, an idea that shall correspond with the description

that is here given of the general idea of a triangle, which is, *neither oblique, nor rectangle, or equilateral, equicrural, nor scalenon, but all and none of these at once?* (Intro., 13)

Although Berkeley called for his reader to introspect and thereby determine whether or not he is capable of forming such an idea of a triangle, this is little more than a rhetorical flourish. Since virtually all Berkeley's readers would grant that inconsistencies cannot be conceived and contradictory things cannot exist,[81] Locke's description of the abstract idea of a triangle should be taken to indicate that one could not conceive of such a triangle and that, even as an idea, nothing corresponding to the description could exist.[82] Although Berkeley's emphasis on the inconsistency of the putative abstract idea of a triangle make it clear that this was his point in considering the passage, in the parallel passage in the *New Theory of Vision* he left no doubt that his objective was to show that in so far as any alleged abstract ideas are composed of inconsistent properties, they are inconceivable and can have no ontological status. There he argued that Locke himself was committed to the inconceivability of his abstract idea of a triangle (that no such idea could exist). After quoting part of *Essay* 4.7.9, Berkeley wrote:

> That author acknowledges it does 'require some pains and skill to form this general idea of a triangle' (*Ibid.*) But, had he called to mind what he says in another place, to wit, 'that ideas of mixed modes wherein any inconsistent ideas are put together cannot so much as exist in the mind, i.e., be conceived (*vide* Bk. III. chap. 10, sec. 33, *ibid.*) — I say, had this occurred to his thoughts, it is not improbable he would have owned it above all the pains and skill he was master of, to form the above-mentioned idea of a triangle, which is made up of manifest staring contradictions. (*NTV*, 125)

Since Locke himself held that inconsistencies are inconceivable, it follows that in so far as an abstract idea is compounded of inconsistent properties, it cannot be conceived (it cannot exist in the mind). Hence, in so far as Locke's description of the abstract idea of a triangle in Book 4, Chapter 7, Section 9 of the *Essay* is a paradigmatic description of an abstract idea, it follows that no such ideas can exist.

It is fairly clear that Berkeley himself considered this his strongest argument against the theory of abstraction and that he believed it to be such throughout his philosophical career. In the *Philosophical Commentaries* he had indicated that the triangle passage from Locke's *Essay* would provide the 'killing blow' against the abstractionists (*PC*, 687). In questioning the need of abstract ideas for communication in Section 14 of the Introduction, he again referred to the alleged need to form an idea composed of inconsistent qualities. There he asked:

> Is it not a hard thing to imagine, that a couple of children cannot prate together, of their sugar-plumbs and rattles and the rest of their little trinkets, till they have first tacked together *numberless inconsistencies* [emphasis added], and so framed in their minds *abstract general ideas*, and annexed them to every common name they make use of? (Intro., 14; cf. Intro., 16)

Again, his point is that in so far as the alleged abstract idea is composed of inconsistent qualities, it is impossible and cannot be conceived. Also, it is fairly clear that he considered this to be his strongest criticism of the doctrine of abstraction throughout his philosophical career, for even in *Siris*, his last work, he described how 'some moderns understand abstraction' as 'an abstract idea compounded of inconsistencies, and prescinded from all real things' (*S*, 323).

It is far from clear, however, that Locke's celebrated triangle passage states his considered opinion on the formation of an abstract idea of a triangle or that any abstractionist held that abstract ideas are composed of inconsistent qualities. When explicitly discussing abstract ideas — something Locke was *not* doing in the fourth book of the *Essay* — Locke provided a different and more plausible account of one's abstract idea of a triangle. There he wrote:

> Thus a Figure including a Space between three Lines, is the real, as well as nominal *Essence* of a Triangle; it being not only the abstract *Idea* to which the general name is annexed, but the very *Essentia*, or Being, of the thing itself, that Foundation from which all its Properties flow, and to which they are all inseparably annexed.[83]

Now if this passage reflects Locke's considered opinion on the formation of an abstract idea of a triangle, it does not require that one explicitly include inconsistent properties in one's abstract idea of a triangle. Indeed, since this might be construed as attending to the general shape of a particular object to the exclusion of all its other properties, it might be consistent with Berkeley's own views on the possibility of selective attention (cf. Intro., 16). None the less, even if his 'killing blow' falls short of its mark, we have seen that this was but one of four distinct types of criticism that Berkeley directed against the doctrine of abstraction in the Introduction to the *Principles*.

An Argument in the Third Edition of the *Alciphron*

So far, we have considered the arguments against abstraction Berkeley developed in the Introduction to the *Principles*. In three of the four arguments, Berkeley appealed to principles accepted by many of the abstractionists and argued that on the basis of those principles either one cannot abstract or there is no good reason to claim that there are abstract ideas. In Sections 10 and 13 of the Introduction, Berkeley argued that because the object allegedly conceived in an abstract idea is something that could not possibly exist as conceived, the principle that whatever is impossible cannot be conceived entails that such objects cannot be conceived. In Sections 11 and 12 he appealed to the principle of parsimony to show that there are no good grounds for positing the existence of abstract ideas as the meanings of sortal terms.

In the third edition of the *Alciphron*, Berkeley developed an additional argument against abstract ideas. This argument, unlike the other arguments, is based upon a principle that is peculiar to Berkeley — the principle that ideas are passive and cannot represent active beings. There Berkeley wrote:

> ***Euphranor.*** Pray tell me, Alciphron, is not an idea altogether inactive?
> ***Alciphron.*** It is.
> ***Euphranor.*** An agent therefore, an active mind or spirit, cannot be an idea, or like an idea. Whence it should seem to follow that those words which denote an active principle, soul, or spirit do not, in a strict and proper sense, stand for ideas. And yet they are not insignificant neither; since I

understand what is signified by the term *I*, or *myself*, or know what it means, although it be no idea, nor like an idea, but that which thinks, and wills, and apprehends ideas, and operates about them. Certainly it must be allowed that we have some notion that we understand, or know what is meant by, the terms *myself, will, memory, love, hate*, and so forth; although, to speak exactly, these words do not suggest so many distinct ideas.

Alciphron. What would you infer from this?

Euphranor. What hath been inferred already — that words may be significant, although they do not stand for ideas. The contrary whereof having been presumed seems to have produced the doctrine of abstract ideas.

(*A*, VII, 5)

If this argument is sound, it shows that the theory of abstract ideas is too narrow to provide the foundation for an adequate semantic theory. Given the principles that ideas are passive and no passive entity can represent an active entity, it follows that one can have no ideas of minds and their operations. Hence, one can have no abstract ideas of minds and their operations. But if it is presumed that having an abstract idea of a thing of a certain kind is a necessary condition for the meaningful use of sortal terms, this entails that one cannot use terms such as 'mind', 'loving', and 'hating' meaningfully. But one can use such terms meaningfully. Hence, having an abstract idea is not a necessary condition for the meaningful use of sortal terms.

This is a fairly weak criticism of the doctrine of abstract ideas, for it rests upon principles peculiar to Berkeley. Berkeleian ideas are nothing but ideas of sensible qualities and the 'feelings' peculiar to the several passions (cf. *PHK*, 1). Only spirits, not ideas, can be causes (*PHK*, 25-26), and given Berkeley's likeness principle, it follows that no idea can be like (resemble) and thereby represent something that is active. Had earlier philosophers accepted these principles, Berkeley's argument would have had some force against the doctrine of abstract ideas, but it is clear that these principles were not generally accepted by earlier philosophers. Although questions concerning one's ideas of substance *qua* substratum might seem to pose problems to proponents of the way of ideas, these philosophers did not deem such problems insuperable. Locke, for example, drew a distinction between positive and relative ideas. He took positive ideas to be ideas of the constitutive properties of things of a kind — they are similar to Berkeleian ideas and might reasonably be deemed mental images. Relative items, on the other hand, are ideas that will allow one to single out a particular object or kind of object, even though they will not allow one to claim knowledge of the constitutive properties of an object of that kind. Relative ideas are *not* mental images and they do not represent by resemblance.[84] Given the distinction between positive and relative ideas, Berkeley's argument in the *Alciphron* can carry little weight against the abstractionists. While it might show that one cannot have *positive* abstract ideas of minds and operations of minds — something the proponents of the way of ideas were willing to grant — it does not even address the question of relative ideas of such objects. Hence, the argument is inadequate.

Berkeley, Abstract Ideas, and Mental Images

Although the argument from the *Alciphron* would seem to require that one construe an abstract idea as a mental image, the same cannot be said for the arguments in the Introduction to the *Principles*. In the Introduction, the strongest grounds for claiming that Berkeley construes an abstract idea as a mental image might be drawn from his argument from introspection in Section 10 and, perhaps, his request that his reader introspect at the end of Section 13. But in neither of these sections does his case rest primarily upon an argument from introspection. His strongest argument in Section 10, the argument which I suggested is compressed into a single sentence, rests upon two principles generally accepted by the abstractionists: (1) that impossible states of affairs are inconceivable; and (2) that it is impossible for qualities of objects to exist in isolation from the objects of which they are qualities (Intro., 7). The principle that inconsistent entities are impossible and therefore inconceivable seems to be at the heart of the criticisms Berkeley raises in Section 13, and there is, therefore, no reason to construe the term 'idea' in that section as referring to a mental image. Finally, the argument based upon the principle of parsimony in Section 11 and 12 is independent of any specific construal of the term 'idea'.[85]

Nor should one find this surprising. Berkeley did not introduce his technical sense of the term 'idea' prior to the first section of the body of the *Principles*, and although Berkeley had introduced a definition of the word 'idea' prior to stating his arguments against abstraction in the *New Theory of Vision*, his definition there is at least as broad as Locke's.[86] Thus, unless it were claimed that all Lockean ideas are mental images,[87] there would be no grounds for attributing such an account to Berkeley.

None the less, Berkeley's arguments in Sections 11 and 12 of the Introduction do require that abstract ideas be understood as existents (or, at least, subsistents) of a kind distinct from that of determinate particular ideas. While such a view is clearly found in the scholastic doctrine of intelligible forms, if it could be shown that neither Locke nor the Cartesians took 'abstract ideas' to be different in kind from determinate particular ideas, Berkeley's arguments in those sections would be inconclusive. The argument implicit in Section 10, however, would still be sufficient to show that, on their own principles, the abstractionists could not consistently claim that it is possible to engage in abstraction.

Notes

1. Many commentators on Berkeley's critique of abstract ideas have proceeded as if his sole objective was to refute Locke's version of that doctrine. Cf. Frederick Copleston, *Modern Philosophy: The British Philosophers: Berkeley to Hume*, vol. 5, pt. 2 of his *A History of Philosophy* (Doubleday Image Books, New York, 1964), pp. 22-5; J.O. Urmson, *Berkeley*, Past Masters Series (Clarendon Press, Oxford, 1982), pp. 25-31; G.J. Warnock, *Berkeley*, Pelican Philosophy Series (Pelican Books, Melbourne 1953), pp. 61ff. A notable exception to this tendency is Julius R. Weinberg's 'The Nominalism of Berkeley and Hume', in his *Abstraction, Relation, and Induction: Three Essays in the History of Thought* (The University of Wisconsin Press, Madison, 1965), pp. 3-32.

2. This argument is also found in the body of the *Principles* and in the *Dialogues*, but in neither of those works is it set forth as a criticism of the doctrine of abstract ideas.

3. One should notice that the doctrine of abstraction did not simply die out after the criticisms of Berkeley and Hume. One finds a doctrine that is in many respects similar to that of John Locke in the writings of Thomas Reid in *Essays on the Intellectual Powers of Man*, Baruch Brody (ed.) (M.I.T. Press, Cambridge 1969), pp. 463-531). On the similarities between Reid's doctrine and Locke's, see Phillip D. Cummins, 'Reid on Abstract General Ideas', in Stephen F. Barker and Tom L. Beauchamp (eds), *Thomas Reid: Critical Interpretations* (Philosophical Monographs, Philadelphia, 1976), pp. 62-76.

4. John Locke, *Essay concerning Human Understanding* (ed. P.H. Nidditch) (Clarendon Press, Oxford, 1975), Book 2, Chapter II, Section 9, p. 159.

5. J.L. Mackie, *Problems from Locke* (Clarendon Press, Oxford, 1976), pp. 109-12; Urmson, *Berkeley*, pp. 25-31.

6. Locke, *Essay*, 1.1.8.
7. As we shall see, one of the grounds upon which Berkeley's critique of the doctrine of abstraction has been criticized is that it allegedly construes all ideas as images.
8. Jonathan Bennett, *Locke, Berkeley, Hume: Central Themes* (Clarendon Press, Oxford, 1971), p. 48.
9. Locke, *Essay*, 3.3.1, p. 6.
10. My division of abstraction into only three levels is, of course, somewhat arbitrary and only approximates the process. There might be intermediate levels of abstraction between what I have called first-order and second-order abstraction, as well as between second-order and third-order abstraction. For example, one might form abstract ideas of a general shade of a color, e.g., scarlet, as well as an abstract idea of a general shade of color that is an intermediate between, e.g., redness and color. None the less, this three-fold division of orders of abstraction provides a convenient means for discussing the process Locke describes.
11. Given Locke's broad notion of an idea as whatever the mind attends to in thinking (*Essay* 1.1.8), there is no systematic reason why one need construe a Lockean abstract idea as a mental image. Whether or not there are good reasons to suggest that his abstract ideas should be construed as mental images is an issue I shall leave for Locke scholars to debate.
12. Locke, *Essay*, 3.6.2.
13. Cf. Locke, *Essay*, 3.6.5. Locke makes the same general claim regarding the essence of mixed modes (*Essay*, 3.5.7), although since a mixed mode is strictly a mental construct, the nominal/real essence distinction collapses with respect to mixed modes (*Essay*, 3.5.3-6).
14. See Locke, *Essay*, 2.8.8-26 on the primary/secondary qualities distinction, where Locke argues that the primary qualities are the constitutive properties of body, Cf. *Essay*, 3.6.5.
15. Cf. Locke, *Essay*, 4.6.9.
16. Locke, *Essay*, 3.3.8; cf. Berkeley, Intro. 9.
17. Aristotle, *Metaphysics* A. 2, 982^a, 23-5 (trans. W.D. Ross), in Richard McKeon (ed.), *The Basic Works of Aristotle*, The Random House Lifetime Library (Random House, New York, 1941), p. 691.
18. Aristotle, *Metaphysics*, K. 3, 1061^a, 29-1061^b, 4, *Basic Works of Aristotle*, p. 855.
19. Cf. Maurice de Wulf, *An Introduction to Scholastic Philosophy, Medieval and Modern* (trans. P. Coffey) (Dover Publications, New York, 1956), p. 133; and Weinberg, 'The Nominalism of Berkeley and Hume', especially pp. 6-11.
20. Cf. *PC*, 779.
21. Thomas Aquinas, *Summa Theologica*, I.P., q.85, a. 1ad1, quoted in John Frederick Peifer, *The Concept in Thomism* (Bookman Associates Inc., 1952), p. 115.
22. Thomas Aquinas, *On the Truth of the Catholic Faith: Summa Contra Gentiles*, 5 vols. (trans. Anton C. Pegis) (Doubleday Image Books, New York, 1955-7), Book I, Chapter 65, para. 2, 1:213; cf. Locke, *Essay*, 3.3.1 and 6.
23. Thomas Aquinas, *Truth*, 3 vols. (trans. Robert W. Molligan) (Henry Regnery Company, Chicago, 1952-4), question 4, article 2, 1:176-81.
24. See Thomas Aquinas, *On Being and Essence* (trans. A.A. Maurer) (Toronto, 1949), ch. 3, p. 40.
25. See J.S. [John Sergeant], *Method to Science* (W. Redamayne, London, 1696), Book 1, Lesson 1, Section 6, page 2; cf. 1.1.10, p. 3.
26. For a more complete discussion of abstraction in the scholastic tradition, see Peifer, *The Concept in Thomism*, pp. 113-79.
27. Nicholas Malebranche, *The Search After Truth*, Book 3, part 2, Chapter 8, Section 1, in *The Search After Truth and Elucidations of the Search After Truth*

Abstraction   49

(trans. Thomas M. Lennon and Paul J. Olscamp) (The Ohio State University Press, Colombus, 1980), p. 242.

28. Letter from Descartes to Clerselier, 12 January 1646, in Elizabeth S. Haldane and G.R.T. Ross (eds), *The Philosophical Works of Descartes*, 2 vols. (Cambridge University Press, London, 1911): 2.134. Further references to *The Philosophical Works of Descartes* will be abbreviated HR.

29. Rene Descartes, *The Principles of Philosophy*, Part 1, Principle 53, HR, 1:240.

30. A difference, of course, is that both Locke and the scholastics maintain that in forming general concepts one abstracts from the phenomenally given, while Descartes held that these ideas are in some sense innate. For our purposes, this difference makes no difference. Cf. *Principles of Philosophy*, Part 1, Principle 59, HR, 1:242-3.

31. Malebranche, *The Search After Truth*, 3.2.8.2, p. 243.

32. Arnauld, *The Art of Thinking: Port-Royal Logic* (trans. James Dirkoff and Patricia James) (Bobbs-Merill, Library of Liberal Arts, Indianpolis, 1964), pp. 47-8. Cf. Arnauld's objections to Descartes' *Meditation*, HR, 2:82.

33. Arnauld, *The Art of Thinking*, p. 48.

34. Ibid.

35. Ibid. As we shall note below, Berkeley made a similar claim (Intro. 10).

36. Ibid.

37. Ibid., p. 48-9.

38. Ibid., p. 49.

39. Ibid., pp. 49-50.

40. Berkeley makes few references to Aquinas and the other medievals by name, although his discussion of analogical meaning in the Fourth Dialogue of the *Alciphron* indicates that at some point in his philosophical career he had become familiar with some of the works of Aquinas and Suarez (A. 4.20-1). Whether Berkeley had extensive first-hand knowledge of the works of the medievals at the time he wrote the *Principles* must be left as an open question.

41. Cf. Descartes, *Principles of Philosophy*, I,45, HR, 1:237.

42. Cf. Malebranche, *Search After Truth*, 1.18.1, pp. 79-80, and 4.11.2, pp. 316-7.

43. Cf. *PC*, 265, 288, 358, 388, 424, 686-686a, 800, and 818. See A.A. Luce, *Berkeley and Malebranche: A Study of the Origins of Berkeley's Thought* (Clarendon Press, Oxford, 1967).

44. I have been unable to find any place where Berkeley explicitly referred to Arnauld or the *Port-Royal Logic*, but as we shall see below, Berkeley's reference to the sense in which he grants that he *can* abstract as opposed to those in which he cannot, and his contention that those senses in which he cannot abstract are the 'proper acceptations of *abstraction*' (Intro., 10) parallel Arnauld's comments on the three kinds of abstraction.

45. The First Draft version of this section is substantially the same. See *Works* 2:122-3.

46. Locke, *Essay*, 2.2.2. Locke, however, did not consistently use the word 'notion' as a technical term. Cf. *Essay*, 3.3.7.

47. Cf. Robert Boyle, 'A Free Inquiry into the Vulgarly Received Notion of Nature', in M.A. Stewart (ed.), *Selected Philosophical Papers of Robert Boyle*, Philosophical Classics (University of Manchester Press, Manchester, 1979), pp. 183 and 184; Joseph Butler, *The Analogy of Religion*, E.C. Mossner (ed.) (Frederick Unger Publishing Co., New York, 1961), pp. 7, 33, and 226.

48. See Peifer, *The Concept in Thomism*, pp. 187-8. The vagueness of the term 'notion' together with its scholastic connotations might explain Berkeley's own hesitance to use the term. As Davis has noted, the first draft of Section 140 of the *Principles* read, 'In a large sense indeed, we may be said to have an idea or rather a

50   Abstraction

notion of *spirit*', but the phrase 'or rather a notion' was not included in the first edition of the *Principles*, but was added again to the second edition. See Davis, 'Berkeley's Doctrine of the Notion', *Review of Metaphysics*, 12 (1959), p. 381.

49. Locke, *Essay*, 3.3.9, Locke's emphasis.

50. Many commentators have taken Berkeley's statement of what is 'agreed on all hands' to mark a point of agreement between Berkeley and the abstractionists. (Cf. Willis Doney, 'Is Berkeley's a Cartesian Mind?' in *Berkeley: Critical and Interpretive Essays* (ed. Colin Murray Torbayne) (University of Minnesota Press, Minneapolis, 1982), pp. 278-9; Harry M. Bracken, *Berkeley* (St. Martin's Press, New York, 1974), p. 39.) We should observe that unless Berkeley's own views changed between the writing of the *Essay toward a New Theory of Vision* and the writing of the *Principles* — and there are good grounds for claiming that there was no significant change — it can only be the abstractionists who are 'agreed on all hands'. Notice that in the final sentence of the section Berkeley asserts that it is impossible for color to exist apart from extension, i.e., that everything that is colored is extended. It is quite clear that, at least in the geometrical sense of the term 'extension', Berkeley did not accept that position. In the *New Theory of Vision* Berkeley introduced the notion of a minimum visible. Claiming that 'There is ... a *minimum visible*, beyond which sense cannot perceive' (*NTV*, 53), he claimed that minimum visibles cannot be divided into parts (*NTV*, 80). Now the geometrical notion of extension holds that anything that is extended is divisible. Thus, if minimum visibles are indivisible, it follows that they are unextended. But since minimum visibles are immediate objects of sight (*NTV*, 81), and since only light and color are immediate objects of sight (*NTV*, 129; cf. *PHK*, 1), minimum visibles are color points (cf. *NTV*, 82). Hence, the position Berkeley advanced in the *New Theory of Vision* entails that there are ideas (existents) that are colored and *not* extended, and since he retained the notion of a minimum sensible in the *Principles* (*PHK*, 132), it follows that he was committed to the claim that there are things that are colored and unextended (cf. *PHK*. 127-32). Further, in Section 7 of the Introduction and, as we shall see, in Sections 8 and 9 as well, Berkeley used the term 'extension' as if it were univocal, i.e., as if there were only one kind of extension, the position assumed by the proponents of the primary/secondary qualities distinction. But again, in the *New Theory of Vision* Berkeley argued that the objects of sight and of touch are distinct, and that visual extension is different from tangible extension (*NTV*, 49, 129; cf. *PHK*, 1). Thus, given these differences between what Berkeley took to be 'agreed on all hands' and the positions for which he argued, one can only understand the agreement to which he alludes to obtain among the abstractionists.

51. Cf. Descartes, *Principles of Philosophy*, 1.56, HR, 1:241-2.

52. This is marked in the scholastics by the substance/accidents distinction. Cf. de Wulf, *An Introduction to Scholatic Philosophy*, pp. 100-1; Thomas Blundevile, *The Art of Logike* (London, 1599; reprint edition Theatrum Obis Terrarum, Ltd. and De Capo Press, Amsterdam and New York: 1969), p. 17; Rene Descartes, *The Principles of Philosophy*, 1.51 and 56, HR, 1:239-40 and 241-2; Arnauld, *The Art of Thinking*, p. 39; and John Locke, *A Letter to the Right Reverend Edward, Lord Bishop of Worcester*, in *The Works of John Locke*, 10 vols. (London, 1823; reprint edition Scientia Verlag Aalen, Darmstadt, West Germany: 1963), 4:21.

53. Cf. Arnauld, *The Art of Thinking*, pp. 49-50; but see also Descartes, *Principles of Philosophy* Part 1, Section 61, HR, 1:244-5.

54. Aristotle, *Metaphysics* K, 1060^a29-1060^b4, *Basic Works of Aristotle*, p. 855.

55. Aristotle, *De Anima*, Bk. 2, Ch. 7 431^b16-17 (trans. J.A. Smith), in *Basic Works of Aristotle*, p. 595.

56. Aristotle, *Physics*, Bk. 1, Ch. 4, 188^a5-12 (trans. R.P. Hardie and R.K.

Gaye) in *The Basic Works of Aristotle*, p. 226.

57. Locke, *Essay*, 2.23.6-7.

58. Cf. Locke, *Essay*, 2.8.9, pp. 124-35; Robert Boyle, 'The Origin of Forms and Qualities According to the Corpuscular Philosophy', in *Selected Philosophical Papers of Robert Boyle*, pp. 18-30.

59. Cf. Locke, *Essay*, 2.8.8-14; Boyle, 'The Origin of Forms and Qualities', pp. 30-2.

60. Cf. Locke, *Essay*, 3.3.7-9 to Section 9 of Berkeley's Introduction to see exactly how Lockean Berkeley's discussion is.

61. The phrase is Berkeley's, Intro., 10. Cf., Arnauld, *The Art of Thinking*, pp. 48-9.

62. At least they are as qualitatively complex as those things one generally perceives on the basis of a particular sense. In Berkeley's more technical sense of 'real thing', there is a lawful relationship between the ideas of a particular sense and among the ideas of the several senses, and one need not assume that the qualitative complexity introduced by the several senses need be included in an idea of the imagination (cf. *PHK*, 30, 33).

63. I am not the first to suggest that this argument is implicit in Section 10 of the Introduction to the *Principles* (cf. Weinberg, 'The Nominalism of Berkeley and Hume', pp. 17-18, and Kenneth W. Winkler, 'Berkeley on Abstract Ideas', *Archiv für Geschichte der Philosophie*, 63 (1983), pp. 63-80). My interpretation differs from that of Weinberg and Winkler, however, in so far as (1) they base their account primarily upon Section 13 of the Introduction and several other works; and (2) they contend that Berkeley's rejection of the doctrine of abstract ideas rests upon the contention that abstract ideas are inconsistent and, therefore, impossible. I shall show that the argument in Section 10 demonstrates that there are latent inconsistencies in the positions accepted by the abstractionists themselves.

64. Aquinas, *Summa Theologica*, I, Q. 25, Art. 3, Reply, in Auton C. Pegis (ed.), *Introduction to St. Thomas Aquinas* (Modern Library, New York, 1948), p. 231.

65. Cf. J.S. [John Sergeant], *Solid Philosophy Asserted, Against the Fancies of the Ideists: Or, The Method to Science Farther Illustrated* (Printed for Roger Clevil, London, 1697), p. 163.

66. Cf. Locke, *Essay*, 3.10.33.

67. Descartes, *Principles of Philosophy*, Part I, Section 60, *The Philosophical Works of Descartes*, 1:243; cf. Rene Descartes, *Philosophical Letters* (ed. and trans. Anthony Kenny) (University of Minnesota Press, Minneapolis, 1970), pp. 90-1. The perceptive reader will notice that is it not properly a *conceivability* criterion that Descartes advanced, rather, it is a *conceiving* criterion, i.e., it is a criterion of possibility that is based upon what one actually (clearly and distinctly) conceives. Nonetheless, since it follows from one's claim to actually conceive that x is Φ that it is conceivable that x is Φ, we need not concern ourselves with this difference.

68. Arnauld, *The Art of Thinking*, p. 323.

69. Thomas Reid, *Essays on the Intellectual Powers of Man*, pp. 430-1. Reid indicates that many eighteenth-century philosophers accepted a stronger version of the principle, viz., a version that replaces the conditional in the statement above with a biconditional, and some commentators have suggested that Berkeley himself accepted this stronger version of the principle (cf. Kenneth Winkler, 'Editor's Introduction, *A Treatise Conceiving the Principles of Human Knowledge* (Hackett edition), p. xvi; Willis Doney, 'Is Berkeley's a Cartesian Mind?' pp. 275-6; Willis Doney, 'Berkeley's Argument Against Abstract Ideas', in Peter A. French, Theodore E. Vehling, Jr., and Howard K. Wettstein (eds), *Midwest Studies in Philosophy VIII, 1983: Contemporary Perspectives on the History of Philosophy*, pp. 295-308). I am unconvinced that an inconceivability criterion plays any role in

Berkeley's construction of an ontological inventory, and I shall discuss my reasons why in Chapter 2.

70. Cf. J.L. Mackie, *Problems from Locke* (Clarendon Press, Oxford, 1976), pp. 107-12; Winkler, 'Berkeley on Abstract Ideas', pp. 74-5; and C.C.W. Taylor, 'Berkeley's Theory of Abstract Ideas', *Philosophical Quarterly*, 28 (1978), pp. 97-115.

71. Arnauld, *The Art of Thinking*, p. 40; cf. Descartes, *Principles of Philosophy*, Part I, Section 61, HR 1:244; Locke, *Essay*, 2.12.4; and Locke, *Letters to the Bishop of Worcester, Works of John Locke*, 4:21. Since this is clearest in Arnauld, I shall focus on his comments.

72. Arnauld, *The Art of Thinking*, p. 40; cf. p. 48.

73. Locke, *Essay*, 3.3.6; cf. Sergeant, *Solid Philosophy Asserted*, p. 33.

74. Locke, *Essay*, 2.11.10-11; crf. Rene Descartes, *Discourse on the Method of Rightly Conducting the Reason and Seeking the Truth in the Sciences*, Part 5, HR, 1:11; Sergeant, *Solid Philosophy Asserted*, p. 15.

75. This seems to be justified in the case of Locke. See Locke's initial discussion of abstraction in *Essay*, 2.11.9; cf. Arnauld's uncritical introduction of the notion of abstraction in *The Art of Thinking*, pp. 47ff.

76. Aristotle, *De Interpretatione*, 16^{a}1-29 (trans. E.M. Edghill) in *The Basic Works of Aristotle*, p. 40; Locke, *Essay*, 3.2.8; Berkeley, *NTV*, 143.

77. See Locke, *Essay* 3.2 and 3.3; cf. Malebranche, *The Search After Truth*, pp. 228-9.

78. In Section 12 of the Introduction Berkeley provides a few more details of his theories of meaning and of universal signs. Since this adds nothing further to his critique of the abstractionists than was provided in Section 11, we may safely ignore it.

79. Cf. James W. Cornman, 'A Reconstruction of Berkeley: Minds and Physical Objects as Theoretical Entities', *Ratio*, 13 (1971), pp. 76-87; and G.A. Johnston, *The Development of Berkeley's Philosophy* (Macmillan and Co., Limited, London, 1923), p. 39. The reader should also notice that throughout the *Second Dialogue* Berkeley considers various accounts of the nature of material substance and the theoretical role that material substance is supposed to play. He rejects each either on the ground that the notion of material substance is unclear or inconsistent, or on the ground that material substance will fulfill no theoretical purpose.

80. My interpretation of Section 11 presupposes that Berkeley assumed ideas, and therefore abstract ideas, to be entities. John W. Yolton has recently argued, however, that in neither Locke nor Arnauld are ideas to be construed as entities (see John W. Yolton, *Perceptual Acquaintance From Descartes to Reid* (University of Minnesota Press, Minneapolis 1984), especially pp. 61-6 and 88-103). While an examination of Yolton's extensive arguments is beyond the scope of this work, one point should be noted. Yolton maintains that Descartes, Arnauld and Locke took ideas to be perceptions or intentional objects, and he maintains that they assigned no ontological status to ideas (*Perceptual Acquaintance*, pp. 89 and 101). If Yolton is correct and my reconstruction of Berkeley's argument is correct, Berkeley's argument in Section 11 is unsuccessful. But Yolton's argument is questionable. Based primarily upon Locke's *An Examination of P. Malebranche's Opinion of Seeing All Things in God*, Yolton argues that Locke held that ideas are neither substances nor modes of substances (*Perceptual Acquaintance*, p. 93), but little follows from that. In particular, it does not follow that ideas are not at least *subsistents*, and if they are subsistents, Berkeley would still obtain a greater ontological economy by denying the need for more than one kind of subsistent idea.

81. Cf. Arnauld, *The Art of Thinking*, p. 323.

82. This point has already been noticed by E.J. Craig, 'Berkeley's Attack on

Abstract Ideas', *Philosophical Review*, 77 (1968), pp. 432-3; Weinberg, 'The Nominalism of Berkeley and Hume', p. 17; and Winkler, 'Berkeley on Abstract Ideas', 69-71.

83. Locke, *Essay*, 3.3.18.

84. See Locke, *Essay* 2.23.3 and John Locke, *Letter to the Bishop of Worcester*, *Works of John Locke*, 4:21-2. For a discussion of relative ideas in Locke, see Robert Ammerman, 'Our Knowledge of Substance according to Locke', *Theoria*, 31 (1965), pp. 1-8, and my 'Locke's Relative Ideas', *Theoria*, 47 (1981), pp. 142-59. As we shall see in Chapter 4, there are certain affinities between Locke's distinction between positive and relative ideas, and Berkeley's distinction between positive and relative notions.

85. Pitcher has recently argued that the entire case against abstract ideas rests upon Berkeley's alleged erroneous assumption that abstract ideas are mental images (George Pitcher, *Berkeley* (Routledge & Kegan Paul, London, 1977), pp. 62-90). But Pitcher has not recognized that there are four distinct arguments in the Introduction to the *Principles*. He conflates what I have called the enthymematic argument in Section 10 with the argument in Section 13 (*Berkeley*, pp. 66-71). Were one to deem this conflation legitimate *and* contend that even in the Introduction Berkeley held that ideas are nothing but mental images, then Pitcher is certainly correct in claiming that Berkeley's argument fails. But I see no reason why one need have so narrow an understanding of 'idea' in the Introduction, and I have argued at some length that it is reasonable to construe the enthymematic argument in Section 10 as distinct from the argument in Section 13. As I have reconstructed the arguments, both are based upon considerations of principles accepted by the abstractionists, and there is no need to construe abstract ideas as mental images. Of course, if I am correct, Berkeley's arguments have basically an *ad hominum* force, but certainly such arguments were needed if Berkeley's arguments were to have any persuasive force against the abstractionists.

86. Cf. Locke's definition of 'idea' in *Essay*, 1.1.8 with Berkeley's definition in *NTV*, 45.

87. Locke's distinction between positive and relative ideas tends to mitigate against any construal of all ideas as mental images (see Locke, *Essay*, 2.23.3, and his *Letter to the Bishop of Worcester*, *Works of John Locke*, 4:21-2). I have discussed this distinction in 'Locke's Relative Ideas'.

2 POSSIBILITY AND IMPOSSIBILITY

In the last chapter we examined Berkeley's criticism of the theory of abstraction. It was argued that Berkeley showed (1) that theories of abstraction are incompatible with both the traditional substance/mode distinction and with any version of the object/quality distinction that holds that qualities are necessarily related to objects; (2) that abstract ideas are not needed to provide the meanings of sortal terms; and (3) that, in so far as abstract ideas are composed of inconsistent qualities, they cannot even 'exist in the mind'. With his rejection of abstract ideas, Berkeley rejected the primacy of intensional (connotative) theories of meaning and, as we saw in examining his argument from parsimony, he suggested that a purely extensional (denotative) theory of meaning provides an adequate account of the meaning of general terms. In examining Berkeley's positive theory of meaning, I hope to show that he proposed an extension theory of meaning ranging over possible, as well as actual, objects. But if Berkeley included possible objects in the extension of a term, we must have a clear grasp of the distinctions between possible and actual (real) objects in Berkeley's ontology and of his criteria of possibility and impossibility. Hence, I shall examine these issues in this chapter and shall postpone a discussion of Berkeley's positive theory of meaning until the next chapter.

In examining Berkeley's criteria of possibility and impossibility, we must address two distinct but related questions. First, there is the question of the metaphysical criterion of possibility, that is, what characteristic distinguishes possible objects from impossible objects? Second, there is the question of the epistemological criterion of possibility, that is what grounds will justify one's claim to know that a certain kind of object is possible? We must also raise these questions with respect to impossibility. It is widely held that Berkeley's answer to one of the questions regarding the criterion of possibility was that he accepted a conceivability criterion of possibility, that is, he accepted, at least, the principle that if it is conceivable that there is an x that is Φ, then it is possible that there is an x that is Φ and, perhaps, the stronger principle that it is conceivable that there is an x that is Φ if and only if it is possible that there is an *x* that is Φ.¹ Sufficient care is seldom taken, however, to indicate whether Berkeley accepted a conceivability criterion as a metaphysical principle, an epistemological principle, or both; nor have commentators examined the several forms that the conceivability criterion might take. In this chapter, I shall begin by considering several general versions of the conceivability criterion of possibility as well as versions of its major competitor — the formal or describability criterion of possibility. Next, I shall examine Berkeley's distinction between possible and real (actual) objects. Third, I shall examine the question of Berkeley's metaphysical criteria of possibility and impossibility. Fourth, I shall examine the question of Berkeley's epistemological criteria of possibility and impossibility. Finally, I shall defend my account by examining the evidence for an alternative interpretation, this interpretation being the contention that Berkeley employed a biconditional form of a conceivability criterion of possibility in constructing his ontology. So let us begin by attempting to clearly state what a philosopher who accepts a conceivability criterion of possibility holds.

Criteria of Possibility and Impossibility

We should notice, first, that conceivability is a modal notion: to claim that it is conceivable that there is an *x* that is Φ is to claim that it is possible to conceive that there is *x* that is Φ.² Because both conceivability and possibility are modal notions, it is reasonable to employ the machinery of modal logic in attempting to explicate conceivability criteria of possibility. Although this will ultimate require the machinery of *quantified* modal logic, since it is only the quantified versions that can state what is involved in claiming that an object of a certain kind is conceivable or possible, we might reasonably begin with the propositional versions of the criterion. By considering the propositional versions of the conceivability criterion of possibility, we shall have a fairly straightforward basis for examining the principles that are entailed by both the conditional and the biconditional versions of the conceivability criterion and, since the entailment relations hold for the quantified versions as well, it will make our later discussions of the quantified versions of the criterion much clearer. It should be stressed that my concern in this section is, primarily, to state the several versions of the conceivability and describability criteria of possibility and to examine some of the propositions entailed by these criteria and, secondarily, to examine the plausibility of accepting some of these propositions as metaphysical or epistemological criteria of possibility. It will be only in the second and subsequent sections of this chapter that I shall examine the semantic issues necessary to provide an interpretation of these criteria and the question of which of them Berkeley accepted.

In its propositional form, where 'P' is a proposition and the issue is the possibility that P is true, the minimum claim made by the conceivability criterion of possibility is that if P is conceivable, then it is possible that P is true. In symbolic notation, where 'C' is a one-place conceiving operator and '$\Diamond$' is a logical possibility operator, this would be stated as follows:

(1) $\Diamond CP \rightarrow \Diamond P$

The conditional form of the conceivability criterion of possibility merely asserts that conceivability is a sufficient condition for possibility and, by transposition, it entails that if it is impossible that P is true, then the truth of P is inconceivable:

(2) $-\Diamond P \rightarrow -\Diamond CP$

A stronger version of the conceivability criterion of possibility holds that the conceivability of the truth of P is a necessary and a sufficient condition for the possibility of the truth of P, that is, it replaces the conditional in (1) with a biconditional. This criterion asserts:

(3) $\Diamond CP \leftrightarrow \Diamond P$

(3) is logically equivalent to:

(4) $(\Diamond CP \rightarrow \Diamond P) \,\&\, (\Diamond P \rightarrow \Diamond CP)$

that is, it is logically equivalent to the conjunction of (1) and the proposition that if it is possible that P is true, then it is conceivable that P is true, that is

(5) $\Diamond P \rightarrow \Diamond CP$

Thus, if anyone asserts (3) he is committed to accepting both (2) and the transposition of (5) that is,

(6) $-\Diamond CP \rightarrow -\Diamond P$

(6) asserts that if it is inconceivable that P is true, then it is impossible that P is true. (6) is the conditional form of the inconceivability criterion of impossibility in propositional modal logic. Although one might also assert a biconditional form of the inconceivability criterion of impossibility, namely,

(7) $-\Diamond CP \leftrightarrow -\Diamond P$

(7) is logically equivalent to (3) and, therefore, we need not give separate consideration to (7).

Given these considerations of the principles entailed by (1) and (3) we can now turn to the quantified versions of the principles. Since the issues with which the philosophers of the seventeenth and eighteenth centuries were concerned were the metaphysical issue of whether some *object* of a particular kind is possible and the epistemological issue whether one can know that some *object* of a particular kind is possible, it is clear we shall be concerned with the quantified versions of the conceivability criterion of possibility in attempting to discover which version or versions of the criterion Berkeley accepted. Further, in our abstract considerations of the conceivability criterion of possibility we shall focus on those forms corresponding to (1) and (3), and we shall provide separate considerations of the quantified versions of the inconceivability criterion of impossibility corresponding to (6). This procedure will allow us to more clearly see the issues that are involved in claiming that a philosopher accepted either of these.

In examining the quantified versions of the conceivability criterion of possibility, we should begin by considering what is implied in claiming that an x of kind Φ is possible. The notion of possibility is open to two interpretations: in claiming that it is possible that there is an x that is Φ, one might be claiming that it is possible that there is an x that is Φ, that is, $\Diamond(\exists x)\Phi x$ (*de dicto* possibility), or one might be claiming that there is an x which is possibly Φ, that is, $(\exists x)\Diamond\Phi x$ (*de re* possibility).[3] *De dicto* possibility does not commit one to the actual existence of an object that is Φ; *de re* possibility commits one to the actual existence of an object that is possibly Φ. Thus, with respect to the claim that it is possible that there is an x that is Φ, there are two possible interpretations of the quantified conceivability criterion of possibility. But the notion of conceivability also includes the notion of possibility. Hence, one must consider both *de dicto* conceivability or *de re* conceivability. One holds either that if it is possible that there is a y such that y conceives that there is an x that is Φ, then it is either *de dicto* or *de re* possible that there is an x that is Φ (*de dicto* conceivability), or one holds that if there is a y such that it is possible that y conceives that there is an x that is Φ, then it is *de dicto* or *de re* possible that there is an x that is Φ (*de re* conceivability). Thus, there are four possible interpretations of the uninstantiated form of the conditional quantified conceivability criterion of possibility. Where 'C' is a two-piece conceiving operator and '◊' is a logical possibility operator, the *de dicto* conceivability criterion of *de dicto* possibility asserts:

(8) $\Diamond(\exists y)Cy(\exists x)\Phi x \to \Diamond(\exists x)\Phi x$

The *de dicto* conceivability criterion of *de re* possibility asserts:

(9) $\Diamond(\exists y)Cy(\exists x)\Phi x \to (\exists x)\Diamond\Phi x$

The *de re* conceivability criterion of *de dicto* possibility asserts:

(10) $(\exists y)\Diamond Cy(\exists x)\Phi x \to \Diamond(\exists x)\Phi x$

Finally, the *de re* conceivability criterion of *de re* possibility asserts:

(11) $(\exists y)\Diamond Cy(\exists x)\Phi x \to (\exists x)\Diamond\Phi x$

Given these four formulations of the quantified conceivability criterion of possibility, we might ask whether any of these versions of the criterion could plausibly function as metaphysical or epistemological criteria of possibility.

If a metaphysical criterion of possibility is intended to mark off the realm of the possible and not to provide an analysis of the nature of possibility, any one of (8), (9), (10) or (11) might plausibly be proposed as a metaphysical criterion of possibility.

None of them, however, is a plausible candidate for an epistemological criterion of possibility. The epistemological issue is whether or not one can know that a particular kind of object is possible (in either sense). If one were to employ either a *de dicto* or a *de re* conceivability criterion of possibility, one question of what is possible would need to be resolved before the criterion could be employed: one would need to know either that it is possible that there is something that conceives that there is an x that is Φ (*de dicto* conceivability) or that there is something that possibly conceives that there is an x that is Φ (*de re* conceivability). But this is one of the issues that should be resolved by the criterion. It will not do simply to claim that the issue can be resolved on the basis of what one actually conceives, for although the fact that one conceives that there is an x that is Φ entails that it is conceivable that there is an x that is Φ in either sense of 'conceivable', the realm of the conceivable in either sense is not limited to what is actually conceived, let alone to what one particular person actually conceives. To put this differently, while actually conceiving that there is an x that is Φ entails that it is conceivable that there is an x that is Φ. The fact that one person does not or, as a matter of fact, cannot conceive that there is an x that is Φ does not entail that it is inconceivable that there is an x that is Φ. As an epistemological criterion of possibility, one could more reasonably employ something comparable to what Hume deemed an 'establish'd maxim in metaphysics', being '*That whatever the mind clearly conceives includes the idea of possible existence, or in other words, that nothing we imagine is absolutely impossible.*'[4] Notice that this is *not* a conceivability criterion, rather, it is what might be called a *conceiving* criterion of possibility. Although the notion of possibility would still be open to both *de dicto* and the *de re* interpretations, one does not confront a similar ambiguity in the antecedent of the criterion. Thus, the general form of the conceiving criterion of *de dicto* possibility would be represented as:

(12) $(\exists y)Cy(\exists x)\Phi x \rightarrow \Diamond(\exists x)\Phi x$

The general form of the conceiving criterion of *de re* possibility would be represented as:

(13) $(\exists y)Cy(\exists x)\Phi x \rightarrow (\exists x)\Diamond\Phi x$

On the basis of an instantiation of one of these criteria for y, namely, in the case in which one conceives that there is an x that is Φ, one could claim to know that it is possible that there is an x that is Φ in the relevant sense of 'possible'.

We shall see later that in attempting to decide which, if any, version(s) of the conceivability criterion of possibility or the conceiving criterion of possibility Berkeley accepted, it will be important to consider the transpositions of (8), (9), (10), (11), (12) and (13). Since we have already considered these transpositions for (1), this will not be difficult. The transposition of (8) is:

(14) $\quad -\Diamond(\exists x)\Phi x \rightarrow -\Diamond(\exists y)Cy(\exists x)\Phi x$

The transposition of (9) is:

(15) $\quad -(\exists x)\Diamond\Phi x \rightarrow -\Diamond(\exists y)Cy(\exists x)\Phi x$

The transposition of (10) is:

(16) $\quad -\Diamond(\exists x)\Phi x \rightarrow -(\exists y)\Diamond Cy(\exists x)\Phi x$

The transposition of (11) is:

(17) $\quad -(\exists x)\Diamond\Phi x \rightarrow -(\exists y)\Diamond Cy(\exists x)\Phi x$

The transposition of (12) is:

(18) $\quad -\Diamond(\exists x)\Phi \rightarrow -(\exists y)Cy(\exists x)\Phi x$

And the transposition of (13) is:

(19) $\quad -(\exists x)\Diamond\Phi x \rightarrow -(\exists y)Cy(\exists x)\Phi x$

Notice that (14), (15), (16) and (17) might be called impossibility criteria of inconceivability, while (18) and (19) might be called impossibility criteria of nonconceiving. In drawing these distinctions one should acknowledge that all four versions of the impossibility criteria of inconceivability make stronger claims than does either version of the impossibility criteria of nonconceiving. If one accepts the claim that there is an x that is Φ is either *de dicto* or *de re* inconceivable, one is committed to the claim that no actual thing

Possibility and Impossibility 61

conceives that there is an x that is Φ, however, if one accepts the claim that no actual thing conceives that there is an x that is Φ, one is not committed to the claim that there is an x that is Φ is either *de dicto* or *de re* inconceivable: the simple fact that no actual thing conceives that there is an x that is Φ entails neither that there is no actual thing that possibly conceives that there is an x that is Φ, nor that it is impossible that there is a thing that conceives that there is an x that is Φ.

Before turning to the various conditional forms of the inconceivability criteria of impossibility, we should mention that some persons would advance *biconditional forms* of the conceivability and conceiving criteria of possibility. These correspond exactly to (8) through (13), simply replacing the conditional with a biconditional. Thus, there are biconditional *de dicto* conceivability criteria of *de dicto* and *de re* possibility:

(20) $\Diamond(\exists y)Cy(\exists x)\Phi x \leftrightarrow \Diamond(\exists x)\Phi x$

(21) $\Diamond(\exists y)Cy(\exists x)\Phi x \leftrightarrow (\exists x)\Diamond \Phi x$

There are biconditional *de re* conceivability criteria of *de dicto* and *de re* possibility:

(22) $(\exists y)\Diamond Cy(\exists x)\Phi x \leftrightarrow \Diamond(\exists x)\Phi x$

(23) $(\exists y)\Diamond Cy(\exists x)\Phi x \leftrightarrow (\exists x)\Diamond \Phi x$

And there are biconditional conceiving criteria of *de dicto* and *de re* possibility:

(24) $(\exists y)Cy(\exists x)\Phi x \leftrightarrow \Diamond(\exists x)\Phi x$

(25) $(\exists y)Cy(\exists x)\Phi x \leftrightarrow (\exists x)\Diamond \Phi x$

Since the biconditional forms of the conceivability criteria of possibility entail conditional forms of the inconceivability criterion of impossibility, we should briefly examine these. The *de dicto/de re* distinctions apply to inconceivability and impossibility as well as conceivability and possibility, of course. Thus, there are four forms of the inconceivability criterion of impossibility. First, there is the *de dicto* inconceivability criterion of *de dicto* impossibility:

(26) $-\Diamond(\exists y)Cy(\exists x)\Phi x \to -\Diamond(\exists x)\Phi x$

Second, there is the *de dicto* inconceivability criterion of *de re* impossibility:

(27) $-\Diamond(\exists y)Cy(\exists x)\Phi x \to -(\exists x)\Diamond\Phi x$

Third, there is the *de re* inconceivability criterion of *de dicto* impossibility:

(28) $-(\exists y)\Diamond Cy(\exists x)\Phi x \to -\Diamond(\exists x)\Phi x$

And, finally, there is the *de re* inconceivability criterion of *de re* impossibility:

(29) $-(\exists y)\Diamond Cy(\exists x)\Phi x \to -(\exists x)\Diamond\Phi x$

Similarly, there is the nonconceiving criterion of *de dicto* impossibility:

(30) $-(\exists y)Cy(\exists x)\Phi x \to -\Diamond(\exists x)\Phi x$

and there is the nonconceiving criterion of *de re* impossibility:

(31) $-(\exists y)Cy(\exists x)\Phi x \to -(\exists x)\Diamond\Phi x$

Just as with the corresponding conceivability criteria of possibility, it might be reasonable to accept any version of the *de dicto* or the *de re* inconceivability criterion, that is, (26), (27), (28) or (29), as a metaphysical criterion of impossibility, but none is a plausible candidate for an epistemic criterion of impossibility. Given that the claims made in the antecedent are either that it is impossible that there is a *y* that conceives that there is an *x* that is Φ (*de dicto* inconceivability) or that there is not a *y* such that it is possible that *y* conceives that there is an *x* that is Φ (*de re* inconceivability), one of the epistemic questions one would want answered by the criterion must be taken as answered in order to apply the criterion, namely, whether it is *impossible* to conceive that there is an *x* that is Φ. Hence, if one is to claim any epistemic insight into the question of what kinds of objects are impossible on the basis of what is not conceived, one could claim nothing more than either (30) or (31).

But even (30) and (31) are too strong, for it is certainly at least a herculean task to establish that no one conceives that there is an x that is Φ. A *prima facie* more plausible epistemic criterion of impossibility based upon what one does not conceive might be an instantiation of (30) or (31), that is to say, one in which one claims that it is impossible that there is an x that is Φ because one does not conceive that there is an x that is Φ. Where 'i' represents the person applying the criterion, these would be:

(32) $-Ci(\exists x)\Phi x \rightarrow -\Diamond(\exists x)\Phi x$

and:

(33) $-Ci(\exists x)\Phi x \rightarrow -(\exists x)\Diamond\Phi x$

Presumably, one could know that one does not conceive that there is an x that is Φ on the basis of introspection.

But neither (32) nor (33) is a plausible epistemic criterion of impossibility, for, from the fact that I do not now and, perhaps, never have and never will conceive of mesons, it hardly follows that it is *impossible* that there are mesons. After all, some people claim to be able to conceive of mesons and there is good scientific evidence that mesons exist. If there is any plausible epistemic criterion of impossibility that is based upon the absence of conception, it must be an instantiation for y of a version of the inconceivability criterion of impossibility, that is, it must contend that it is impossible for me to conceive that there is an x that is Φ. One should notice that while the rules of quantified modal logic allow one to instantiate claims of *de re* possibility, they will not allow one to instantiate claims of *de dicto* possibility, since in the case of a *de dicto* claim there is no guarantee that there is an *actual* object in terms of which the formulae can be instantiated. Thus, there are only two instantiated versions of the inconceivability criterion of impossibility. There is, first, the instantiated *de re* inconceivability criterion of *de dicto* impossibility:

(34) $-\Diamond Ci(\exists x)\Phi x \rightarrow -\Diamond(\exists x)\Phi x$

Second, there is the instantiated *de re* inconceivability criterion of *de re* impossibility:

(35) $-\Diamond Ci(\exists x)\Phi x \rightarrow -(\exists x)\Diamond\Phi x$

But (34) and (35) will also prove to be inapplicable in practice, for there would never be sufficient introspective evidence to show that it is impossible for me to conceive that there is an x that is Φ. The fact that I do not presently conceive that there is an x that is Φ provides only weak inductive evidence that it is impossible for me to conceive that there is an x that is Φ. Indeed, even making a very serious attempt to conceive of that there is an x that is Φ and finding that, in fact, I consistently fail to do so provides nothing more than somewhat stronger inductive evidence that it is impossible for me to conceive that there is an x that is Φ. As I mentioned above, an epistemic criterion of impossibility is intended to provide grounds for the justificiation of the claim that a certain kind of object or state of affairs is impossible, and if one must know that it is *impossible to conceive* that there is an x that is Φ in order to justify the claim that it is impossible that there is an x that is Φ, that is, if one must know that a certain state of affairs is impossible in order to establish that another object or state of affairs is impossible, one of the questions to be decided by an inconceivability criterion of impossibility must already be settled if one is to apply the criterion.

Thus, it is implausible to take inconceivability to provide epistemic grounds for a claim of impossibility. None the less, one might advance (26), (27), (28), (29), (30) or (31), or some instantiation of (28), (29), (30) or (31) as a metaphysical principle. One might contend, for example, that if God cannot conceive that there is an x that is Φ, then it is *de dicto* or *de re* impossible that there is an x that is Φ, that is, one might accept:

(36) $-\Diamond Cg(\exists x)\Phi x \rightarrow -\Diamond(\exists x)\Phi x$

or:

(37) $-\Diamond Cg(\exists x)\Phi x \rightarrow -(\exists x)\Diamond\Phi x$

Or one might contend simply that if God does not conceive that there is an x that is Φ, then it is *de dicto* or *de re* impossible that x is Φ, that is, one might accept:

(38) $-Cg(\exists x)\Phi x \rightarrow -\Diamond(\exists x)\Phi x$

or:

(39) $-Cg(\exists x)\Phi x \to -(\exists x)\Diamond\Phi x$

But if any of these principles were advanced as something more than a matter of faith, one would need good theoretical reasons to accept it. However, as we shall see later, Berkeley seems to have accepted either (36) or (38) as a metaphysical criterion of impossibility.

So far we have seen that even though one might advance a conceivability criterion of possibility or an inconceivability criterion of impossibility as a metaphysical principle, there appear to be difficulties with the several versions of these criteria of possibility and of impossibility as epistemic criteria. These are, of course, not the only metaphysical and epistemological criteria one might advance. One might also base one's claims of the possibility or impossibility that there is an x that is Φ upon considerations of the consistency or inconsistency of a description or putative real definition of an x that is Φ, that is, questions of possibility and impossibility might be based upon formal considerations. The several versions of the describability criteria of possibility and impossibility correspond in form to the several versions of the conceivability criterion with this difference: while one can reasonably draw a distinction between *de dicto* and *de re* conceivability, in the case of describability one is limited to *de dicto* describability. The reason for this should be clear enough. A claim of *de dicto* describability asserts that it is possible that there is a consistent description of an x that is Φ, while a claim of *de re* describability would assert that there there is a possibly consistent description of an x that is Φ. Since descriptions either are consistent or they are not, it is questionable whether one can make sense of any talk of an actual description of an x that is Φ that is possibly (though perhaps not actually?) consistent. In so far as one can make sense of this claim, one's logical intuitions suggest that a description can be possibly consistent only if it is actually consistent and, consequently, *de re* describability criteria would be extensionally equivalent to what I shall call *describing* criteria, that is, criteria based upon actual consistent descriptions. Thus, we need not concern ourselves with considerations of *de re* describability.

There are four possible versions of the *de dicto* describability criterion of possibility. Where the expression '$Dy(\exists x)\Phi x$' reads as

'y is a consistent description of an x that is Φ', the conditional form of the *de dicto* describability criterion of *de dicto* possibility asserts:

(40) $\Diamond(\exists y)Dy(\exists x)\Phi x \rightarrow \Diamond(\exists x)\Phi x$

The conditional form of the *de dicto* describability criterion *de re* possibility asserts:

(41) $\Diamond(\exists y)Dy(\exists x)\Phi x \rightarrow (\exists x)\Diamond\Phi x$

The biconditional form of the *de dicto* describability criterion of *de dicto* possibility asserts:

(42) $\Diamond(\exists y)Dy(\exists x)\Phi x \leftrightarrow \Diamond(\exists x)\Phi x$

And the biconditional form of the *de dicto* describability criterion of *de re* possibility asserts:

(43) $\Diamond(\exists y)Dy(\exists x)\Phi x \leftrightarrow (\exists x)\Diamond\Phi x$

(42) and (43) entail *de dicto* indescribability criteria of impossibility:

(44) $-\Diamond(\exists y)Dy(\exists x)\Phi x \rightarrow -\Diamond(\exists x)\Phi x$

(45) $-\Diamond(\exists y)Dy(\exists x)\Phi x \rightarrow -(\exists x)\Diamond\Phi x$

Similarly, both (40) and (42) entail the following impossibility criteria of indescribability:

(46) $-\Diamond(\exists x)\Phi x \rightarrow -\Diamond(\exists y)Dy(\exists x)\Phi x$

And both (41) and (43) entail the following impossibility criterion of indescribability:

(47) $-(\exists x)\Diamond\Phi x \rightarrow -\Diamond(\exists y)Dy(\exists x)\Phi x$

One should notice that (40), (41), (42) and (43) are plausible as metaphysical principles, although, for basically the same reasons we considered in examining the corresponding versions of the conceivability criteria, they are not plausible epistemic criteria. Similarly, unless it is given that it is impossible that there is a consistent description of an x that is Φ, or it is given that it is *de dicto* or *de re* impossible that there is an x that is Φ, (44), (45), (46) and (47) could play no role in epistemic contexts. There are, however, describing correlates of the conceiving criteria that are plausible epistemic criteria of possibility and impossibility, and it is to these we shall now turn.

Although epistemic questions of possibility and impossibility are raised with respect to particular descriptions of an x that is Φ, the criteria remain general in form. In the conditional form, the describing criterion of *de dicto* possibility asserts:

(48) $(\exists y)Dy(\exists x)\Phi x \rightarrow \Diamond(\exists x)\Phi x$

The biconditional form of the describing criterion of *de dicto* possibility asserts:

(49) $(\exists y)Dy(\exists x)\Phi x \leftrightarrow \Diamond(\exists x)\Phi x$

The conditional form of the describing criterion of *de re* possibility asserts:

(50) $(\exists y)Dy(\exists x)\Phi x \rightarrow (\exists x)\Diamond\Phi x$

The biconditional form of the describing criterion of *de re* possibility asserts:

(51) $(\exists y)Dy(\exists x)\Phi x \leftrightarrow (\exists x)\Diamond\Phi x$

In practice, one would employ particular instances of (48), (49), (50), or (51) instantiating y in terms of a particular description of an x that is Φ. Similarly, what might be called, for lack of a better term, the nondescribing criterion of *de dicto* impossibility asserts:

(52) $-(\exists y)Dy(\exists x)\Phi x \rightarrow -\Diamond(\exists x)\Phi x$

(52), of course, is entailed by (49). Finally the nondescribing criterion of *de re* impossibility asserts:

(53) $-(\exists y)Dy(\exists x)\Phi x \rightarrow -(\exists x)\Diamond\Phi x$

(53) is entailed by (51). Since there are fairly straightforward logico-semantic tests of consistency, (48), (49), (50), (51), (52) and (53) would qualify as plausible epistemic criteria of possibility and impossibility.

So far we have seen that although one might accept it as a metaphysical principle that whatever is conceivable is possible or that whatever is inconceivable is impossible, it is implausible to take conceivability or inconceivability as epistemic criteria of possibility or impossibility. As an epistemic criterion, it is more plausible to accept a conceiving criterion of possibility, and even if one would claim either a *de dicto* or a *de re* conceivability criterion of possibility, the actual test of the possibility that there is x that is Φ would be in conceiving that there is an x that is Φ. Inconceivability is not a plausible epistemic criterion of impossibility, since to apply the criterion, that is, to establish that it is impossible that there is an x that is Φ, one would already need to know that it is inconceivable that there is an x that is Φ and no empirical evidence is sufficient to establish either the *de dicto* or the *de re* inconceivability that there is an x that is Φ. On the other hand, the describing and nondescribing criteria of possibility and impossibility can plausibly function as epistemic criteria of possibility and impossibility. Further, it is plausible that a philosopher would accept a conceiving criterion as an epistemic criterion of possibility and a nondescribing criterion as an epistemic criterion of impossibility.[5] Similarly, one might hold that conceivability is the metaphysical mark of possibility and inconceivability is the metaphysical mark of impossibility, while accepting a describing criterion of possibility and a nondescribing criterion of impossibility in one's epistemology.[6] Indeed, a given philosopher might accept any combination of the several versions of these criteria in his metaphysics and epistemology. Thus, in examining Berkeley on possibility and impossibility, we shall raise the question of criteria with respect to both his metaphysics and his epistemology, and we must not assume that once we have discovered his criteria in one philosophical discipline, that we have also discovered his criteria in the other. If our considerations of Berkeley's criteria are to be intelligible, however, we must first consider his distinction between existents and 'real objects'. The distinctions we shall draw here will prove invaluable in making sense of the *de dicto/de re* distinction in Berkeley's writings.

Berkeley's Distinction between Ideas and 'Real Objects'

One of the recurrent themes in Berkeley's works is that sensible real things are composed of ideas of the several senses (cf. *PHK*, 1). But if 'real things' are themselves composed of ideas, how are they to be distinguished from ideas? This is an issue Berkeley considers in Sections 29 through 34 of the *Principles*. There he considers two kinds of distinction: the distinction between ideas of the sense and ideas of the imagination and the distinction between real things and ideas. In turning to these sections we shall see that Berkeley tends to blur these two distinctions, since he provides three criteria for drawing them. I hope to show that one of these criteria is superfluous and, consequently one is left with reasonable grounds for drawing the ideas of sense/ideas of the imagination and the real things/ideas distinctions.

In Section 29, Berkeley presents what might be called the volitional criterion, namely, ideas of the imagination are dependent on one's own will, while ideas of the senses are independent of one's own will. Having noted in Section 28 that 'I find I can excite ideas in my mind at pleasure, and vary and shift the scene as oft as I think fit' (*PHK*, 28), he contrasted the ideas of sense to those of the imagination in Section 29. There he wrote:

> But whatever power I may have over my own thoughts, I find the ideas actually perceived by sense have not a like dependence on my will. When in broad daylight I open my eyes, it is not in my power to choose whether I shall see or no, or to determine what particular objects shall present themselves to my view; and so likewise as to the hearing and other senses, the ideas imprinted on them are not creatures of my will. (*PHK*, 29)

My ideas of the imagination are dependent upon my will, while my ideas of the senses are independent of my will. This criterion was also found in Locke, who took the independence of one's will to indicate that the ideas of sense have an external cause.[7] While Berkeley agreed that all ideas of sense were caused by something outside one's own mind, he, of course, differed from Locke regarding the nature of that cause.

In Section 30, he provided two more criteria for distinguishing between ideas of the imagination and ideas of the senses. These might be called the phenomenological criterion and the lawful criterion. There he wrote:

> The ideas of sense are more strong, lively, and distinct than those of the imagination; they have likewise a steadiness, order, and coherence, and are not excited at random, as those which are the effects of human wills often are, but in a regular train or series, the admirable connexion whereof sufficiently testifies the wisdom and benevolence of its Author. Now the set rules or established methods, wherein the mind we depend on excites in us the ideas of sense, are called *Laws of Nature*: and these we learn by experience, which teaches us that such and such ideas are attended with such and such other ideas, in the ordinary course of things. (*PHK*, 30)

Ideas of the sense differ phenomenologically from ideas of the imagination in so far as they 'are more strong, lively, and distinct' than ideas of the imagination. Ideas of sense also differ from ideas of the imagination in so far as they have a greater 'steadiness, order, and coherence' than those of the imagination, that is, sequences of them are describable by the laws of nature. It is the fact that most of the ideas of sense are lawfully ordered that 'gives us a sort of foresight, which enables us to regulate our actions for the benefit of life' (*PHK*, 31), and which in general makes the prediction of events possible (cf. *PHK*, 59).

One should notice that in Sections 29 and 30 Berkeley does not introduce the notion of 'real things': the distinction with which he is concerned appears to be the distinction between ideas of the imagination and ideas of the senses. The distinction between 'real things' and 'images of things' (mere ideas) is introduced in Section 33, and the class of real things is a subclass of the class of ideas of the senses. There he wrote, 'The ideas imprinted on the senses by the Author of Nature are called *real things*: and those excited by the imagination being less regular, vivid and constant, are more properly termed *ideas*, or *images of things*, which they copy and represent' (*PHK*, 33). The same point is made again in Section 34:

> Whatever we see, feel, hear, or any wise conceive or understand, remains as secure as ever, and is as real as ever. There is a *rerum nature*, and the distinction between realities and chimeras retains its full force. This is evident from *Sect.* 29, 30, and 33,

where we have shewn what is meant by *real things* in opposition to *chimeras*, or ideas of our own framing; but they both equally exist in the mind, and in that sense are alike *ideas*. (*PHK*, 34)

In these passages, Berkeley appears to be appealing to his previous distinction between ideas of the imagination and ideas of sense, suggesting that the same criteria can be used to distinguish images of things from real things. But if Berkeley intended to claim that the realm of 'real things', that is, the realm of what we ordinarily consider to be spatially and temporally complex objects, is the same as the realm of ideas of sense, then even if one would allow that these objects can be reduced to ideas of sense, there are some serious difficulties that confront Berkeley. I shall first spell out the nature of these difficulties and then argue that, if the criteria are properly understood, Berkeley can avoid these difficulties. Then I shall argue that the phenomenological criterion does not play a significant role either in distinguishing between ideas of sense and ideas of the imagination or in distinguishing between real things and images of things.

Ignoring the phenomenological criterion for the moment, the issues we should consider are these. Assuming that ordinary objects are composed of ideas of the senses, is Berkeley redundant in proposing both a volitional criterion and a lawful criterion? If he is, then all the ideas of the senses are components of ordinary objects. If he is not redundant in proposing two criteria, then (although all ordinary objects are composed (solely) of ideas of the senses) not all ideas of the senses are components of ordinary objects, and the two criteria play distinct roles in Berkeley's philosophy. As I shall show, one might plausibly suggest that the volitional criterion is intended to distinguish ideas of the sense from ideas of the imagination, while the lawful criterion is intended to distinguish 'real things' (ordinary objects) from both imaginary objects and ideas of the sense that are not components of ordinary objects. To see that this is plausible, let us consider the following case.

If one retains Berkeley's contention that ideas are the immediate objects of thought, common sense suggests that some of the ideas of which one is aware are caused by finite persons other than oneself.[8] If I seem to hear John say, 'Good morning', for example, my common sense assumption is that John is the cause of the auditory ideas of which I am aware. By Berkeley's volitional criterion, these auditory ideas would count as ideas of sense, since my awareness of these ideas is independent of any action of my will. But if the lawful criterion is *also* intended to mark the distinction between ideas of the imagination and ideas of sense, I would be unable to distinguish these auditory ideas from ideas of the imagination. To draw such a distinction, it would be necessary for me to be able to make certain predictions from those auditory ideas to other ideas. In the case of human speech, however, such predictions are difficult, if not impossible, to make: John might say virtually anything after his initial 'Good morning'. Berkeley's own suggestion that ideas excited by human wills are often random — and therefore unpredictable — is certainly consistent with this (cf. *PHK*, 30). Although one might not be able to predict what auditory ideas of human speech will follow those of which one is aware at any given time, there might still be a lawful correlation among ideas of two different kinds, for example, auditory ideas of a kind one might call John's voice (ideas having those properties peculiar to John's voice) might be correlated with certain visual ideas (ideas that are components of John's body). Even this latter correlation, however might be less than lawful: it might happen, for example, that what I take to be ideas of John's voice are actually caused by some talented impressionist.

The case of hearing words might be contrasted with other types of ideas of sense, namely, those one takes to be components of ordinary objects. In seeing the table in my kitchen, for example, I am able to make various predictions. I can predict that at a later time under similar circumstances I will be aware of another idea that is similar to the one of which I am presently aware, that is, an idea that is a component of the same table or what I take to be the same table. I could also predict that if I would visually perceive my hand placed on top of the table, then I would have a tactual idea of resistance. If at a later time I would visually perceive a pile of ashes where my table previously had been, I would be able lawfully to explain what had happened to my table. These considerations suggest that the volitional criterion and the lawful criterion are intended to yield different distinctions. The volitional criterion alone is sufficient to allow one to distinguish between ideas of sense and ideas of the imagination: an idea is an idea of the sense if and only if my awareness of it is independent of an action of my will. The lawful criterion, on the other hand, allows one to distinguish those ideas of the sense that are components of 'real things' (ordinary objects) from those ideas of sense which are not components of ordinary objects: an idea which, by the volitional criterion, is an idea of sense is 'real' (a component of an ordinary object) if and only if it is possible to correctly predict the occurrence of other ideas of sense on the basis of it (if and only if it is part of a lawfully describable sequence of ideas). Notice that using the lawful criterion to delineate the class of 'real things' presupposes that ideas of sense are already distinguished from ideas of the imagination on the basis of the volitional criterion. Apart from a distinction between ideas of sense and ideas of the imagination, the lawful criterion would not allow one to distinguish 'real things' from imaginary things, since it is possible to construct a world composed of lawfully ordered imaginary objects (a fictitious world).

My reconstruction of Berkeley's distinctions between ideas of sense and ideas of the imagination, and between 'real things' and images of things, is based upon his volitional and lawful criteria alone. This indicates that one can properly claim that the phenomenological criterion is, at best, of little significance in drawing these distinctions. But if we reflect a bit further, we shall find that the phenomenological criterion is unreliable, and Berkeley would be well-advised to exclude it from the criteria he presented to draw these distinctions. Remember, Berkeley's phenomenological criterion holds that 'The ideas of sense are more strong, lively, and distinct than those of the imagination' (*PHK*, 30). In basing the grounds for his distinction on the phenomenological characteristics of the ideas of which one is aware, his proposed criterion corresponds in both intent and content to Hume's phenomenological criterion for drawing the distinction between impressions and ideas on the basis of their relative force and vivacity.[9] But even Hume recognized that the phenomenological criterion provides nothing more than a rough and ready means of distinguishing between these two types of perceptions: it is properly neither a metaphysical nor an epistemic criterion, because it does not provide conclusive grounds for drawing the distinction. As Hume wrote:

> The common degrees of these are easily distinguished; tho' it is not impossible but in particular instances they may very nearly approach to each other. Thus in sleep, in a fever, in madness, or in any very violent emotions of the soul, our ideas may

approach to our impressions: As on the other hand it sometimes happens that our impressions are so faint and low, that we cannot distinguish them from our ideas.[10]

If it is possible for one to apply a putative metaphysical or epistemic criterion and yet to fail to accurately distinguish between two kinds of things, one's putative criterion is inadequate. Hume is certainly correct in suggesting that there are cases in which the phenomenological criterion will not allow one to correctly distinguish between impressions (ideas of sense) and ideas (ideas of the imagination) and, consequently, it is at least inadequate as an epistemic criterion. If one of my soft-spoken students asks me a question, the impression (idea of sense) that is caused in my mind might be so weak that I would be unable to distinguish it from an idea of the imagination on the basis of the phenomenological criterion alone. Nonetheless, it could be distinguished from an idea of the imagination on the basis of Berkeley's volitional criterion. It is because the phenomenological criterion is neither a wholly reliable epistemic criterion, nor is it needed for Berkeley to draw either metaphysical or epistemological distinctions between ideas of sense and ideas of the imagination, that one can safely ignore it.

Berkeley's Metaphysical Criteria

Having examined Berkeley's distinction between real sensible objects and mere ideas, we are now in a position to draw the *de dicto/de re* distinction in terms of the kinds of objects in Berkeley's ontology. Since real sensible objects are composed of ideas, and since there is no intrinsic difference between an idea of sensation and an idea of the imagination, any existent idea is a possible component of a real thing, that is, ideas are *de re* possible objects. Any idea of sensation is a component of some real sensible object, although one might not know of which particular object it is a component. No idea of the imagination is a component of a real object, but since it differs from an idea of sensation only with respect to its causal origin, it is in principle possible that it could be a component of a real sensible object. Similarly, *de dicto* possibility is to be construed as the possible existence of a *real x* that is Φ. Given the *de dicto/de re* distinction in Berkeley, we may now consider the metaphysical criteria he employs to distinguish *de dicto* and *de re* possible objects from *de dicto* and *de re* impossible objects.

In the case of *de re* possible objects (ideas), discovering the metaphysical criterion is not at all difficult. Since the *esse* of ideas is *percipi*, there is an idea (a *de re* possible object, a possible component of a real object) if and only if it is perceived (conceived) by some mind. Hence, Berkeley's metaphysical criterion of *de re* possibility and impossibility is (25): there is an x that is possibly Φ (a possible component of an x that is Φ) if and only if there is something that conceives that there is an x that is Φ.

The case is not quite so clear with respect to Berkeley's criteria of *de dicto* possibility and impossibility, although I shall show that the evidence suggests that his metaphysical criterion of possibility is either (22) instantiated for God, that is:

(54) $\Diamond Cg(\exists x)\Phi x \leftrightarrow \Diamond(\exists x)\Phi x$

or it is (24) instantiated for God, i.e.,

(55) $Cg(\exists x)\Phi x \leftrightarrow \Diamond(\exists x)\Phi x$

I shall also argue that given Berkeley's philosophical theology, it makes little difference whether one attributes (54) or (55) to him. To see that this is plausible, we should begin by examining the question whether God creates real objects or merely ideas.

Berkeley's most systematic discussion of creation occurs in the *Third Dialogue between Hylas and Philonous* and the evidence there suggests that God creates real objects. Focusing on the question of the sensible objects that God created, Philonous is made to say:

> Moses mentions the sun, moon, and stars, earth and sea, plants and animals: that all these things do really exist, and were in the beginning created by God, I make no question. If by *ideas*, you mean fictions and fancies of the mind, then these are no ideas. If by *ideas*, you mean immediate objects of the understanding, or sensible things which cannot exist unperceived, or out of a mind, then these things are ideas. But whether you do, or do not call them *ideas*, it matters little. The difference is only about a name. And whether that name be retained or rejected, the sense, the truth and reality of things continue the same. In

common talk, the objects of the senses are not termed *ideas* but *things*. Call them so still: provided you do not attribute to them any absolute external existence, and I shall never quarrel with you for a word. The Creation therefore I allow to have been a creation of things, of *real* things. (*DHP*, III, 250-1)

Continuing, Philonous indicates that the creation of sensible things consists in making these things perceivable to finite minds, and that these things have an eternal existence in the mind of God. In Philonous' words:

When things are said to begin or end their existence, we do not mean this with regard to God, but His creatures. All objects are eternally known by God, or which is the same thing, have an eternal existence in his mind: but when things before imperceptible to creatures, are by a decree of God, made perceptible to them; then are they said to begin a relative existence, with respect to the created minds. Upon reading therefore the Mosaic account of the Creation, I understand that the several parts of the world became gradually perceivable to finite spirits, endowed with proper faculties; so that whoever such were present, they were in truth perceived by them. (*DHP*, III, 251-2)

There are several points to notice in these passages. First, the things God creates (causes to exist) are *real* things. Second, in claiming that all objects are eternally known by God, Berkeley seems to be claiming that all objects that could exist — whether or not God causes them to exist — are conceived by God, that is, it seems that Berkeley accepted (12) instantiated for God. Further, his suggestion that '*All* objects are eternally known by God' (*DHP*, III, 251, my emphasis), suggests that if God does not conceive that there is an x that is Φ, then God cannot create an x that is Φ. That is, it seems that Berkeley also accepted (30) instantiated for God. Thus, these texts suggest that Berkeley's metaphysical criterion of *de dicto* possibility and impossibility is (55): it is possible that there is an x that is Φ if and only if God conceives that there is an x that is Φ.

But the texts do not appear to be consistent on this point. In the First Draft of the Introduction to the *Principles*, Berkeley seems to have proposed an instance of a *de re* conceivability criterion of *de dicto* possibility, rather than a conceiving criterion. As Berkeley wrote: 'It is, I think, a receiv'd axiom that an impossibility cannot be conceiv'd. For what created intelligence will pretend to conceive, that which God cannot cause to be?' (*Works* 2:125). This suggests that if God cannot create an x that is Φ, then it is *impossible* for God to conceive that there is an x that is Φ and, therefore, that Berkeley's metaphysical criterion of *de dicto* possibility and impossibility is that it is *de dicto* possible that there is an x that is Φ if and only if it is *possible* for God to conceive that there is an x that is Φ, that is, (54). Is the difference between divine conceiving and divine conceivability of any significance?

It seems not. Berkeley seems to grant as a tenet of philosophical theology that, with respect to God's conceptions, the distinction between what is conceivable for God and what God conceives collapses. In ascribing omniscience to God (*DHP*, II 257; cf. *PHK*, 146), Berkeley seems to be claiming that God is eternally aware of all that he could create, that is, of all *de dicto* possibilities. Hence, whether one ascribes (54) or (55) to Berkeley is of little consequence: when instantiated for God, the distinction between (22) and (24) collapses.

Before turning to Berkeley's epistemological criteria of possibility and impossibility, one further point should be noted. Berkeley's metaphysical criteria do nothing more than specify what is *de dicto* and *de re* possible and impossible. They provide little guidance regarding what can be *known* to be possible or impossible. In the case of *de re* possibility, one can know that those ideas of which one is aware are possible components of real objects, but the criterion provides one with no guidance regarding *de re* impossibility: the fact that one does not conceive that there is an x that is Φ provides little evidence that there is no other spirit that conceives that there is an x that is Φ. In the case of *de dicto* possibility, the criteria provide one with no direct guidance regarding what is or is not *de dicto* possible, for one cannot directly know what God can or cannot conceive (cf. *DHP*, III, 233). Thus, Berkeley's metaphysical criteria of possibility provide one with little guidance regarding epistemological issues and, for the same reasons, they provide one with little guidance regarding the construction of an ontological inventory.

Berkeley's Epistemological Criteria

In turning to Berkeley's epistemic criteria of possibility and impossibility, we should remember that any epistemic criterion of possibility or impossibility that is based upon conceivability or inconceivability is *prima facie* implausible. Even though the fact that one actually conceives that there is an x that is Φ, the fact that at any given time one does not conceive that there is an x that is Φ entails neither that it is *de dicto* or *de re* inconceivable that there is an x that is Φ nor that one will not conceive that there is an x that is Φ at some other time. It is for this reason that it would be more reasonable to advance a *conceiving* criterion of possibility as an epistemic criterion of possibility.

Turning to Berkeley's works, one finds evidence that Berkeley himself accepted a conceiving criterion of possibility. This is fairly clear from his comment in Section 5 of the *Principles* that 'my conceiving or imagining power does not extend beyond the possibility of real existence or perception'. Indeed, this theme is repeated throughout the *Principles* (cf. Intro., 10; *PHK*, 22). Even though it is fairly clear that Berkeley took one's actual conceiving to be the epistemic mark of possibility, we must inquire further into nature of Berkeley's epistemic criterion. In particular, we must ask whether it is an instance of (12) or (13).

Berkeley quite clearly holds that when one conceives that there is an x that is Φ, one's immediate object of awareness is an idea.[11] Now those ideas of which the mind is aware exist *qua* ideas. Real things, as we have seen, are composed of lawfully ordered ideas of the several senses. Although the ideas of which one is aware when one conceives that there is an x that is Φ are ideas of the imagination and, therefore, differ in causal origin from ideas of the senses, they do not differ intrinsically from ideas of the senses. Hence, it remains possible in principle that any idea one conceives (imagines) could be part of the lawfully ordered sequence of ideas that constitutes a real object. Any given idea one would conceive, however, would correspond to an idea of a particular sense, and given Berkeley's further claim that time is nothing but the succession of ideas (*PHK*, 98; cf. *PHK*, 110-12), any idea one would conceive is nothing more than a possible temporal slice of a real object. Recognizing that what is conceived is an existent and a possible component of a real object shows that Berkeley's epistemic criterion of *de re* possibility is an instance of (13):

if one conceives that there is an x that is Φ, there is a thing that is possibly Φ, that is, there is an x that is possibly a component of a real thing that is Φ.

Notice that what one can know on the basis of Berkeley's conceiving criterion of *de re* possibility is severely limited. In knowing that there is something that is possibly a component of a real object, one does not know what real objects could exist. Those sensible objects that Berkeley deemed real are combinations of ideas of the several senses, while typically what one conceives in applying the conceiving criterion of *de re* possibility is an idea of a kind peculiar to a specific sense, for example an idea of light and colors (an idea of the imagination that corresponds to one's ideas of sight). While one might be able simultaneously to conceive of ideas peculiar to several senses and thereby construct a qualitatively rich idea (cf. *PHK*, 1), such an idea still would be no more than a possible temporal slice of a real object. Real *sensible* objects, at least, are temporally complex and lawfully describable. Hence, in claiming that it is possible that there is a real sensible object x of kind Φ, one would need to concern oneself, at least in part, with considerations regarding what laws are laws that describe possibly real objects, and this would *seem* to require something other than a conceiving criterion of possibility. Similarly, with respect to nonsensible objects, for example, substances, since one's conceptions are at best indirect, one could justify one's claim that it is possible that there is an x that is Φ only on the basis of a consideration of the relations that might obtain between an idea and an object,[12] and again, this does not seem to be something that is available to a conceiving criterion. As we shall see, there is evidence that Berkeley accepted a describing criterion of *de dicto* possibility, that is, an instance of (48), but since the same evidence indicates that he accepted a nondescribing criterion of *de dicto* impossibility, that is, an instance of (52), we may reasonably begin by examining Berkeley's epistemic criteria of impossibility.

The clearest evidence that Berkeley rejected epistemic criteria of impossibility that are based upon inconceivability is found in Philonous' reply to Hylas' argument that the grounds for accepting the doctrine of material substance are the same as those for accepting the doctrine of immaterial substance. Notice what Berkeley made Philonous say:

I say in the first place, that I do not deny the existence of material substance, merely because I have no notion of it, but because the notion of it is inconsistent, or in other words, because it would be repugnant that there should be a notion of it. Many things, for ought I know, may exist, whereof neither I nor any other man hath or can have any idea or notion whatsoever. But then those things must be possible, that is, nothing inconsistent must be included in their definition. (*DHP*, III, 232-3; cf. *PHK* 81)

In claiming that things might exist of which no human being can conceive, Berkeley clearly rejected the use of either an inconceivability or a nonconceiving criterion as an epistemic criterion of impossibility, that is, he rejected the contention that one can know that a certain state of affairs is impossible simply because one does not or cannot conceive of it. Although this is a rejection of inconceivability as an epistemic criterion of impossibility, it remains consistent with the text to claim that the class of those things that Berkeley would consider properly inconceivable, that is, those things of which even God does not or cannot conceive, is coextensive with the class of impossible things. Berkeley's point in this passage, however, is not merely to reject an inconceivability or nonconceiving criterion of impossibility, it is also to advance a nondescribing criterion of *de dicto* impossibility. He held that if a given description of an x that is Φ is inconsistent, then it is impossible for there to be a real x (as described) that is Φ, that is, Berkeley accepted (52) as an epistemic criterion of *de dicto* impossibility.

We should also notice that this passage suggests Berkeley accepted a describing criterion of *de dicto* possibility, that is, (48). In claiming that anything that exists 'must be possible, that is, nothing inconsistent must be included in their definition' (*DHP*, III, 232-3), Berkeley suggests that anything that can be consistently described (or which has a consistent real definition) is a possible existent. In so far as a thing is subject to description or definition, it must be either complex or, in the case of spirits, knowable only on the basis of its relations to a thing of which one is immediately aware. Therefore, objects that could be real are either complex collections of ideas or things (internally) related to ideas. It is for this reason that this passage suggests that Berkeley accepted (48) as an epistemic criterion of possibility and, therefore, that he accepted (49) as an epistemic criterion of *de dicto* possibility and impossibility.

This is not the only passage in which Berkeley appears to have accepted (52) as an epistemic criterion of *de dicto* impossibility. In the first two editions of the *Alciphron*, one also finds Euphranor asking Alciphron, 'Which are those things you would call absolutely impossible?' and Alciphron replying, 'Such as include a contradiction' (*A*, VII 6, 333-4). Similarly, in the *Second Dialogue* one finds the following exchange between Hylas and Philonous:

Philonous. When is a thing shewn to be impossible?
Hylas. When a repugnancy is demonstrated between the ideas comprehended in its definition.

(*DHP*, II, 225)

Both of these passages support my contention that Berkeley accepted (52) as an epistemic criterion of impossibility.

If my contention is correct that Berkeley accepted (49) as an epistemic criterion of *de dicto* possibility and impossibility, it seems plausible that he accepted (53) as an epistemic criterion of *de re* impossibility. To see this, we should consider what is involved in accepting (49) as an epistemic criterion of *de dicto* possibility and impossibility. If one is to show that it is possible that there is a real x that is Φ, one must give a complete description of that x, that is, one must give a description of each of the temporal phases of that x (ideas that compose that x), and one must state the laws that unite the various temporal phases into an object. If such a description is consistent, then it is possible that there is an x that is Φ; if the description is inconsistent, then it is impossible that there is an x that is Φ. If the description is *inconsistent*, then either the description of one or more of the temporal phases of the object is inconsistent, or one or more of the natural laws describing the sequences of temporal phases of the object is inconsistent, or there are inconsistent descriptions of both kinds. This is the intent of (52). If it is impossible that there is a real object x that is Φ in virtue of the fact that it is impossible that there is a temporal phase of that object — in the case of a sensible real object, in virtue of the fact that it is impossible that there is an idea falling under a particular description — it is reasonable to suggest that if a description of a temporal phase of an object (an idea) is inconsistent, then there is no x that is possibly Φ, that is, it is reasonable to suggest that

Berkeley accepted (53) as his epistemic criterion of *de re* impossibility. The positive evidence for this is to be drawn from the *Third Dialogue*, since in claiming that it is impossible that there is a notion of material substance because the definition is inconsistent, 'or in other words, it is repugnant that there should be a notion of it' (*DHP*, III, 232), Berkeley seems to be taking indescribability as the general mark of impossibility: if a description of an x that is Φ is inconsistent, then it is both *de dicto* and *de re* impossible that there is an x that is Φ. Further evidence for this might be drawn from consideration of conceiving. The fact that a particular person *does not* conceive that there is an x that is Φ does not entail that it is inconceivable that there is an x that is Φ and, consequently, it can provide no more than *prima facie* evidence for the inconceivability and impossibility that there is an x that is possibly Φ. Hence, if criteria of impossibility are limited to indescribability (and nondescribing) criteria and inconceivability (and nonconceiving) criteria, it is only a nondescribing criterion that can provide a plausible epistemic criterion of impossibility. Hence, just as (52) appears to be the most plausible candidate for Berkeley's criterion of *de dicto* impossibility, (53) appears to be the most plausible candidate for Berkeley's criterion of *de re* impossibility.[13]

Thus, we have seen that there is evidence that Berkeley accepted a conceiving criterion as an epistemic criterion of *de re* possibility, that is, (13), and he accepted a describing criterion as an epistemic criterion of *de dicto* possibility and impossibility, that is, he accepted both (48) and (52), and therefore he accepted (49). We have also seen that there is evidence that Berkeley accepted (53) as an epistemic criterion of *de re* impossibility. The evidence we have considered, however, shows neither that Berkeley accepted these criteria throughout his philosophical career nor that he consistently rejected epistemic criteria based upon conceivability or inconceivability. At most it shows that from 1713 onward he set forth describing criteria of *de dicto* possibility and impossibility. Since most of the putative evidence that he proposed an inconceivability criterion of impossibility is drawn from the *Principles*, we must now turn to that work.

Possibility and Impossibility in the *Principles*

Willis Doney has recently suggested that an inconceivability criterion of impossibility 'is clearly implied in Part I of the *Principles*, Sections 5, 6, 10, 22, and 23'.[14] If, in examining these sections, it can be shown (1) that Berkeley did not explicitly claim that he accepted an inconceivability criterion of impossibility; and (2) that his claims of impossibility in those sections can be justified on the basis of a nondescribing criterion of impossibility, for example (52), I shall take this to be sufficient to show that Berkeley consistently accepted a nondescribing criterion as an epistemic criterion of *de dicto* impossibility.[15] So let us turn to those sections.

If Berkeley employed an inconceivability criterion of impossibility in Sections 5 and 6 of the *Principles*, then those sections must be construed as providing arguments for the principle that the *esse* of sensible objects is *percipi*. If one is to show that Sections 5 and 6 were intended to provide arguments for the principle that *esse* is *percipi*, then Berkeley should there claim that it is impossible for sensible objects to exist unperceived. What I shall show is that there are no grounds for taking the argument in Section 5 as an independent argument for *esse* is *percipi*, and that there are few grounds for taking the argument in Section 6 to be such an argument. Further, in so far as either section might be construed as providing an argument for *esse* is *percipi*, the argument rests upon a nondescribing criterion of impossibility.

Before looking at Sections 5 and 6, however, we should notice the context in which they are found. In Section 3 of the *Principles* Berkeley proposed his primary argument for the principle that the *esse* of sensible objects is *percipi*. In Section 4 he continued, but his support for the principle rests upon the claim that the contention that 'all sensible objects have an existence real or natural, distinct from their being perceived by the understanding' is inconsistent. In his words:

> But with how great an assurance and acquiescence soever this principle [that sensible objects exist unperceived] may be entertained in the world; yet whoever shall find it in his heart to call it in question may, if I mistake not, perceive it to involve a manifest contradiction. For what are the forementioned objects but things we perceive by sense, and what do we perceive besides our own ideas or sensations; and is it not plainly repugnant that any of these or any combination should exist unperceived? (*PHK*, 4)

Similarly, in Section 7 he claimed that 'for an idea to exist in an unperceiving thing, is a manifest contradiction' (*PHK*, 7). Hence, it is clear that *one* of the grounds upon which Berkeley supported *esse* is *percipi* is that the position of the 'materialists' is formally inconsistent. The issue is, then, whether there is an independent argument for *esse* is *percipi* in Sections 5 and 6 that is based upon claims of inconceivability.

Section 5 reads as follows:

> If we thoroughly examine this tenet, it will, perhaps, be found at bottom to depend on the doctrine of *abstract ideas*. For can there be a nicer strain of abstraction than to distinguish the existence of sensible objects from their being perceived, so as to conceive them existing unperceived. Light and colours, heat and cold, extension and figures, in a word the things we see and feel, what are they but so many sensations, notions, ideas or impressions on the sense; and is it possible to separate, even in thought, any of these from perception? For my part I might as easily divide a thing from it self. I may indeed divide in my thoughts or conceive apart from each other those thing which, perhaps, I never perceived by sense so divided. Thus I imagine the trunk of a human body without the limbs, or conceive the smell of a rose without thinking on the rose itself. So far I will not deny I can abstract, if that may properly be called *abstraction*, which extends only to the conceiving separately such objects, as it is possible may really exist or be actually perceived asunder. But my conceiving or imagining power does not extend beyond the possibility of real existence or perception. Hence as it is impossible for me to see or feel anything without an actual sensation of that thing, so it is impossible for me to conceive in my thoughts any sensible thing or object distinct from the sensation or perception of it. (*PHK*, 5)

Notice how Berkeley begins his discussion. He does *not* claim to be developing an argument for *esse* is *percipi*, rather the first sentence suggests that he intends to *explain* how the confusion of the 'materialists' rests upon another philosophical error, namely, the doctrine of abstact ideas. His discussion is largely a reiteration of his argument in Section 10 of the Introduction, for, as in the earlier section, he indicates the (improper) sense in which he is able to engage in abstraction and then claims that his abstracting power 'does not extend beyond the possibility of real existence or perception', that is, impossible states of affairs are inconceivable (cf. *Works* 2:125). Hence, since it is impossible for a sensible object to exist unperceived, 'so it is impossible for me to conceive in my thoughts any sensible thing or object distinct from the sensation of perception of it'. If this is the correct interpretation of this section, then Section 5 does not provide an argument for *esse* is *percipi*, rather, it presupposes that principle and explains the possibility of such a philosophical error on the basis of another philosophical error, that is to say, the doctrine of abstract ideas.

Section 5, however, is open to at least two alternative interpretations. One might suggest that it poses a challenge to the reader to conceive of an unperceived object. Assuming that the reader accepts either a conceiving or a conceivability criterion of possibility, if the reader could actually conceive of an unperceived object, this would be sufficient to show that it is either *de dicto* or *de re* possible that there are unperceived objects. But it is impossible to meet such a challenge. Berkeley's notion of the perceiving relation is extremely broad: perceiving is simply a relation that obtains between a mind and an object (idea).[16] Thus, the state of affairs Berkeley describes, namely, perceiving of an unperceived object, is contradictory and therefore impossible. Notice, however, this does not show that it is impossible for a sensible object to exist unperceived, rather, it shows that if one takes conceivability to be the mark of possibility, one cannot show that it is possible for x to exist unperceived.

On the other hand, one might claim that Berkeley makes an implicit appeal to either an inconceivability criterion of impossibility or, at least, to an inconceivability criterion of inseparability.[17] If Berkeley accepted either of these criteria, then if he claimed that the existence of a sensible object cannot be conceived apart from being perceived, this would be taken to show that it is impossible for a sensible object (idea) to exist unperceived (apart from a relation to a mind). Berkeley's argument, however, does not make so strong a claim. He suggests that *he* cannot conceive of a sensible object apart from its being perceived, and the fact that *he* cannot conceive of such a separation does not show that there is no (perhaps divine) mind that could conceive of such a state of affairs. At best, the argument he advances provides inductive evidence that it is impossible to conceive of a sensible object apart from a relation to a mind — it cannot conclusively show that such a state of affairs is inconceivable — and, consequently, even if he accepted either an inconceivability criterion of impossibility or inseparability, the argument would, at best, provide limited evidence that it is impossible for a sensible object to exist unperceived. Further, as we saw above, his claim that 'my conceiving or imagining power does not extend beyond the possibility of real existence' suggests that Berkeley already accepted it as established that unperceived ideas are impossible and *therefore* inconceivable. Thus, unless one were to claim that Berkeley advances a very weak argument in Section 5, that is, an argument based upon inductive evidence drawn from introspection, or that he drew conclusions that went far beyond the evidence available, it makes little sense to suggest that an inconceivability criterion is found in Section 5 of the *Principles*. Since we have already seen that there are at least two alternative interpretations of the passage that yield a stronger argument and that do not appeal to an inconceivability criterion, it is unreasonable to suggest that Berkeley's argument in Section 5 presupposes an inconceivability criterion.

Much of the same can be said regarding Section 6 of the *Principles*. The bulk of that section is nothing more than a reiteration of the principle that the *esse* of a sensible object is *percipi* together with the claim that this principle is necessarily true. If one were to claim that he appeals to an inconceivability criterion at any point in this section, the only place one might plausibly find it is in the last sentence: 'To be convinced of which, the reader need only reflect and try to separate in his own thoughts the being of a sensible thing from its being perceived' (*PHK*, 6). But here again, if there is an implicit appeal to an inconceivability criterion, the argument is either a weak inductive argument or a deductive argument with an unwarranted conclusion. It seems more plausible to interpret this sentence in accordance with the second interpretation of Section 5 above, namely, that there is no evidence to support the contention that it is even possible for sensible objects to exist unperceived.

Although neither Section 5 nor Section 6 can be reasonably understood as presupposing an inconceivability criterion of impossibility, one might more reasonably contend that the argument in Section 10 of the *Principles* presupposes an inconceivability criterion of impossibility. There, after indicating that the proponents of the primary/secondary qualities distinction claim that color, sounds, heat and cold and 'such like secondary qualities' exist only in the mind, Berkeley proceeds to argue that extension also exists only in the mind. He wrote:

> Now if it be certain, that those original qualities are inseparably united with the other sensible qualities, and not, even in thought, capable of being abstracted from them, it plainly follows that they exist only in the mind. But I desire any one to reflect and try, whether he can by any abstraction of thought, conceive the extension and motion of a body, without all other sensible qualities. For my own part, I see evidently that it is not in my power to frame an idea of a body extended and moved, but I must withal give it some colour or other sensible quality which is acknowledged to exist only in the mind. In short, extension, figure, and motion, abstracted from all other qualities are inconceivable. Where therefore the other sensible qualities are, there must these be also, to wit, in the mind and no where else. (*PHK*, 10)

It might *appear* that Berkeley is here providing an argument that is based upon an inconceivability criterion of impossibility. His putative argument may be reconstructed as follows:

> (1) If extension is inseparably united with color (or some other secondary quality), then if color exists only in the mind, then extension also exists only in the mind;
> (2) I am incapable of conceiving of extension apart from color;
> (3) therefore extension apart from color is inconceivable;
> (4) what is inconceivable is impossible;
> (5) therefore, extension cannot exist apart from color (or some other secondary quality);
> (6) color exists only in the mind;
> (7) therefore, extension exists only in the mind.

If this is Berkeley's argument, then his argument is unsound. It does not follow from the claim that I am, in fact, unable to conceive of extension apart from color that it is impossible for anyone to conceive of extension apart from color. Is there, some other ground upon which Berkeley could claim that extension is inseparably united with color or some other secondary quality? Yes. Given the account of minimum visibles that he developed in the *New Theory of Vision*, Berkeley could argue that it is impossible for there to be an extension that does not possess a color or some other secondary quality, and his argument would be independent of the inconceivability criterion of impossibility. A minimum visible is an indivisible point of color, and since it is indivisible, it is unextended (*NTV*, 80-1).[18] Since one can conceive of a minimum visible, Berkeley's conceiving criterion of *de re* possibility, that is, (13), allows one to infer that there are possible components of real objects that are colored and unextended. Extensions are at once inherently divisible and composed of indivisible points. Hence, a visible extension must be composed of visible points of color (minimum visibles). If visible extensions are *composed* of indivisible points of color, it is impossible to conceive of visible extensions that are not colored. Thus, one cannot conceive of (visible) extension apart from color, although one can conceive of color (color points) apart from extension. The same argument holds, *mutatis mutandis*, for tangible extensions (cf. *NTV*, 54). Thus, Berkeley could claim that it is inconceivable for there to be an extension apart from some secondary qualities, but this is because extensions are composed of points possessing only secondary qualities. Since it is *given* that secondary qualities exist only in the mind and since extensions are *composed* of things containing only secondary qualities, it follows that extension exists only in the mind: inconceivability plays no part in the argument.

Finally, neither Section 22 nor Section 23 shows that inconceivability plays any role in Berkeley's argument against the doctrine of material substance. In Section 22 he invites his readers to look into their 'own thoughts, and so trying whether you can conceive it possible for a sound, or figure, or motion, or colour, to exist without the mind, or unperceived. This easy trial may make you see that what you contend for is a downright contradiction' (*PHK*, 22). Similarly, in Section 23 he argued that to show that it is possible for objects to exist unperceived (apart from a relation to the mind) 'it is necessary that you conceive them existing unconceived or unthought of, which is a manifest repugnancy' (*PHK*, 23). In both of these sections Berkeley claims that it is impossible for there to be any evidence for the *possibility* of the existence of sensible objects that are not related to a mind, for it is conceiving that provides the grounds for judgments of *de re* possibility, and it is a contradiction to claim that it is possible to conceive of an *x* that is, at the time of one's conceiving, unconceived.

Thus, the evidence that Berkeley seriously entertained an inconceivability criterion of impossibility in epistemic contexts appears to be weak at best. Given the textual evidence, it appears that his concerns with conceivability and inconceivability proper were limited to metaphysical contexts, and there he was concerned solely with what it is possible or impossible for God to conceive and create (*de dicto* possibility and impossibility). Actual conceiving provides the basis for the metaphysical distinction between *de re* possibility and impossibility. In the epistemic realm, Berkeley appears to have limited himself to a conceiving criterion of *de re* possibility, a nondescribing criterion of *de re* impossibility and a describing criterion of *de dicto* possibility and impossibility, and it is his epistemic criteria of possibility and impossibility that direct the construction of his ontological inventory.

Notes

1. Kenneth Winkler, 'Editor's Introduction', in *A Treatise Concerning the Principles of Human Understanding* (Hackett edition), p. xvi; Willis Doney, 'Berkeley's Argument Against Abstract Ideas', in Peter A. French, Theodore E. Vehling, Jr and Howard K. Nettstein (eds), *Midwest Studies in Philosophy VIII, 1983: Contemporary Perspectives on the History of Philosophy*, pp. 295-308; cf. Willis Doney, 'Is Berkeley's a Cartesian Mind?' in *Berkeley: Critical and Interpretive Essays* (ed. Colin Murray Turbayne) (University of Minnesota Press, Minneapolis, 1982) pp. 276-9; Edwin B. Allaire, 'Berkeley's Idealism', *Theoria*, 1963, reprinted in *Essays in Ontology*, Iowa Publications in Philosophy, vol. 1 (Martinus Nijhoff, The Hague, 1963): p. 102.

2. Should someone object to my construal of 'conceivability' as the possibility of conceiving, suggesting that it should be construed as the ability to conceive, the following considerations should alley such doubts. To claim one has the ability to do x entails that it is possible for one to do x and that, in the appropriate situation, it is probable that one would actually do x (cf. Lawrence H. Davis, *Theory of Action*, Foundations of Philosophy (Prentice-Hall, Englewood Cliffs, New Jersey, 1979), pp. 42-56). To justify the claim that it is probable that a given individual i would conceive that there is an x that is Φ, presupposes that at some earlier time either i or some individual that is exactly similar to i has conceived that there is an x that is Φ. But in applying the criterion, it is an open question whether anyone has the ability to conceive that there is an x that is Φ, and the only way in which one could provide a positive answer to the question is by *actually conceiving* that there is an x that is Φ. Hence, although construing 'conceivability' as the ability to conceive is a weaker construal than a claim of actual conceiving and a stronger claim than one finds in construing 'conceivability' as the possibility of conceiving, since to justify the claim the one has the ability to conceive that there is an x that is Φ requires that someone actually conceive that there is an x that is Φ, nothing is gained by including this as an additional construal of the criterion.

3. Since the *de dicto/de re* distinction can be traced back at least as far as the fourteenth-century philosopher Jean Buridan (cf. A.N. Prior, 'Logic, Modal', in Paul Edwards (ed.), *The Encyclopedia of Philosophy*, 8 vols (Macmillan, New

York, 1967), 5:9-10), it seems reasonable to employ these distinctions in discussing Berkeley's criteria of possibility and impossibility.

4. David Hume, *A Treatise of Human Nature* (ed. L.A. Selby-Bigge, 2nd ed. rev. by P.H. Nidditch) (Clarendon Press, Oxford, 1978), p. 32. Cf. Descartes, *Principles of Philosophy*, Part I, Section 60, HR, I:243-4; Descartes, *Meditations*, HR I: 185; and Arnauld, *The Art of Thinking: Port-Royal Logic* (trans. James Dickoff and Patricia James) (Bobbs-Merrill, Library of Liberal Arts, Indianapolis, 1964), p. 323. The reader should notice that Hume, like Descartes and Arnauld, requires that something be *clearly* conceived if it be deemed possible. This seems to indicate that one conceive of the whole on the basis of the relations among the parts of the whole, that is, that one conceive of an object analyzed in terms of its components, for if one's conception of an object were not clear, it might happen that it would include inconsistent properties. While the clarity requirement might be needed to make conceiving an adequate ground for deeming an object possible, it will be sufficient simply acknowledge this and not explicitly include this stipulation in our discussions of the conceivability criteria.

5. Arnauld might be cited as a case in point. See Arnauld, *The Art of Thinking*, p. 323.

6. Hume might be a case in point. In his discussion of the necessity of the causal maxim in the *Treatise* he appealed to the conceivability criterion of possibility to show that any two causally related objects are not necessarily conjoined (*Treatise* I.iii.3, pp. 79-80; David Hume, *An Enquiry concerning Human Understanding*, L.H. Selby-Bigge (ed.), *Enquiries concerning the Human Understanding and concerning the Principles of Morals* 3rd edn, rev. by P.H. Nidditch (Clarendon Press, Oxford, 1975), p. 25), although in the same passages he appeals to a formal criterion of possibility. An examination of the question whether or not Hume employed separate criteria of metaphysical and epistemic possibility is, however, beyond the scope of this study.

7. John Locke, *An Essay concerning Human Understanding* (ed. P.H. Nidditch) (Clarendon Press, Oxford, 1975) 4.11.5.

8. Cf. *PHK*, 145. Even if God causes all ideas of which we are aware that we do not cause ourselves, it is consistent with Berkeley's concern with God's lawful ordering of ideas to suggest that if I cause my arm to move, God will cause an idea of my moving arm in you.

9. Hume, *Treatise*, I.i.1, p. 1.

10. Ibid., I.i.1, p. 2.

11. Cf. *PHK*, 1. This holds equally for sensible and nonsensible objects (e.g., minds), although in the case of the latter there is more to one's conception than a positive idea (see my 'Berkeley's Notions', *Philosophy and Phenomenological Research*, 45 (1985) pp. 407-25, or Chs 4 and 5 below).

12. Cf. *PHK*, 16-17. We shall discuss this at length in Ch. 4.

13. Although this chapter provides nothing more than a preliminary study of the quantified modal logic that is implicit in Berkeley's philosophy, one point that is germane to a more complete elucidation of that logic should be clear, namely, that Berkeley accepted neither the Barcan Formula, i.e., $[\diamond(\exists x)\Phi \rightarrow (\exists x)\diamond\Phi]$, nor the Converse Barcan Formula, i.e., $[(\exists x)\diamond\Phi \rightarrow \diamond(\exists x)\Phi]$ in the epistemic realm. Although from the fact that one knows that it is *de dicto* possible that there is an x that is Φ one can know that there are divine ideas of an x that is Φ, divine ideas are not *de re* possible objects, i.e., they are not possible components of real objects that are Φ. *De dicto* possible objects have an archetypical existence, while real objects have an ectypical existence (cf. *DHP*, III, 254-5), and for this reason God's ideas are not possible components of real objects. To deny this would be inconsistent with Berkeley's repeated rejection of occasionalism (cf. *PHK* 67-69; *DHP*, II, 213-15 and 219-20). Hence, it would be unreasonable to attribute the Barcan Formula to Berkeley. Not would it be reasonable to attribute the Converse Barcan

Formula to Berkeley. If Berkeley accepted the Converse Barcan Formula, then he would hold that *de re* possibility entails *de dicto* possibility, but this cannot be. *De dicto* possible objects are objects that could be real, whether or not there are such objects. As we have seen, to have epistemic grounds for claiming that it is possible that there is a real x that is Φ requires not merely a consistent description of the temporal slices of those objects — the ideas that would compose them — it also requires a consistent statement of the laws of nature that unite those temporal slices into a real object. To claim that there is an x that is possibly Φ (*de re* possibility) is to claim merely that there is a possible component (temporal slice) of a real x that is Φ, and since such a consideration pays no attention to any laws of nature that might unite such components into a real object, considerations of *de re* possibility show little regarding *de dicto* possibility.

14. Willis Doney, 'Berkeley's Argument Against Abstract Ideas', p. 306, note 3.

15. Since those who attribute an inconceivability criterion of impossibility to Berkeley pay little or no attention to the distinctions between *de dicto* and *de re* conceivability and possibility, we need not concern ourselves with these distinctions for the purposes of this discussion.

16. Cf. Colin M. Turbayne, 'Lending a Hand to Philonous: The Berkeley, Plato, Aristotle Connection', in Colin Morray Turbayne (ed.), *Berkeley: Critical and Interpretive Essays* (University of Minnesota Press, Minneapolis, 1982), pp. 295-310.

17. Cf. Willis Doney, 'Is Berkeley's a Cartesian Mind?', pp. 273-82.

18. Cf. David Raynor, '"*Minima Sensibilia*" in Berkeley and Hume', *Dialogue*, 19 (1980), pp. 196-200. Although Bracken has argued that minimum sensibles are extended (cf. Harry M. Bracken, *Berkeley* (St. Martin's Press, New York, 1974), p. 27 and Harry M. Bracken, 'Hume on the "Distinction of Reason"', *Hume Studies*, 10 (1984), pp. 94-5, 106 n. 14), I find his arguments unconvincing. Commenting on entry 276 of the *Philosophical Commentaries* — Berkeley's claim that 'It seems all lines can't be bisected in 2 equall parts ...' — Bracken writes: 'That is, it seems a line of an unequal number of *minima* could not be divided equally. Hence each *minimum visible* is extended' ('Hume on the "Distinction of Reason"', p. 95). The conclusion that minimum sensibles are extended simply does not follow from this. The mark of being extended was divisibility. If a minimum sensible is indivisible, this would indicate that it is *un*extended, not that it is extended.

Appendix

Propositional Functions in Chapter 2

(1) $\Diamond CP \to \Diamond P$
(2) $-\Diamond P \to -\Diamond CP$
(3) $\Diamond CP \leftrightarrow \Diamond P$
(4) $(\Diamond CP \to \Diamond P) \,\&\, (\Diamond P \to \Diamond CP)$
(5) $\Diamond P \to \Diamond CP$
(6) $-\Diamond CP \to -\Diamond P$
(7) $-\Diamond CP \leftrightarrow -\Diamond P$
(8) $\Diamond(\exists y)Cy(\exists x)\Phi x \to \Diamond(\exists x)\Phi x$
(9) $\Diamond(\exists y)Cy(\exists x)\Phi x \to (\exists x)\Diamond\Phi x$

(10) $(\exists y)\Diamond Cy(\exists x)\Phi x \to \Diamond(\exists x)\Phi x$
(11) $(\exists y)\Diamond Cy(\exists x)\Phi x \to (\exists x)\Diamond \Phi x$
(12) $(\exists y)Cy(\exists x)\Phi x \to \Diamond(\exists x)\Phi x$
(13) $(\exists y)Cy(\exists x)\Phi x \to (\exists x)\Diamond \Phi x$
(14) $-\Diamond(\exists x)\Phi x \to -\Diamond(\exists y)Cy(\exists x)\Phi x$
(15) $-(\exists x)\Diamond \Phi x \to -\Diamond(\exists y)Cy(\exists x)\Phi x$
(16) $-\Diamond(\exists x)\Phi x \to -(\exists y)\Diamond Cy(\exists x)\Phi x$
(17) $-(\exists x)\Diamond \Phi x \to -(\exists y)\Diamond Cy(\exists x)\Phi x$
(18) $-\Diamond(\exists x)\Phi x \to -(\exists y)Cy(\exists x)\Phi x$
(19) $-(\exists x)\Diamond \Phi x \to -(\exists y)Cy(\exists x)\Phi x$
(20) $\Diamond(\exists y)Cy(\exists x)\Phi x \leftrightarrow \Diamond(\exists x)\Phi x$
(21) $\Diamond(\exists y)Cy(\exists x)\Phi x \leftrightarrow (\exists x)\Diamond \Phi x$
(22) $(\exists y)\Diamond Cy(\exists x)\Phi x \leftrightarrow \Diamond(\exists x)\Phi x$
(23) $(\exists y)\Diamond Cy(\exists x)\Phi x \leftrightarrow (\exists x)\Diamond \Phi x$
(24) $(\exists y)Cy(\exists x)\Phi x \leftrightarrow \Diamond(\exists x)\Phi x$
(25) $(\exists y)Cy(\exists x)\Phi x \leftrightarrow (\exists x)\Diamond \Phi x$
(26) $-\Diamond(\exists y)Cy(\exists x)\Phi x \to -\Diamond(\exists x)\Phi x$
(27) $-\Diamond(\exists y)Cy(\exists x)\Phi x \to -(\exists x)\Diamond \Phi x$
(28) $-(\exists y)\Diamond Cy(\exists x)\Phi x \to -\Diamond(\exists x)\Phi x$
(29) $-(\exists y)\Diamond Cy(\exists x)\Phi x \to -(\exists x)\Diamond \Phi x$
(30) $-(\exists y)Cy(\exists x)\Phi x \to -\Diamond(\exists x)\Phi x$
(31) $-(\exists y)Cy(\exists x)\Phi x \to -(\exists x)\Diamond \Phi x$
(32) $-Ci(\exists x)\Phi x \to -\Diamond(\exists x)\Phi x$
(33) $-Ci(\exists x)\Phi x \to -(\exists x)\Diamond \Phi x$
(34) $-\Diamond Ci(\exists x)\Phi x \to -\Diamond(\exists x)\Phi x$
(35) $-\Diamond Ci(\exists x)\Phi x \to -(\exists x)\Diamond \Phi x$
(36) $-\Diamond Cg(\exists x)\Phi x \to -\Diamond(\exists x)\Phi x$
(37) $-\Diamond Cg(\exists x)\Phi x \to -(\exists x)\Diamond \Phi x$
(38) $-Cg(\exists x)\Phi x \to -\Diamond(\exists x)\Phi x$
(39) $-Cg(\exists x)\Phi x \to -(\exists x)\Diamond \Phi x$
(40) $\Diamond(\exists y)Dy(\exists x)\Phi x \to \Diamond(\exists x)\Phi x$
(41) $\Diamond(\exists y)Dy(\exists x)\Phi x \to (\exists x)\Diamond \Phi x$
(42) $\Diamond(\exists y)Dy(\exists x)\Phi x \leftrightarrow \Diamond(\exists x)\Phi x$
(43) $\Diamond(\exists y)Dy(\exists x)\Phi x \leftrightarrow (\exists x)\Diamond \Phi x$
(44) $-\Diamond(\exists y)Dy(\exists x)\Phi x \to -\Diamond(\exists x)\Phi x$
(45) $-\Diamond(\exists y)Dy(\exists x)\Phi x \to -(\exists x)\Diamond \Phi x$
(46) $-\Diamond(\exists x)\Phi x \to -\Diamond(\exists y)Dy(\exists x)\Phi x$
(47) $-(\exists x)\Diamond \Phi x \to -\Diamond(\exists y)Dy(\exists x)\Phi x$
(48) $(\exists y)Dy(\exists x)\Phi x \to \Diamond(\exists x)\Phi x$
(49) $(\exists y)Dy(\exists x)\Phi x \leftrightarrow \Diamond(\exists x)\Phi x$
(50) $(\exists y)Dy(\exists x)\Phi x \to (\exists x)\Diamond \Phi x$

(51) $(\exists y)Dy(\exists x)\Phi x \leftrightarrow (\exists x)\Diamond \Phi x$
(52) $-(\exists y)Dy(\exists x)\Phi x \rightarrow -\Diamond(\exists x)\Phi x$
(53) $-(\exists y)Dy(\exists x)\Phi x \rightarrow -(\exists x)\Diamond \Phi x$
(54) $\Diamond Cg(\exists x)\Phi x \leftrightarrow \Diamond(\exists x)\Phi x$
(55) $Cg(\exists x)\Phi x \leftrightarrow \Diamond (\exists x)\Phi x$

3 BERKELEY'S THEORY OF MEANING

Having examined his objections to the doctrine of abstract ideas and his criteria of possibility and impossibility, we may now turn to Berkeley's positive theory of meaning. My concern will be *solely* with the use of language for communication and not with such alternative uses of language as the rousing of emotion (cf. Intro, 19). We have already seen that in developing one of his objections to the doctrine of abstract ideas Berkeley argued that an extensional theory of meaning provides adequate grounds for the meaning of sortal terms, and, therefore, on grounds of parsimony, one should not posit abstract ideas as the meanings of sortal terms. In this chapter we shall see that Berkeley included both *de dicto* and *de re* possible objects in the extension of a term.[1] Indeed, we shall see that Berkeley's theory of meaning is more consistently extensional than Locke's is intensional (connotative), for while Locke held that abstract ideas provide the meanings of sortal (categorematic) terms but not of syncategorematic terms, Berkeley's theory will allow one to treat both categorematic and syncategorematic terms extensionally.

I shall begin by drawing several distinctions that will prove germane to the elucidation of an extensional theory of meaning. Next, I shall examine Berkeley's discussions of the meaning of sortal terms. Third, I shall show that Berkeley's extensional theory of meaning pertains to syncategorematic terms as well as to categorematic terms. Since Berkeley held that meaning is purely conventional, I shall examine, fourth, the question of how the relevant conventions come to be known. Finally, I shall briefly examine Berkeley's discussions of analogical and metaphorical meaning.

Extensions and Paradigms

In discussions of meaning a distinction is commonly drawn between extensional or denotative theories of meaning and intensional or connotative theories of the meaning of sortal terms. Proponents of an extensional theory of meaning hold that a sortal term refers distributively to all objects to which the term correctly applies, and it is each of these objects in all their particularity that the term means. Thus, it is all cats that provide the meaning of the term 'cat'. Proponents of an intensional theory of meaning hold that it is all and only those properties that objects of a certain kind (in the extension of a term) have in common that provide the meaning of a sortal term. Thus, the meaning of the term 'cat' consists of all and only the properties that are common to all cats. It should be clear that the theory of meaning implicit in Locke's discussion of abstract ideas is an intensional theory of meaning.[2] In the next section we shall see that Berkeley's theory of meaning is an extensional theory.

With respect to an intensional theory of meaning, a distinction is commonly drawn between the subjective intension or connotation of a term, the objective intension of a term and the conventional intension of a term. The *subjective* intension of a term consists of all and only those properties of objects of a certain kind that a particular speaker of a language considers to be possessed by all the objects in the extension of a term. The subjective connotation of a term is subject to change as a language user's knowledge of the objects in the extension of a term increases. A Lockean nominal essence might reasonably be taken to express the subjective intension of a term.[3] The *objective* intension of a term consists of all and only those properties of objects of a certain kind that are actually possessed by all the objects in the extension of a term. The objective intension of a term does not vary among speakers, and one might reasonably compare it with a Lockean real essence or a scholastic essential form. As Locke indicates, however, at least the real essence of substances cannot be known, or can be known only by an omniscient mind and, consequently, real essences (objective intensions) can play little or no role in a theory of meaning.[4] Finally, the *conventional* connotation of a term consists of all and only those properties of objects of a certain kind that are generally accepted by the speakers of a certain language as distinguishing objects of one kind from objects of all other kinds. The conventional intension of a term is public in the sense that it might be stated in a lexical definition. Like the subjective intension of a term, the conventional intension of a term might change or become enriched as the majority of the speakers of the language become more knowledgeable of properties of objects of a certain kind, but such changes are slow and gradual *vis-à-vis* changes in the subjective intension of any given speaker. For example, as a child learns a language, his or her subjective intension of a term will approach the conventional intension of the term — this is what is taken to be involved in coming to know the meaning of a word — but if the child-now-adult specializes in a particular area of study, his or her subjective intension of a given term might eventually include many more properties than does the conventional intension of a term.

A similar set of distinctions can be drawn with respect to the extensions of a term. The *subjective* extension of a term consists of all and only those objects that a particular speaker of a language includes in the extension of a term. Since any given speaker of a language has a very limited range of experience, the speaker's subjective extension of a term will always be relatively limited, and the number of objects in the subjective extension will increase as the speaker becomes acquainted with additional objects of a particular kind. The number of objects in the speaker's subjective extension will also decrease if the speaker is somewhat forgetful. In any case, the subjective extension of a term will be subject to almost constant change. The *objective* extension of a term consists of all and only those objects that are actually included in the extension of a term. As in the case of the objective *intension*, the objective extension could be known only by an omniscient speaker of a language and it is, therefore, of little interest to us. Finally, the *conventional* extension of a term consists of all and only those objects that the majority of speakers of a particular language include in the extension of a term.

Now it should be noticed that there is an imperfect parallel between the conventional *intension* of a term and the conventional *extension* of a term. While the conventional *intension* of a term consists of all and only those properties of objects of a kind that the majority of speakers of a language deem constitutive of a thing of a kind, one cannot reasonably claim that the conventional *extension* of a term consists of all and only those particular objects that the majority of speakers of a language include in the extension of a particular term, for there are few particular objects with which the majority of the speakers of a language are familiar. If one can reasonably speak of the conventional extension of a general term, it is plausible to do so only in terms of *paradigms* together with a rule of resemblance indicating that anything will count as a thing of that kind if it resembles the paradigms at least as much as the paradigms resemble one another. For example, most speakers of

American English might deem the Empire State Building, the Sears Tower, the World Trade Center and the Hancock Building paradigmatic skyscrapers, even though any given speaker of the language might use only one or two of these buildings as his or her subjective paradigm(s). By comparing other objects with these paradigms, for example, my house or the University of Texas Tower, one would have grounds for deciding whether or not the term 'skyscraper' is properly applied to those objects, that is, whether those objects are properly to be included in the extension of the term 'skyscraper'.[5] If this is an accurate account of conventional meaning according to an extensional theory of meaning, then learning the meaning of sortal terms consists of learning what at least some of the conventional paradigms of things of a kind are and developing the ability to make comparisons between the paradigms and other objects that result in classifications that are consistent with those of the majority of speakers of the language.

There are several reasons why philosophers might consider extensional theories of meaning attractive. First, if one proposes an *intensional* theory of meaning, some philosophers will assign a distinct ontological status to the intension of a term, and, consequently, such an intensional theory of meaning will assume a richer ontology than is required for an extensional theory of meaning. We have already seen that one of Berkeley's criticisms of Locke's theory of meaning was based upon such a consideration: if abstract ideas are a distinct kind of entity and it is possible to construct a theory of meaning that does not posit abstract ideas, the latter theory is philosophically preferable on grounds of parsimony.[6] Second, and related to the first, some extensional theories of meaning allow one to avoid charges of essentialism.[7] Finally, and related to the second, an extensional theory of meaning will allow that very different kinds of things can be classified under the same sortal term. Since there is nothing essential signified by the term 'Christmas tree', the term can signify both evergreen trees that are decorated with lights and ornaments at Christmas and the arrangement of pipes and values used to direct the flow of oil and natural gas at an oil well. We shall see that this last fact regarding extensional theories of meaning is of some importance to Berkeley.

One further point should be noticed. Even if one proposes an extensional theory of meaning, this does not preclude one from giving an intensional definition of a term. In such a case, the definition consists of nothing more than a listing of all the known classes of objects in which a thing of a certain kind is found. We shall see that Berkeley himself recognized this fact.

Given this as a conceptual background, let us now turn to Berkeley's discussion of meaning.

Berkeley and Categorematic Terms

There can be little question that Berkeley accepted an extensional theory of the meaning of sortal or categorematic terms. As we saw in Chapter 1, the criticism of the abstractionists that he raised in Section 11 of the Introduction to the *Principles* was intended to show that there are no grounds for positing abstract ideas in grounding the meaning of sortal terms, for it is possible to develop an adequate account of the meaning of sortal terms without the introduction of abstract ideas. As used by an individual speaker of a language, a sortal term does not pick out an abstract idea that specifies the (subjective) intension of that term, rather, 'a word becomes general by being made a sign, ... of several particular ideas, any one of which it indifferently suggests to the mind' (Intro., 11). While his passage might suggest that Berkeley was concerned merely with the subjective extension of a term, many other discussions provide overwhelming evidence that he took meaning in general to be based upon the extension of a term. In Section 12 of the Introduction, one finds this:

> And as that particular line becomes general, by being made a sign, so the name *line* which taken absolutely is particular, by being a sign is made general. And as the former owes its generality, not to its being the sign of an abstract or general line, but of all particular right lines that may possibly exist, so the latter must be thought to derive its generality from the same cause, namely, the various particular lines which it indifferently denotes. (Intro., 12)

In Section 15 of the Introduction, one finds this:

> It is I know a point, much insisted on, that all knowledge and demonstration are about universal notions, to which I fully agree: but then it doth not appear to me that those notions are formed by *abstraction* in the manner premised; *universality*, so

far as I can comprehend not consisting of the absolute, positive nature or conception of any thing, but in the relation it bears to the particulars signified or represented by it: in virtue whereof it is that things, names, or notions, being in their own nature *particular*, are rendered *universal*. (Intro., 15)

In Section 18 of the Introduction, Berkeley wrote, 'Whereas, in truth, there is no such thing as one precise and definite signification annexed to any general name, they all signify indifferently a great number of particular ideas' (Intro., 18; cf. First Draft, *Works* 2: 127-9). Notice that in each of these passages Berkeley claims, contrary to the abstractionists, that a word does not signify or denote an abstract general idea; rather, it signifies an indeterminably large number of determinate particular ideas. Further, this account of the meaning of sortal terms was retained at least through the first two editions of the *Alciphron*. There one finds this:

Euphranor. But may not words become general by being made to stand indiscriminately for all particular ideas which from a mutual resemblance belong to the same kind, without the intervention of any abstract general idea?
Alciphron. Is there then no such thing as a general idea?
Euphranor. May we not admit general ideas, though we should not admit them to be made by abstraction, or though we should not allow of general abstract ideas? To me it seems a particular idea may become general by being used to stand for or represent other ideas; and that general knowledge is conversant about signs or general ideas made such by their signification, and which are considered rather in their relative capacity, and as substituted for others, than in their own nature or for their own sake. A black line, for instance, an inch long, though in itself particular, may yet become universal, being used as a sign to stand for any line whatsoever.
Alciphron. It is your opinion, then, that words become general by representing an indefinite number of particular ideas?
Euphranor. It seems so to me.

(*Works*, 3.334-5)

Berkeley's point is, again, that sortal terms conjunctively signify all of the many things of a particular sort, that is, his theory of the meaning of sortal terms is extensional.

These passages leave little question that Berkeley proposed an extensional theory of the meaning of sortal terms. Each passage refers to the signification of an object by a word, and if we are to understand Berkeley's theory of meaning, we must become clear on the nature of the signification relation. In an attempt to elucidate the nature of Berkeley's relation of signification, I shall examine Section 12 of the Introduction in some detail. By examining the claims made there in the light of several passages from the *New Theory of Vision*, we shall discover the extent to which Berkeley took the relation of signification to be arbitrary and the methods by which he divided objects into sorts.

In Section 12 of the Introduction, Berkeley wrote:

> By observing how ideas become general, we may the better judge how words are made so. And here it is to be noted that I do not deny absolutely there are *general ideas*, but only that there are any *abstract general ideas*. For, in the passages we have quoted wherein there is mention of general ideas, it is always supposed that they are formed by abstraction, after the manner set forth in sections 8 and 9. Now if we will annex a meaning to our words, and speak only of what we can conceive, I believe we shall acknowledge, that an idea, which considered in itself is particular, becomes general, by being made to represent or stand for all other particular ideas of the same sort. To make this plain by an example, suppose a geometrician is demonstrating the method, of cutting a line in two equal parts. He draws, for instance, a black line of an inch in length, this which in itself is a particular line is nevertheless with regard to its signification general, since as it is there used, it represents all particular lines whatsoever; for that which is demonstrated of it, is demonstrated of all lines or, in other words, of a line in general. And as that particular line becomes general, by being made a sign, so the name *line* which taken absolutely is particular, by being a sign is made general. And as the former owes its generality, not to its being the sign of an abstract or general line, but of all particular lines that may possibly exist, so the latter must be thought to derive its generality from the same cause, namely, the various particular lines which it indifferently denotes. (Intro., 12)

Notice Berkeley claims that a determinate particular idea becomes general by being made to represent all ideas of the same sort. The relation that obtains between a particular idea functioning as a general idea and other particular ideas of that sort is the relation of signification: a determinate particular idea of a line *signifies* all lines, and Berkeley indicates that, similarly, a term such as 'right line' signifies 'all particular right lines that may possibly exist'. None the less, his contention that either a particular idea or a particular word can represent all things of a sort raises two questions. First how does Berkeley divide the world into sorts? Second, is the signification relation that obtains between a general Berkeleian idea and all things of a sort the same kind of relation that obtains between a word and all things of a sort? Once we have answered these questions we may more profitably examine the evidence supporting my claim that Berkeley's theory of meaning is purely extensional and questions regarding the kinds of objects included in the extension of a term.

Consider the right line (or line segment) Berkeley's geometrician draws on a piece of paper. It is a straight line an inch in length drawn with black ink on white paper. This line is said to signify *all* right lines. How can this be? In one sense, the answer is quite straightforward: assuming that the things in the world are already divided into sorts of things, the geometrician's line is presented as a paradigm of a line as such, and any claim that will be true of that line as a line will be true of any other line as such. As a paradigm of a line, one is not concerned with the color of the line, its length, or the fact that all lines drawn with a pen have some breadth. The knowledgeable speaker of a language has been acquainted with straight lines of many lengths, drawn on objects of various kinds with instruments of various kinds, and he or she will understand what the geometrician will mean in claiming that the line drawn signifies or represents any line whatsoever. The geometrician is suggesting that one should not attend to the length of the line, the color of the line, the fact that it was drawn with a broad-tipped pen, and the consequent fact that it has some breadth: there are other things that are classified as lines which have none of these characteristics. The line that has been drawn represents all lines regardless of its accidental characteristics.[8] But while this might be clear enough for a person who already understands what sort of thing a line is, we still must inquire into the grounds upon which Berkeley divides things into sorts.

While Berkeley's discussion of the solitary man in the First Draft of the Introduction to the *Principles* seems to suggest that one is able to engage in a limited amount of sorting apart from language (cf. *Works* 2: 141), for our purposes it will be easier to discuss the division of things into sorts on the assumption that there is already a conventional language in place. Let us assume I am attempting to teach my son Tristan the meaning of the word 'line'. In doing so I might use a broad-tipped pen to draw a black line of one inch on a piece of white paper, a narrow-tipped pen to draw a red line of six inches on a piece of white paper, a green crayon to draw a line of six inches on a piece of red paper, piece of blue chalk to draw a twelve inch line on a blackboard, and so forth, pointing to each line after I draw it and clearly saying, 'Line'. Since I know the conventions of the English language, each of the lines to which I would point would be correctly identified as a line, and as Tristan learns the meaning of the term 'line' he would also point at various things speakers of English call lines and say, 'Line'. One would become confident that he had learned the meaning of the term 'line' when he was able to point to lines he had not seen before and consistently could say 'line', rather than 'circle' or 'duck'. In learning the meaning of the term, it would seem that all he is doing is noticing or attending to the respect in which the lines he sees are similar to those I have shown him in the past, that is, that his sorting of kinds of things in to the classes of lines and non-lines is based upon the resemblances between those things he sees and the paradigmatic lines I have shown him. Let us assume that Tristan has now learned what sort of things visible lines are. One day we go for a walk. As we walk down the sidewalk, Tristan gleefully points to a division between one slab of concrete and another and says, 'Line'. He then sits down and runs his finger along the division between the two slabs of concrete and 'feels the line'. Now assuming that one can plausibly speak of tangible lines, a good Berkeleian would contend that the visible line between the two slabs of concrete is distinct from the tangible line between them, indeed, it is a major theme in the *New Theory of Vision* that the objects of sight and the objects of touch are distinct (see *NTV*, 132-7). Thus, Berkeley would claim that there is literally no similarity between the visible lines Tristan has learned to identify and the tangible lines with which he is becoming acquainted as he sits on the sidewalk. Some visible things might be classified as lines on the basis of the resemblances among them, and some tangible things might be classified as lines on the basis of the resemblances among them, but visible and tangible lines are distinct sorts of lines.

But if visible and tangible lines are distinct sorts of lines, why are they both placed under the appellation 'line'? Berkeley provides an answer to this question in his *New Theory of Vision*. In discussing this issue regarding visible and tangible figures in general, he wrote:

> It is customary to call written words and the things they signify by the same name; for, words not being regarded in their own nature, or otherwise than as they are marks of things, it has been superfluous and beside the design of language to have given them names distinct from those of the things marked by them. The same reason holds here also. Visible figures are the marks of tangible figures; and, for sec. 59, it is plain that in themselves they are little regarded, or upon any other score than for their connection with tangible figures, which by nature they are ordained to signify. And, because this language of nature does not vary in different ages or nations, hence it is that in all times and places visible figures are called by the same names as the respective tangible figures suggested by them; and not because they are alike, or of the same sort with them. (*NTV*, 140)

Given that visible figures and tangible figures are distinct kinds of things, Berkeley indicates that visible figures are naturally signs of tangible figures. What does he mean by this? He means, at least in part, that visible figures and tangible figures are united together by natural laws (are constantly conjoined in experience). As a matter of fact, in many cases — although presumably not all — when one is aware of a visible figure, there is a specifiable procedure one might undertake in order to be aware of a tangible figure. For example, if one sees a cube, then if one visibly places one's hand on the cube, one will become aware of the tangible figure. Now, unless one has a very acute sense of touch, it is unlikely that one could become tactually aware of a line consisting of a mound of graphite on a piece of paper and it is clear that one cannot become tactually aware of a line on the monitor of a computer, so in the case of two-dimensional tangible figures there is only a partial conjunction between the visible and tangible figures of which one is aware. It is worthy of note, however, that the paragraph from the

New Theory of Vision is presented in the context of a discussion of the Molyneux Problem, and, consequently, it was concerned with the correlation between a two-dimensional visual image and the three dimensions of which one is aware on the basis of touch. Since, in fact, any line one would visually perceive has some breadth and any line one would tactually perceive has both some breadth and some depth, there is a close correlation between lines and other figures, and the natural tendency to take a visual object to be a sign of a tangible object would apply in the case of lines as well.

Now that we have seen that Berkeley maintains that visible and tangible lines are different in kind but includes both under the term 'line', we are in a position to discuss the relation of signification both with respect to words and Berkeleian general ideas, that is, determinate ideas that are general in function. As we noticed above, in Section 12 of the Introduction Berkeley claimed that the 'black line of an inch in length' that a geometrician draws as an illustration for a proof, though 'a particular line is nevertheless *with regard to its signification* general' (Intro., 12). Given that the particular black line 'represents all particular lines whatsoever' (Intro., 12), it follows that the relation of signification is not based *solely* upon resemblance. While all visual lines will, to a greater or lesser degree, resemble the geometrician's line, no tangible lines will resemble it. Hence, resemblance between a particular idea taken as general and all the other particular ideas it is taken to signify is not a necessary condition for signification. It is merely a matter of fact that human beings take both visual and tangible lines to be lines, and, in this sense, the signification of all lines of all kinds by a particular determinate line or idea of a line is arbitrary: if human psychology were different, the signification relation would be different as well.[9]

If the relation of signification is arbitrary when one takes a particular idea of a line to represent all lines, it is still more arbitrary in the case of words, for while an idea of a line might resemble some lines, for example, visible lines, there is no resemblance between a word and any of the objects in the extension of a term. Indeed, the introduction of words increases both the degree of arbitrariness and the number of kinds of signification relations. Words are of two kinds: there are spoken words and written words, and consequently there is a signification relation that obtains between these two kinds of words. In the *New Theory of Vision*, Berkeley indicates that the relation between written letters and particular sounds is purely conventional and arbitrary prior to the establishment of a convention among the speakers of a language, although this relation is no longer arbitrary once a convention has been established. As Berkeley wrote:

> To illustrate this, I observe that visible figures represent tangible figures much after the same manner that written words do sounds. Now, in this respect, words are not arbitrary; it not being indifferent what written word stands for any sound. But it is requisite that each word contain in it so many distinct characters as there are variations in the sound it stands for. Thus, the single letter *a* is proper to mark one simple uniform sound; and the word *adultery* is accommodated to represent the sound annexed to it — in the formation whereof there being eight different collisions or modifications of the air by sound, it was fit the word representing it should consist of as many distinct characters, thereby to mark each particular difference or part of the whole sound. And yet nobody, I presume, will say the single letter *a*, or the word *adultery*, are alike unto or of the same species with the respective by them represented. *It is indeed arbitrary that, in general, letters of any language represent sounds at all; but, when that is once agreed, it is not arbitrary what combination of letters shall represent this or that particular sound* [emphasis added]. I leave this with the reader to pursue, and apply it in his own thoughts. (*NTV*, 143)

Notice that Berkeley here indicates that there is a signification relation that obtains between a sound and a written letter — in virtue of several such relations, a signification relation that obtains between a spoken word and a written word. Ultimately, this relation is arbitrary. In so far as it is determinate, the signification relation is established merely on the basis of the conventions of a particular language. It should be remembered, of course, that Berkeley understood kinds extensionally, and consequently, any instance of the letter 'a' signifies *all* the instances of each of the several kinds of sounds conventionally associated with that letter, and each of these particular sounds of each kind signifies *all* instances of the written letter 'a'. Similarly, any written instance of a word such as 'adultery' signifies all instances of those combinations of sounds that are, by convention, deemed spoken instances of that word, and vice versa.[10]

Turning now to the signification of words, it should be clear, given our considerations to this point, that the number of distinct kinds of objects that will be included in the extension of a term will vary with the term in question. In the case of the term 'red', for example, the extension of the term includes all things that are red in color and all these things are objects of sight (cf. *PHK*, 1). With respect to other terms, however, many different kinds of object can be included in the extension of a particular word. If, as Berkeley suggests, the objects available to each of the several senses are distinct in kind, then the term 'rose' must be understood to signify a class of certain resembling visual objects of certain shapes, certain resembling objects of smell, certain resembling objects of touch, and, perhaps, certain resembling objects of taste. Since there are various conventions governing the use of the term 'rose', that is, one would want to distinguish between 'real roses' growing in the garden, plastic roses, pictures of roses and rose water perfume, the precise kinds of visual, tactual, and olfactory objects included in the extension of the term would vary with the sense of the term 'rose' in question and the conventions that govern that sense of the term. In each case, however, there are distinct kinds of sensible objects (ideas) that fall within the extension of the term, and although there might be resemblances among all objects of one sensible mode that are included in the extension of a term, there neither is nor need be any resemblance among the objects of distinct sensible modes that fall under the extension of any one sense of the term 'rose': Berkeley would contend that it is all of the objects of each of those distinct sensible modes that are included in the extension of the term, and it is, therefore, all the objects of each of those sensible modes that one 'means' by the term 'rose'.[11] Although all of Berkeley's discussions of the meanings of sortal or categorematic terms focus on nouns and adjectives, the same considerations apply in the case of verbs and adverbs. Verbs would be treated as gerunds and adverbs would be treated as adjectives modifying gerunds. In a case of a verb such as 'walk', for example, the extension of the term would include at least certain visible objects (ideas of walking) and the kinesthetic sensations that one has when one walks. Thus, there are good grounds for contending that Berkeley treated the meaning of all categorematic terms extensionally.

So far we have seen that Berkeley proposed an extensional

theory of the meaning of categorematic terms, that he divided the world into sorts on the basis of the resemblances among objects of a sort, and that the division of objects into sorts is independent of language at least in the sense that objects of more than one sort can be included in the extension of a term. Before we turn to Berkeley's treatment of syncategorematic terms, we should ask another question regarding the kinds of objects Berkeley includes in the extension of a term: whether Berkeley includes possible objects in the extension of a term.

If my discussions in the last chapter of Berkeley's distinction between ideas and real objects and his distinction between *de dicto* and *de re* possible objects is correct, it follows that Berkeley included at least *de re* possible objects in the extension of a term, for it was shown that ideas are *de re* possible objects, and it is unquestionable that Berkeley included ideas in the extension of a term. The latter theme is found at several places in the Introduction to the *Principles*. In Section 11, for example, Berkeley wrote, 'But it seems that a word becomes general by being made a sign, not of an abstract general idea, but of *several particular ideas*, any one of which it indifferently suggests to the mind' (Intro., 11; emphasis added). In Section 18, one finds, 'Whereas, in truth, there is no such thing as one precise and definite signification annexed to any general name, they all signify indifferently *a great number of particular ideas*' (Intro., 18; emphasis added). In the First Draft of the Introduction, the same theme is repeated:

> From which it must necessarily follow, that one word be made of sign of *a great number of particular ideas*, between which there is some likeness, & which are said to be of the same sort. (*Works* 2:128; emphasis added)

> Any name may be used indifferently for the sign of *any idea, or any number of ideas*, it not being determin'd by any likeness to represent one more than another. (*Works* 2:129; emphasis added)

The theme was raised again in the first two editions of the *Alciphron*:

> **Euphranor.** But may not words become general by being made to stand indiscriminately for *all particular ideas* which from a

mutual resemblance belong to the same kind, without the intervention of any abstract general idea?
(*Works* 3:334; emphasis added; cf. *FTM*, 47)

Thus, there can be little question that Berkeley included ideas, that is, *de re* possible objects, in the extension of a term. Nor is this surprising. Throughout his works, Berkeley takes ideas and minds to be the two most fundamental categories in his ontology. Real sensible objects are themselves composed of lawfully ordered ideas and a real sensible object is an object of a particular kind in virtue of the several kinds of sensible ideas of which it is composed. Given the status of ideas in his ontology together with his contention that all ideas are particulars (cf. Intro, 11, 12), the inclusion of ideas, that is, *de re* possible objects, in the extension of a term is what one would expect from Berkeley.

By including *de re* possible objects in the extension of a term, his extensional theory of meaning falls more squarely within the domain of common sense than do the theories of many of the twentieth-century proponents of an extensional theory of meaning. Most recent proponents of an extensional theory of meaning include only 'real objects' in the extension of a term.[12] This yields a consequence that seems contrary to common sense. Since there are neither real unicorns nor real centaurs, the meaning of the terms 'unicorn' and 'centaur' is the same: both terms denote the null set (both terms are meaningless). But anyone who has perused the pictures in the unabridged edition of the *Random House Dictionary of the English Language*, or has read *Bullfinch's Mythology*, might find this contention quite surprising. 'Surely,' they would say, 'what I mean by the term 'unicorn' is something resembling that depicted in the second column on page 1,552 of the *Random House Dictionary*, while what I mean by the term 'centaur' is something resembling that depicted in the first column on page 239 of the *Random House Dictionary*. While there is a limited resemblance between these two things — the bodies of both resemble bodies of horses — there are also significant differences between the unicorn depicted and the centaur depicted. It makes little sense to claim that the meaning of the terms 'unicorn' and 'centaur' are the same, that is to say that both terms are meaningless. At the very least, I have limited grounds for distinguishing between what would be a unicorn from what would be a centaur, if either of these mythical beasts were real.' By including ideas (*de re* possible objects) in the extension of a term, Berkeley's extensional theory of meaning is consistent with this common sense objection to more recent examples of extensional theories of meaning. One should notice, however, that the inclusion of *de re* possible objects (ideas) in the extension of a term entails that it is sufficient for a term to have meaning even if only objects of one kind of sensible modality are included in the extension of a term. While the term 'horse' includes in its extension ideas derived from at least four senses, terms such as 'unicorn' and 'centaur' would seem to include only ideas corresponding to vision: certainly few people would contend that there are olfactory or auditory ideas of a kind peculiar to unicorns or centaurs.

Having seen that Berkeley includes *de re* possible objects (ideas) in the extension of a term, we must ask whether he also included *de dicto* possible objects in the extension of a term. Here the textual evidence is somewhat less clear, although there are good grounds for suggesting that he did so. One of the few texts that suggests that he included *de dicto* possible objects in the extension of a term might be drawn from Section 12 of the Introduction. There Berkeley wrote:

> And as the former [the particular idea of a line that functions as a general idea] owes its generality, not to being the sign of an abstract or general line, but of all particular right lines that *may possibly exist* [my emphasis], so the latter must be thought to derive its generality from the same cause, namely, the various particular lines which it indifferently denotes. (Intro., 12)

Since Berkeley's example in this section concerned a real line drawn upon a piece of paper, his claim that a particular-idea-taken-as-general or a word is a sign of 'all particular rights lines that may possibly exist' suggests that *de dicto* possible objects are included in the extension of a term. Further, if one remembers that one of Berkeley's objectives in developing an extensional theory of meaning was to provide a criticism of the abstractionists by showing that it is possible to provide an adequate theory of meaning without positing abstract ideas, he is virtually committed to the inclusion of *de dicto* possible objects in the extension of a term. For, given Berkeley's epistemic criterion of *de dicto* possibility, it follows that Locke allowed that *de dicto* possible objects can be included in the extension of a term. Notice what Locke wrote:

And though there neither were, nor had been in Nature such a Beast as an *Unicorn*, nor such a Fish as a *Mermaid*; yet supposing those Names to stand for complex abstract *Ideas*, that contained no inconsistency in them; the *Essence* of a *Mermaid* is as intelligible, as that of a *Man*; and the *Idea* of an *Unicorn*, as certain, steady, and permanent, as that of a Horse.[13]

There are two things to notice here. First, Locke was concerned with the essences of things that do not exist but could exist. Since, unlike Berkeley, Locke did not analyze real sensible objects in terms of ideas, one's abstract idea of the essence of a unicorn is not a possible component of a real unicorn — it is not a *de re* possible object in Berkeley's sense — rather, it is a representation of what would be a unicorn if there were any unicorns. Second, notice that Locke suggests that one's abstract idea of a unicorn must be consistent, and he indicates elsewhere that inconsistent ideas cannot represent real objects.[14] Thus, it seems that a consistent abstract idea of an object represents something that could exist: it is a representation of a *de dicto* possible object.[15] Now insofar as Locke held that abstract ideas can represent *de dicto* possible objects, one would expect that Berkeley would also include *de dicto* possible objects in the extension of a categorematic term, for if Berkeley did not include *de dicto* possible objects in the extension of a term, he would have no grounds for claiming that his theory of meaning is an adequate replacement for Locke's. It is also worth noting that there are similarities between Locke's apparent criterion of *de dicto* possibility and Berkeley's epistemic criterion. Locke seems to hold that it is possible that there is an x that is Φ if there is a consistent *idea* of x as Φ, while we have seen that Berkeley held that one can know that it is possible that there is an x that is Φ if a given *description* of x as Φ is consistent.

Thus, we have seen that Berkeley proposed an extensional theory of the meaning of categorematic terms. He included not only real objects in the extension of a term, he also included both *de re* possible objects (particular ideas of sense) and *de dicto* possible objects in the extension of a term. While the textual evidence supporting my contention that he included *de dicto* possible objects in the extension of a term is less than conclusive, I have argued that since Locke seems to have allowed that one can have abstract ideas representing *de dicto* possible objects, and, since Berkeley's objective in developing an extensional theory of meaning was to establish that it is possible to provide an adequate theory of the meaning of categorematic terms without positing abstract ideas, I concluded that Berkeley's objectives commit him to the inclusion of *de dicto* possible objects in the extension of a term.

Having seen that Berkeley developed an extensional theory of meaning that will account for the meaning of categorematic terms, we must now ask whether the same theory can be extended to account for the meaning of syncategorematic terms. In so far as his theory of meaning will account for the meaning of categorematic terms without positing abstract ideas, Berkeley has shown that his theory of meaning is superior to that of the abstractionists on the grounds of parsimony. If it can also be shown that his extensional theory of meaning can account for the meaning of syncategorematic terms, this will show that Berkeley's theory is also superior to that of the abstractionists on grounds of scope and consistency.

Berkeley and Syncategorematic Terms

As Norman Kretzmann has noted, while Locke proposed his theory of abstract ideas to provide the meaning of sortal or categorematic terms, Locke himself acknowledged that there is another class of words, the class of 'particles' or syncategorematic terms, whose meaning cannot be based upon abstract ideas.[16] Examples of syncategorematic terms are 'all', 'some', conjunctions, negation and the copula. Of these Locke wrote:

> Besides Words, which are names of *Ideas* in the Mind, there are a great many others that are made use of, to signify the *connexion* that the Mind give to *Ideas*, or *Propositions, one with another*. The Mind, in communicating its thought to others, does not only need signs of the *Ideas* it has then before it, but others also, to shew or intimate particular action of its own, at that time, relating to those *Ideas*. This it does several ways; as, *Is*, or *Is not*, are the general marks of the Mind, affirming or denying. But besides affirmation, or negation, without which, there is in Words no Truth or Falsehood, the Mind does, in declaring its Sentiments to others, connect, not only the parts of Propositions, but whole Sentences one to another, with their

several Relations and Dependencies, to make a coherent Discourse.[17]

> They [particles] are all *marks of some Action, or Intimation of the Mind*; and therefore to understand them rightly, the several views, postures, stands, turns, limitations, and exceptions, and several other Thoughts of the Mind, for which we have either none, or very deficient Names, and diligently to be studied. Of these, there are a great variety, much exceeding the number of Particles, that most Languages have, to express them by: and therefore it is not to be wondered, that most of these Particles have diverse, and sometimes almost opposite significations. In the Hebrew Tongue, there is a Particle consisting but of one single Letter, of which there are reckoned up, as I remember, seventy, I am sure above fifty several significations.[18]

There are several things to notice here. First, particles (syncategorematic terms) do *not* signify ideas. This claim entails that, for Locke, not all terms obtain their meaning on the same basis: there is one theory of meaning that applies to categorematic terms; there is another theory of meaning that applies to syncategorematic terms. Second, syncategorematic terms signify actions of the mind. Finally, there are many distinct kinds of actions of the mind that can be signified by a single syncategorematic term, as Locke's example of a particle in Hebrew aptly illustrates. Notice that by allowing that there are many different kinds of actions of the mind that can be signified by a single syncategorematic term, Locke implictly grants that while the signification of a categorematic term can be made determinate on the basis of an idea, the meaning of a syncategorematic term cannot be made determinate on the same basis. Locke's theory of the meaning of syncategorematic terms is similar to Berkeley's theory of the meaning of categorematic terms, for just as Berkeley would allow that objects of many different kinds can be subsumed under a single categorematic term, Locke allowed that many different kinds of actions of the mind can be subsumed under a single syncategorematic term. There still appears to be a difference between Locke's theory of the meaning of syncategorematic terms and Berkeley's theory of the meaning of categorematic terms, for Locke seems to claim that syncategorematic terms directly signify *kinds* of actions of the mind and only indirectly signify individual actions of the mind, while

Berkeley held that categorematic terms directly signify individual objects and indirectly signify kinds of things in virtue of the several resemblances among things of a kind.

Does Berkeley also draw a distinction between his account of the meaning of categorematic (sortal) terms and syncategorematic terms? That is, does he also develop two distinct theories of meaning? Or does his extensional theory of meaning cover syncategorematic terms as well? I hope to show that such evidence as there is suggests his extensional theory of meaning is germane to syncategorematic terms as well as categorematic terms.

While the meaning of categorematic terms is a recurrent theme in Berkeley's published writings, he provided no systematic discussion of the meaning of syncategorematic terms. None the less, there are several remarks regarding particles in the *Philosophical Commentaries*, remarks that were almost certainly occasioned by Berkeley's readings of Locke. In these early notebooks one finds this:

S   Some words there are wch do not stand for Ideas, v.g. particles Will etc (*PC*, 661)

S   particles stand for volitions & their concomitant Ideas (*PC*, 661a)

I   All our knowledge is about particular ideas according to Locke. All our sensations are particular Ideas as is evident. w^t use then do we make of general Ideas, since we neither know, nor perceive them. (*PC*, 666)

S   Tis allow'd that Particles stand not for Ideas & yet they are not said to be empty sounds. The truth on't is they stand for the operations of the mind i.e. volitions (*PC*, 667)

Mo. Mr. Locke says all our knowledge is about Particulars. if so, pray w^t is the following ratiocination but a jumble of words Omnis Homo est animal, omne animal vivit, ergo omnis Homo vivit. it amounts (if you annex particular Ideas to the Words animal & vivit) to no more than this. Omnis Homo est Homo, omnis Homo est Homo, ergo omnis Homo est Homo. A mere Sport & trifling with sounds. (*PC*, 668)

In his note on entries 666, 667 and 668, Luce wrote, 'Locke's position in IV xvii 8 (*cf.* III iii) inconsistent with his doctrine of abstract ideas,'[19] and it seems probable that it was at the point that Berkeley wrote entries 661 through 668 that he recognized that Locke's treatment of the meaning of syncategorematic terms is inconsistent with his treatment of the meaning of categorematic terms. But do these passages tell us anything about Berkeley's own treatment of the meaning of syncategorematic terms? It would seem so. Given his extensive criticism of those theories of the meaning of categorematic terms that are based upon abstract ideas, if Berkeley had found Locke's discussion of the meaning of syncategorematic terms (particles) objectionable, one would expect that he would have at least noted his criticisms in passing. The absence of such criticism together with the absence of an alternative account of the meaning of syncategorematic terms *suggests* that Berkeley was willing to allow that 'particles stand for volitions & their concomitant Ideas' (*PC*, 661a), that is, that just as a categorematic term denotes all real and possible objects of a certain kind (or of several kinds), a syncategorematic term denotes all volitions (and their concomitant ideas) of a certain kind (or of several kinds).[20] Further, given that Berkeley recognized the inconsistency between Locke's account of the meaning of categorematic terms and his account of the meaning of syncategorematic terms, the inconsistency being Locke's contention that the meaning of syncategorematic terms is not based upon abstract ideas, I consider it quite probable that Berkeley recognized that in so far as syncategorematic terms denote actions of the mind, he could consistently deal with the meanings of these terms extensionally. Nor should one find this surprising. Even at the level of categorematic (sortal) terms, it was incumbent upon Berkeley to provide an account of the meaning of terms such as 'spirit', 'love', and 'hate'. It is a recurrent theme in Berkeley's writings that it is neither the case that one has ideas of spirits or such operations of the mind as loving or hating nor the case that spirits and operations of the mind can be analyzed solely in terms of ideas (cf. *PHK*, 27, 89, 140, 142). Consequently, it was incumbent upon him to provide a non-ideational account of one's conception of spirits (minds) and their several operations: this was provided by his doctrine of notions. Thus, in so far as syncategorematic terms denote actions of the mind, providing an extensional account of the meaning of syncategorematic terms raises no problems that were not already present at the level of categorematic terms.

Thus, we may reasonably conclude that Berkeley's extensional a matter of convention. In Section 77 of the *New Theory of Vision*, for example, he wrote, 'All which visible objects are only in the mind; nor do they suggest aught external, whether distance or magnitude, otherwise than by habitual connection, as words do things.' This indicates that it is only a habitual union between a word and various objects that make a word a sign of things of a certain kind, although, as he indicated in Section 51, once this habit is established, 'No sooner do we hear the words of a familiar language pronounced in our ears but the ideas corresponding thereto present themselves to our minds; ... so closely are they united that it is not in our power to keep out the one except we exclude the other also.' None the less, while this indicates that the signification relation between a word and the things it signifies, like the relation of signification between visible objects and tangible objects, is based upon a mental habit, neither of these passages points to the differences between the sources of these habits.

This topic is addressed in Section 144. There Berkeley wrote:

It must be confessed that we are not so apt to confound other signs with the things signified, or to think them of the same species, as we are visible and tangible ideas. But, a little consideration will shew us how this may well be, without our supposing them of a like nature. These signs are constant and universal; their connexion with tangible ideas has been learnt at our first entrance into the world; and ever since, almost every moment of our lives, it has been occurring to our thoughts, and fastening and striking deeper on our minds. *When we observe that signs* [words] *are variable, and of human institution; when we remember there was a time they were not connected in our minds with those things they now so readily suggest, but that their signification was learned by the slow steps of experience: this preserves us from confounding them.* But, when we find the same signs suggest the same things all over the world; when we know they are not of human institution, and cannot remember that we have learned their signification, but think that at first sight they would have suggested to us the same things they do now: all this persuades us they are of the same species as the things respectively represented by them, and that it is by a natural resemblance they suggest them to our minds. (*NTV*, 144, emphasis added; cf. *A*, 4,11)

In this section Berkeley contrasts the conventions governing natural signs (visible objects) with the conventions governing words. Visible objects are natural signs of tangible objects: there is a tendency among all human beings to take visible objects to be signs of tangible objects. Among the marks of this natural signification relation are the following: (1) There is a universal tendency to take visible objects to be signs of tangible objects, indeed, there is a tendency to conflate these two kinds of objects. (2) One is not conscious of having learned that visual objects signify tangible objects, since this was 'learned at our first entrance into the world' and the association has been uniformly reinforced ever since. Therefore, (3) they are 'not of human institution'. In contrast, the signification of a word is 'of human institution', that is, is based upon conventions for (a) the signification relation between a word-type and a class of objects is not subject to universal agreement among human beings, and (b) one remembers having learned the conventions that govern the signification of words in a spoken or written language. Thus, in contrast to visible objects, the signification of words is strictly a matter of human convention.

Berkeley's commitment to the conventionality of human language is stated more explicitly in Section 40 of the *Theory of Vision Vindicated*. There Berkeley wrote: 'A great number of arbitrary signs, various and apposite, do constitute a language. If such arbitrary connexion be instituted by men, it is an artificial language; if by the Author of nature, it is a natural language' (*TVV*, 40; cf. *A*, 4, 7). Berkeley's point is once again that in the case of the language of vision there is a natural relation of signification between a visible object and a tangible object: all human beings take visible objects to be signs of tangible objects. Only God can be the cause of the 'conventions' governing such a 'natural language'. In the case of an artificial language such as English, the conventions governing the signification of terms are of purely human contrivance. One comes to 'know the language' as one discovers the conventions governing the significations of the words in the language.[21] Since Berkeley took the signification of words in an 'artificial' language to be based upon human conventions, one question remains to be considered — how does one come to know the conventions governing the signification of words in an artificial language? In answering this question, we should first notice two points. First, as we have seen, the signification relation is nothing more than a habitual association of a sign with the objects signified. Secondly, in so far as both the signification of objects by words and the signification of tangible objects by visible objects are grounded upon certain psychological habits, there is no significant epistemic difference between these two kinds of signification relations: while there is greater certainty regarding the signification of tangible objects by visible objects due to greater constancy of the conjunction between these two kinds of object than one finds in the linguistic realm, this has no bearing on the nature of the signification relation involved. Indeed, the signification relation in the natural realm is not limited to that between visible and tangible objects; rather, it is a metaphor intended to provide insight into the nature of natural laws: one comes to have knowledge of a law of nature when one idea is taken as a sign of another, and ideas of the second kind are, in fact, constantly conjoined with ideas of the first kind (cf. *PHK* 30-3, 60-5, and 105-10). Given this, we may now turn to a consideration of how one gains knowledge of the conventions governing the signification of a word in a language.

Since the conventions governing the signification of a word in a language are learned, let us consider again an example of teaching the meaning of a word to a young child. If I were teaching the convention regarding the signification of the word 'dog' to my young son, Tristan, I would begin by pointing to various objects — for example, real dogs, pictures of dogs and stuffed animals — and saying the word 'dog'. After some time, Tristan will begin to notice the resemblances among the things to which I have pointed and will himself start pointing at objects and saying 'dog'. At first, we can imagine, not all the things at which he points will be things normally signified by the term 'dog' (for example he might point at cats while saying the word 'dog') and I will say to him, 'No, Tristan, that is a cat.' On those occasions in which he points at a dog and says 'dog', I will smile and say, 'Yes, Tristan, that is a dog', or something comparable. After a time his ability to distinguish dogs from other things will improve and those things at which he points while saying the word 'dog' quite consistently will be objects conventionally signified by that term. At this point, one will claim that he has learned the convention governing the signification of the term 'dog'. What has happened? He has developed a habit of associating a particular kind of sound with objects of a certain kind. In so far as learning the signification of a word is similar to learning a natural law, his pointing to various objects while saying the word 'dog' can be seen as predictions (cf. *PHK*,

59): when pointing to an object and saying 'dog', he expects his parent to smile and say, 'Yes, that is a dog.' On some occasions his predictions fail, as when he points at the neighbor's cat, Josephine, and says 'dog', but as time goes on more and more of his 'predictions' prove to be successful, and at a certain point one will grant that he has learned the convention governing the signification of the term 'dog', which is when he quite consistently picks out objects that normal speakers of English call 'dogs'.

Although I believe the example we have considered provides a clear enough illustration of what Berkeley may take to be involved in coming to know the conventional signification of a term, that is to say, one knows the conventional signification of a term when one can predict with accuracy the reactions of speakers of the language when one uses a term, it might be useful to consider another example. Since college professors are often wont to supplement their normal incomes with some kind of work during the summer, let us assume that one summer I take on a job as an unskilled laborer in an oil field. As one who was raised in the north central portion of the United States, let us assume I have neither had any experience in an oil field, nor have I gained familiarity with some of the terminology peculiar to the petroleum industry. I report to work the first day and the foreman says to me, 'Go check the Christmas tree on Well Number One.' I note that beside a large pump there is a sign that says 'Well Number One', but I do not see a Christmas tree, that is, given my limited knowledge of the conventions governing the word 'Christmas tree' and the fact that I do not see an evergreen tree that is decorated with lights and ornaments, I look at the foreman with a puzzled expression on my face and say, 'What Christmas tree?' At that point the foreman patiently explains the convention governing the signification of the term 'Christmas tree' in the petroleum industry: a Christmas tree is the arrangement of pipes and valves on the casing head of the well that is used for controlling the flow of oil and gas. He then points to such an arrangement of pipes and valves at Well Number One and says, 'Now check it!' Having had the convention governing the signification of this sense of the term 'Christmas tree' explicated and having been provided with a paradigm case of a Christmas tree, I am now in a position to recognize the Christmas trees at each of the wells and to use the term in a manner consistent with that of persons in the petroleum industry. From this point on, at least in the relevant contexts, my use of the term 'Christmas tree' will yield neither puzzled expressions in the faces of my hearers nor questions such as 'What do you mean?' The kinds of thing that I would include in my subjective extension of the term 'Christmas tree' would be similar to those that any person in the petroleum industry would include in his subjective extension of the term.[22]

We have seen that Berkeley considered the signification of a term within a language to be a matter of convention. In explicating the meaning of a term, one is generally concerned with listing the several classes of things in which any object found in the conventional extension of a term is also found. Such an explication of the convention provides one with a criterion for including objects in one's subjective extension of that term. Finally, we have seen that coming to know the convention governing the signification of a term in a language is largely to be construed as the ability to correctly predict the reaction of knowledgeable speakers of a language to one's use of a term.

Analogical and Metaphorical Meaning

Although I have now examined the major aspects of Berkeley's semantics, we should briefly examine his discussions of analogical meaning in the *Alciphron* and the *Theory of Vision, Vindicated*, for we shall see that considerations of the limits of analogical meaning are germane to his contention that one neither has nor can have a notion of material substance. As we shall see, Berkeley contended that it is only among ideas, relations among ideas, and actions of the mind that one can legitimately claim an analogy. So let us begin by examining Berkeley's discussion in the *Theory of Vision, Vindicated*.

In Section 46 of the *Theory of Vision, Vindicated*, Berkeley wrote:

> More and less, greater and smaller, extent, proportion, interval are all found in time, as in space; but it will not therefore follow that these are homogeneous quantities. No more will it follow from the attribution of common names that visible ideas are homogeneous with those of feeling. It is true that terms denoting tangible extension, figure, location, motion, and the like are also applied to denote the quantity, relation, and order

of the proper visible objects or ideas of sight. But this proceeds only from experience and analogy. There is a *higher* and *lower* in the notes of music. Men speak in a high or low key. And this, it is plain, is no more than metaphor or analogy. So likewise to express the order of visible ideas the words *situation, high* and *low, up* and *down* are made use of, and their sense, when so applied, is analogical. (*TVV*, 46)

As we saw above, one of Berkeley's main themes throughout his writings on vision was that the objects of sight are properly of a different kind from those of touch. Hence, although the term 'extension' includes both visible and tangible things in its extension (it denotes both visible and tangible extensions), extended visible objects are properly objects of a different kind from extended tangible objects. If the objects of each of the senses are properly distinct, then so are the relations that obtain among the objects of each of the senses, and it is primarily the latter with which Berkeley is concerned in this section. Throughout his works on vision, Berkeley wrote as if the sense of touch is epistemically fundamental and it is with analogies grounded upon ideas of touch that Berkeley is concerned here. Fundamentally, the meaning of terms such as 'high' and 'low' are based upon the sense of touch. On the basis of that sense, one can discover that the tangible ear of an elephant is higher (farther above the ground) than the tangible foot of an elephant. But the terms 'higher' and 'lower' are not used only to denote tangible spatial relations. In the case of visible spatial relations, one's use of the same term is based primarily upon one's experience of certain visible objects corresponding to tangible objects: in most cases when one is tangibly aware that the ear of an elephant is higher than the foot of an elephant one is also aware of a visible elephantine ear and foot. It is because there is a constant conjunction between these two kinds of experience, that one takes the spatial relation to be the same (cf. *TVV*, 47), although, Berkeley contends, they are merely 'analogous'.

Berkeley's use of 'analogous' here is somewhat puzzling. Generally, the term 'analogous' is intended to mark some similarity between objects or states of affairs, but there are *prima facie* reasons why it seems he cannot here understand 'analogy' in terms of similarity. In claiming that visible and tangible objects are distinct in kind, Berkeley is denying that visible objects and tangible objects are similar; hence, they cannot be similar or 'analogous' in that sense of the term. Indeed, in so far as visible and tangible objects would be deemed analogous to one another, Berkeley can surely mean little more than that they are constantly conjoined in experience. But in the paragraph above, he was primarily concerned with analogies between different kinds of *relations*. Does analogy with respect to kinds of relations come to anything more than an experienced constant conjunction of different kinds of relations?

There is a sense in which we are not prepared to examine this issue, for the nature of Berkeleian relations among ideas is one of the topics we shall consider in the next chapter. There I shall argue that Berkeley reduced relations among ideas to actions of the mind (volitions). If this is correct, his contention that there are ideas that are concomitant with volitions (*PC*, 661a) provides the basis for accounting for the sense in which the relations are analogous (similar). To understand this, however, we should begin by considering how Berkeley divides relations into kinds.

Consider the case of the 'higher than' relation in music. The G above middle-C is higher than middle-C. Although this is a relation that obtains between nonspatial objects (sounds), it is represented spatially in a published piece of music. Now if the relations of 'higher than' that obtain between tangible, visible and auditory objects are merely analogous, and not properly the same in kind, this suggests that properly the *kind* of relation involved in each case is determined by the relata, and there is some evidence for this in the 1734 edition of the *Principles*. There he wrote:

> In like manner, we know and have a *notion* of relations between things or ideas; which relations are distinct from the ideas or things related, inasmuch as the latter may be perceived by us without our perceiving the former. To me it seems that *ideas*, *spirits*, and *relations* are all in their respective kinds the object of human knowledge and subject of discourse; and that the term *idea* would be improperly extended to signify *everything* we know or have any notion of. (*PHK*, 89)

This indicates that the relata in a relation are epistemically more fundamental than the relation that joins them together. Now, in so far as the relata are more fundamental than the relation itself, it is quite plausible to suggest that relations are classified on the basis of the objects they relate. Thus, a 'higher than' relation among tangible objects is distinct from a 'higher than' relation that obtains among visible objects, both of which are distinct from a 'higher than' relation that obtains among the auditory notes in the musical scale. Each kind of 'higher than' relation obtains only among objects of a particular kind. None the less, these several kinds of 'higher than' relation are similar (analogous). If, as we shall see in the next chapter, relations among ideas are nothing but actions of the mind, it is reasonable to claim that certain relations are similar, even if they are properly relations obtaining among different kinds of object. Relations might be deemed similar (analogous) if the concomitant ideas of reflection produced by the act of relating are similar. Thus, Berkeley might well claim that 'higher than' relations obtain both among tangible objects and among notes in the musical scale, and that these relations, though distinct in kind, are analogous in so far as the ideas of reflection they produce are similar to one another.

In attempting to understand Berkeley's discussion in Section 46 of the *Theory of Vision Vindicated*, we have treated the meaning of 'higher than' in nontangible contexts as if it were known by analogy. But if one examines the passage closely, one finds that Berkeley distinguished between analogical and metaphorical meaning: speaking of a high or low musical key 'is no more than *metaphor or analogy*' (*TVV*, 46, emphasis added). If my account of Berkeley's discussion of the analogical or metaphorical meaning of relational terms is correct, the sole basis for claiming similarity among relations is that relations among ideas, as actions of the mind, produce ideas of reflection that are similar to one another: the relations themselves remain distinct in kind due to the differences in their relata. To ask seriously whether the several meanings are analogical or metaphorical, we must turn to Berkeley's more explicit discussion of the distinction in the *Alciphron*.

In the Fourth Dialogue of the *Alciphron*, the several disputants discuss the sense in which one can attribute properties to God. In particular, they are concerned with the question whether the properties one can properly attribute to God are properties of the same kinds as one attributes to human beings. After Lysis argued that the sense of the term 'God' is highly ambiguous (*A*, 4, 16) and rehearsed the arguments of Diagoras (Anthony Collins) that it is possible to reconcile the several attributes of God only if one understands these in terms of an analogy to human attributes, noting that the position of Diagoras entails that one can properly know nothing regarding the nature of God (*A*, 4, 17-18), Crito defended the contention that one can analogically or metaphorically attribute properties to God. Since we are concerned with the distinction between analogical and metaphorical meaning, we shall focus solely upon Crito's discussion of that distinction. Crito is made to say:

> For the further clearing of this point [regarding the similarity of relations or habitudes between man and God], it is to be observed that a twofold analogy is distinguished by the Schoolmen — metaphorical and proper. Of the first kind there are frequent instances in Holy Scripture, attributing human parts and passions to God. When He is represented as having a finger, an eye, or an ear; when He is said to repent, to be angry, or grieved; every one sees that analogy is metaphorical. Because those parts and passions, taken in the proper signification, must in every degree necessarily, and from the formal nature of the thing, include imperfection. When, therefore, it is said — the finger of God appears in this or that event, men of common sense mean no more but that it is as truly ascribed to God as the works wrought by human fingers are to man: and so of the rest. But the case is different when wisdom and knowledge are attributed to God. Passions and senses, as such, imply defect; but in knowledge simply, or as such, there is no defect. Knowledge, therefore, in the proper formal meaning of the word, may be attributed to God *proportionately*, that is, preserving a proportion to the infinite nature of God. We may say, therefore, that as God is infinitely above man, so is the knowledge of God infinitely above the knowledge of man, and this is what Cajetan calls *analogia proprie facta*. And after this same analogy we must understand all those attributes to belong to the Deity which in themselves simply, and as such, denote perfection. (*A*, 4,21)

In examining this paragraph, one should remember that the problem with which the disputants in this part of the *Alciphron* are concerned is neither what the name 'God' denotes nor, properly, the explication of that term. The issue is, rather, whether the terms in the explicans are themselves intelligible. Thus, it makes little difference whether the definition of the term 'God' is drawn from either religious or philosophical writings.[23] The issue is whether the terms used in explicating the meaning of the term 'God' denote the same kinds of objects they denote when applied to human beings, and whether and how the several scriptural ascriptions of properties to God can be made consistent with this explication of the term. It is in this context that the distinction between properly analogical meaning and metaphorical meaning is introduced. So let us begin with metaphorical meaning.

At various points in the Old Testament, God is described as having passions or bodily parts.[24] Such claims are inconsistent with the religious-philosophical stance on the nature of God; in particular, they are inconsistent with the presumption that God is perfect. In claiming that in those passages the ascription of passions or bodily parts to God is to be understood metaphorically, Berkeley holds that neither passions nor bodily parts are properly to be ascribed to God. Although the writers of the scriptures might have suggested that God is jealous, for example, since jealousy is an imperfection, it is not properly ascribable to God. None the less, certain aspects of divine justice might be remotely similar to jealousy — perhaps God pursues justice with the same rigor that a jealous man pursues his love — and when the writers of the scriptures wrote *as if* God were jealous, it is to this aspect of divine justice that they refer. In claiming that the ascription of a passion or a bodily part to God is metaphorical, Berkeley is claiming that one cannot properly ascribe either of these to God, although certain aspects of God's nature or actions can be understood as being remotely similar to the passions or actions of human beings.

But how is one to understand such 'remote similarity'? Remember, Berkeley basically divides the world into kinds on the basis of similarity or resemblance. Since visible and tangible extension do not resemble one another, they are properly different kinds of extension, even though these two kinds of extension are placed under a single linguistic term. The division of the world into kinds on the basis of resemblance yields kinds based upon greater and lesser degrees of similarity; objects are divided into *specific* kinds on the basis of a great deal of similarity and into *generic* kinds on the basis of a lesser degree of similarity. In those cases in which two objects are placed in the same genus, they are merely 'remotely similar'. To place these considerations in the context of Berkeley's discussion of the explication of the meaning of the name 'God', one should recall that it is a religious tenet that human beings are made in the image of God, that is, there is a similarity between human beings and God: both God and humans are 'persons'. One's paradigms of persons are human beings, that is, beings to whom both mental and physical properties are ascribed. But, assuming with Berkeley that physical characteristics are 'imperfect', God is a being who has no physical characteristics. Hence, the ascription of physical characteristics to God is consistent with the contention that both God and human beings are persons — it is consistent with considerations of generic identity — but although God and humans are generically identical, that is, 'remotely similar', they are specifically different. Hence, in ascribing properties to God, one must pay close attention to the respects in which God is specifically different from human beings. It is considerations of these differences that allow one to determine which ascriptions of properties to God are merely metaphorical. If God is perfect and both bodily attributes and some emotions imply imperfection, this places strict limits on the respects in which one can ascribe properties to God. Given this, we can understand how metaphorical meaning is to be contrasted with analogical meaning.

Analogical meaning presupposes specific identity, and differences to which one might allude are merely differences in proportion. While the notion of a passion might imply a defect, the notion of knowledge or wisdom does not imply a defect. In ascribing knowledge or wisdom to God, one is ascribing the same specific kind of property to God; however, the ascription is analogical insofar as human knowledge or wisdom is limited, while divine knowledge or wisdom is not limited. The ascription of these properties to God is proportional to the perfection of God: while both God and humans possess wisdom, God's wisdom is perfect or complete, while human wisdom is limited.

Thus, both analogical and metaphorical meaning rest upon considerations of similarity. In the case of analogical meaning one can properly ascribe the same specific kind of property to more than one kind of object, while claiming that in the case of the second kind of object the property is to be understood as being proportionately greater or smaller. For one to ascribe a property to an object analogically, there must be an overriding presumption, or set of presumptions, regarding ther object to which one ascribes the properties that guides one's considerations of proportionality, for example, that the object to which one ascribes these properties analogically is perfect. In the case of metaphorical meaning, one is ascribing a property to an object that can properly be ascribed to some objects in a particular genus, although, perhaps, not to objects in the species in question. One's contention is merely that there is at least some remote (generic) similarity between a property in the object and that property one metaphorically ascribes to it.

Given the nature of the distinction between analogical meaning and metaphorical meaning, it should be clear that the issues in Section 46 of the *Theory of Vision, Vindicated* are more properly concerned with metaphorical than analogical meaning. In so far as the several kinds of 'higher than' relations are specifically distinct, the similarities among them can be only remote. Indeed, in so far as relations are to be construed as actions of the mind, the known similarities among these actions are limited to the ideas of reflection that they produce. Hence, there is no basis for comparison of degrees of a relation: the meaning of the term 'higher than' when applied to something other than spatial relations known on the basis of touch must be metaphorical.

Conclusions

In this chapter we have seen that Berkeley's rejection of abstract ideas is intended to mark a general rejection of intensional theories of linguistic meaning. Berkeley argued that it is the particular objects of a kind (or, in some cases, of several distinct kinds) that provide the meaning of a categorematic term. We have also seen that, given Locke's account of the meaning of syncategorematic terms (particles), it is probable that Berkeley intended his extensional theory of meaning to provide an account of the meaning of syncategorematic as well as categorematic terms. We have seen that Berkeley held language is a sign system based upon social conventions, and we briefly examined the mechanism by which he seems to have believed one learns these conventions. Finally, we have seen that while Berkeley allowed that in some cases terms are used metaphorically or analogically, he at least sketched an account of the nature and limits of such meaning.

Notes

1. To put it differently, Berkeley proposed a possible worlds semantics, although since he rejected essentialism and there is no evidence that he provided

Berkeley's Theory of Meaning 131

any grounds for transworld identity, we may safely ignore an extended discussion of possible worlds semantics.

2. It is beyond the scope of this discussion to examine Margaret Atherton's recent contention that Locke's account of abstraction was not intended to provide a theory of meaning. (See Margaret Atherton, 'The Inessentiality of Lockean Essences', *Canadian Journal of Philosophy* 14 (1984) pp. 277-93.) I shall take the fact that Berkeley considered Locke's account of abstraction to provide the foundation for a theory of meaning (Intro, 11-12) as sufficient to show that this is at least a plausible reading of Locke.

3. Cf. John Locke, *An Essay concerning Human Understanding* (ed. P.H. Nidditch) (Clarendon Press, Oxford, 1975), 3.3.16, 3.6.2-6 and 28-9.

4. Cf. Locke, *Essay*, 3.3.17, and 3.10.17-21.

5. This decision-procedure is not fool-proof, since there might be disagreements among the speakers of a language regarding the sufficiency of the degrees of resemblance between an object and one's paradigms; similar problems can arise if one attempts to classify some objects on the basis of the conventional intension of a term, as Locke's discussions of 'monstrous Productions' of nature make clear. Cf. Locke, *Essay*, 3.6.23 and 3.6.26.

6. Cf. W.V. Quine, 'Two Dogmas of Empiricism', in his *From a Logical Point of View*, 2nd edn (Harper Torchbooks, New York 1961), pp. 20-46.

7. The rejection of essentialism does not follow immediately from the positing of a basically extensional theory of meaning. While the account of names Saul Kripke developed in his *Naming and Necessity* (Harvard University Press, Cambridge, 1980) is basically an extensional theory of the meaning of names, he retained a doctrine of individual essences to allow him to identify individuals over possible worlds.

8. In the second edition of the *Principles* Berkeley indicates in section 16 of the Introduction that such selective attention is possible, and we saw in Chapter 1 that this fact does not mitigate against his critique of abstraction. We shall examine the phenomenon of selective attention in Berkeley further below.

9. We shall see later in this chapter and in the next chapter that the presumption of a high degree of psychological uniformity among human beings plays a significant role in Berkeley's theory of relations.

10. Since meaning is an asymmetrical relation, it is more proper to suggest that there are two meaning or signification relations: a sound signifies a written mark in one relation and a written mark signifies a sound in the other.

I am concerned, here, solely with the signification relation of words to sounds within a language. It is clear, however, that Berkeley could consistently extend this to include other kinds of conventions, e.g., conventions regarding translation from one language to another. Here there would be a convention indicating that all written instances of the English term 'house', for example, would signify all written instances of the German term 'Haus', and vice versa, and all spoken instances of the English term 'house' would signify all spoken instances of the German term 'Haus', and vice versa. There would, however, be no signification relation between the spoken English word 'house' and the written German word 'Haus', since the conventions related written words to certain sounds is a convention *within* a language. Further, as Quine has indicated (cf. W.V. Quine, *Word and Object* (M.I.T. Press, Cambridge, 1960, pp. 26-79), the questions whether the extension of the English word 'house' is the same as that of the German word 'Haus' and whether it is possible ever to know that the two extensions are or are not the same are different and very difficult questions.

11. The recognition that a sortal term might be used in more than one sense poses no problem for an extensional theory of meaning so long as it is possible to explicate the conventions governing each sense. We shall return to this topic in Section 4 of this chapter.

12. Cf. Quine, 'Two Dogmas of Empiricism', pp. 20-46; Quine, *Word and Object*, pp. 238-57.
13. Locke, *Essay*, 3.3.19.
14. Cf. Locke, *Essay*, 3.10.33.
15. Like Berkeley, Locke provided no extended discussion of his criteria of possibility and impossibility, and it is beyond the scope of the present work to develop an account of Locke's criteria of possibility and impossibility. None the less, it is fairly clear that he held that inconsistent ideas cannot represent possible existents, and it is at least plausible to contend that any consistent idea represents an object that could exist.
16. Norman Kretzmann, 'The Main Thesis of Locke's Semantic Theory', *Philosophical Review*, 77 (1968) pp. 175-96.
17. Locke, *Essay*, 3.7.1
18. Locke, *Essay*, 3.7.4. See also the remainder of the chapter.
19. A.A. Luce, 'Editor's Notes on the Entries to the *Philosophical Commentaries*', in *Works* 1: 132.
20. As we shall see in the next chapter, these concomitant ideas play a significant role in Berkeley's account of one's notion of volitions (actions of the mind).
21. For an extended discussion of the analogy between language and the natural realm, see Colin Murray Turbayne, *The Myth of Metaphor*, rev. edn (Yale University Press, New Haven, 1970).
22. For an extended discussion of the notion of convention and how conventions come to be known, see David K. Lewis, *Convention: A Philosophical Study* (Harvard University Press, Cambridge, 1969). Although Lewis's discussion of one's knowledge of conventions does not focus on Berkeley's account, the general outlines of his discussion are consistent with Berkeley's limited comments on that topic.
23. In those writings Berkeley most probably had in mind, there were few differences between philosophical and theological accounts of the nature of God. Cf., for example, the first article of the Anglican 'Thirty-Nine Articles of Religion', in John H. Leith (ed.), *Creeds of the Churches: A Reader in Christian Doctrine from the Bible to the Present* (Doubleday Anchor Books, Garden City, New York 1963), p. 266, with Descartes' descriptions of the idea of God in *Meditations* III and V (HR I: 162 and 180). Cf. *PHK*, 146.
24. Cf., for example, Exodus 20:5 and 31:18.

4 THE EPISTEMIC INTENT OF BERKELEIAN NOTIONS

Our examination of Berkeley's theory of linguistic meaning in the past three chapters was intended to provide a background for an examination of his doctrine of notions, for one of the few clues Berkeley repeatedly provides for understanding this doctrine is that 'we have some notion of soul, spirit, and the operations of mind, such as willing, loving, hating, in as much as we know or understand the meanings of those words' (*PHK*, 27; cf. *PHK* 140 and 142; *DHP*, III, 231; *A*, 7, 5). Since Berkeley proposed an extensional theory of meaning, to claim that one knows the meaning of the terms 'mind' or 'spirit' and of such terms as 'willing', 'loving' and 'hating' implies (1) that one can conceive of minds and their operations and (2) that it is minds themselves and their operations upon which the mind focuses rather than something that represents them. Now, Berkeley repeatedly claimed that notions neither are ideas nor can be analyzed solely in terms of ideas (cf. *PHK*, 27, 89, 140, 142; *DHP* III, 231-3; *A*, 7, 5). So how does one conceive of minds and their operations, and what is involved in claiming that one has knowledge of them?

In this chapter I shall focus upon the epistemic issues germane to the doctrine of notions. I shall begin by examining a distinction that has been largely overlooked in the literature, which is Berkeley's distinction between positive and relative notions.[1] I shall attempt to elucidate Berkeley's positive/relative notions distinction by examining Thomas Reid's distinction between direct and relative conceptions. Second, focusing on relative notions, I shall argue that knowledge based upon relative notions is analogous to what Bertrand Russell called knowledge by description. I shall call this 'the describing model of relative notions'. Third, I shall show that the describing model of relative notions is consistent with Berkeley's accounts of one's notions of substance. Finally, I shall argue that the describing model of relative notions allows one to have notions of operations of minds and relations among ideas, provided that one has positive notions of perception and causality. To show my claim is plausible, I shall examine the nature of Berkeleian relations among ideas.

Positive and Relative Notions

At several places in his discussions of material substance, Berkeley alludes to a distinction between positive and relative notions. In Section 80 of the *Principles*, for example, he wrote:

> In the *last* place, you will say, What if we give up the cause of material Substance, and stand to it that Matter is an unknown *Somewhat* — neither substance nor accident, spirit nor idea — inert, thoughtless, indivisible, immovable, unextended, existing no place? For, say you, whatever may be urged against *substance* or *occasion*, or any other positive or relative notion of Matter, hath no place at all, so long as this relative definition of matter is adhered to. (*PHK*, 80; cf. *PHK*, 16; *DHP*, I, 197-9, *DHP*, II, 223; and *DHP*, III, 242-3)

Although Berkeley himself provided scant elucidation of the distinction between positive and relative notions, this type of distinction seems to have been generally recognized by the major figures in eighteenth century British philosophy. For example, Locke contended that one has merely 'An obscure and relative *Idea* of Substance in general',[2] and Hume later wrote 'The farthest we can go towards a conception of external objects, when suppos'd *specifically* different from our perceptions, is to form a relative idea of them, without pretending to comprehend the related objects.'[3] Although we shall see later that Locke provides a fairly detailed discussion of one's relative ideas of substance in his first *Letter to the Bishop of Worcester*, it is in the works of Berkeley's sometime-disciple Thomas Reid that one finds one of the clearest accounts of the distinction between positive and relative notions or conceptions written in the eighteenth century. Thus, by briefly examining Reid's discussion of the distinction between direct and relative conceptions, we shall be in a better position to understand Berkeley's positive/relative notions distinction.

In his *Essays on the Active Powers of the Human Mind*, Reid drew a distinction between direct and relative conceptions. He wrote:

> Of some things, we know what they are in themselves; our conception of such things I call *direct*. Of other things, we know not what they are in themselves, but only that they have certain

properties or attributes, or certain relations to other things; of these our conception is only *relative*.⁴

Reid's distinction between direct and relative conception is the distinction between conceiving of a thing as it is in itself and conceiving of a thing on the basis of its properties or the relations in which it stands to things conceived directly. Reid's paradigms of things conceived directly include primary qualities and operations of mind, while his paradigms of things conceived relatively include minds, bodies and powers.⁵ Notice that a relation is essential to a relative conception. Even when one conceives of a thing in terms of its properties or attributes, it is only because there is a presumed relation between the directly conceived property and that thing x of which one has a relative conception that one can claim to have a relative conception of x. The concept of a property is inherently relative: a property is always relative to an object, although the nature of the relation between a property and an object — whether it is a relation of inhesion, a part-whole relation, or some other kind of relation — will vary with philosophical accounts of the nature of properties. None the less, it is clear that Reid held that the thing of which one has a relative conception is distinct from both the directly conceived object and the relation(s) on which the relative conception is based.

Having distinguished between direct and relative conception, Reid proceeds to give an example of a relative conception. In his words:

> To illustrate this by some examples: in the university library, I call for the book, press L, shelf 10. No. 10. the library keeper must have such a conception of the book I want, as to be able to distinguish it from ten thousand that are under his care. But what conception does he form of it from my words? They inform him neither of the author, nor the subject, nor the language, nor the size, nor the binding, but only its mark and place. His conception of it is merely relative to these circumstances; yet this relative notion enables him to distinguish it from every other book in the library.⁶

Notice that this relative conception of the book provides one with no knowledge of the peculiar characteristics of the book: it is virtually no more than a conception of the location of the book. None the less, by determining the location of the book one is able to distinguish that particular book from all others in the library. In the sense that it allows one to single out exactly one thing, one's relative conception of the book is distinct and Reid seems to have held that relative conceptions often are more distinct than direct conceptions of an object.[7]

Having briefly examined Reid's distinction between direct and relative conception, we are in a position to ask whether Berkeley's distinction between positive and relative notions was drawn along the same lines. The answer seems to be that it was. In the *First Dialogue*, after Hylas concedes that he has no 'proper positive idea' of matter, Philonous asks whether he has a relative notion of it. Notice the exchange:

> **Philonous.** It seems you have only a relative notion of it [matter], or that you conceive it not otherwise than by conceiving the relation it bears to sensible qualities.
> **Hylas.** Right.
> **Philonous.** Be pleased therefore to let me know wherein that relation consists.
> (*DHP*, I, 197-8; cf. *PHK*, 16-17 and 68)

Upon examination, however, Philonous convinces Hylas that he has no notion of the putative relation of support between matter and its attributes. Philonous then states the following conclusion: 'It seems then you have no idea at all, neither relative nor positive of matter; you know neither what it is in itself, nor what relation it bears to accidents' (*DHP*, I, 199).

This theme is repeated in the *Second Dialogue*. There Philonous is made to say:

> That from a cause, effect, operation, sign, or other circumstance there may reasonably be inferred the existence of a thing not immediately perceived, and that it were absurd for any man to argue against the existence of that thing from his having no direct and positive notion of it, I freely own. But there is nothing of all this; where neither reason nor revelation induce us to believe in the existence of a thing; where we have not even a relative notion of it; where an abstraction is made from perceiving and being perceived, from spirit and idea: lastly, where

there is not so much as the most inadequate or faint idea pretended to: I will not indeed thence conclude against the reality of any notion or existence of any thing: but my inference shall be, that you mean nothing at all: that you employ words to no manner of purpose, without any design or signification whatsoever. And I leave it to you to consider how mere jargon should be treated.(*DHP*, II, 223)

There are several things to notice here. First, in concerning himself with one's alleged notion of material substance, Berkeley was concerned with how one conceives of matter. Second, an alleged positive notion or idea of matter is a conception of what a thing is in itself (cf. *DHP*, III, 242-3). Third, Berkeley allowed that it is sometimes possible to have a relative notion of things that are not directly perceived, and when one has a relative notion of a thing, such a notion is based upon a relation between an idea and the thing of which one has a relative notion. Fourth, since a relation is essential to a relative notion, one can claim to have a relative notion of an object only if one has a clear and determinate notion of the relation involved. It is due to his contention that one has no notion of the relation of support obtaining between matter and its qualities that Berkeley denies that one has a relative notion of matter.[8] Finally, if my account of Berkeley's theory of meaning is correct, this implies that one's definition of matter is inconsistent (cf. *DHP*, III, 232-3), and, therefore, it cannot even pick out a *de dicto* possible object. It is for this reason that Berkeley's contention that the term 'matter' is meaningless constitutes a significant criticism of the doctrine of material substance.

The Describing Model of Relative Notions

Although not all notions are of a single kind, an examination of Berkeley's discussions of one's notions of minds, actions of minds and relations among ideas will show that these notions are relative notions. Consequently, it is imperative that one have a clear understanding of the doctrine of relative notions. In this section I hope to show that if one takes seriously Berkeley's claims to have notions of minds, operations of mind and relations to the extent that one understands the meanings of these words and others like them (*PHK*, 27, 140, 142; *DHP*, III, 231; *A*, 7, 5) and Berkeley's occasional use of the words 'notion' and 'definition' as synonyms (cf. *DHP*, III, 233), one can construct a plausible model for relative notions through a consideration of the doctrine of real definitions. In the two subsequent sections I shall show that this describing model of relative notions is consistent both with Berkeley's discussions of the doctrines of material and immaterial substance and with a plausible account of Berkeley's theory of relations among ideas.

At several places in his discussion of notions, Berkeley suggested that the doctrine of notions plays an important role in his account of the meanings of those 'names' (expressions that refer) that do not denote ideas. His most commonly cited statement to this effect is from Section 27 of the *Principles*. There, after denying that one has an idea of the soul, Berkeley wrote: 'Though it must be owned at the same time, that we have some notion of soul, spirit, and the operations of mind, such as willing, loving, and hating, in as much as we know or understand the meaning of those words' (*PHK*, 27).[9] Similarly, in the *Third Dialogue* he seems to use the words 'notion' and 'definition' synonymously in claiming that 'In the very notion or definition of material substance there is included a manifest repugnance and inconsistency' (*DHP*, III, 233). Further, at several places Berkeley made it quite clear that one knows the meaning of some 'names' of things that are not perceived on the basis of that thing's relations to something known directly, that is, some words are meaningful only because one has relative notions of some things. Notice what he wrote in Section 16 of the *Principles*:

> It is said extension is a mode or accident of matter, and that matter is the *substratum* that supports it. Now I desire that you would explain what is meant by matter's *supporting* extension: say you, I have no idea of matter, and therefore cannot explain it. I answer, though you have no positive, yet if you have any meaning at all, you must have at least a relative notion of matter; though you know not what it is, yet you must be supposed to know what relation it bears to accidents, and what is meant by its supporting them. It is evident *support* cannot here be taken in its usual or literal sense, as when we say that pillars support a building: in what sense therefore must it be taken? (*PHK*, 16)

Finally, in *De Motu* Berkeley reiterated the claim that all things designated by names are known by qualities or relations. In his words:

> But in very truth since it is most certain that all things which we designate by names are known by qualities or relations, at least in part (for it would be stupid, to use a words to which nothing known, no notion, idea or concept, were attached), let us diligently inquire whether it be possible to form any idea of that pure, real, and absolute space continuing to exist after the annihilation of all bodies. (*DeM*, 54)

Since Berkeley repeatedly claimed that one has a notion of a thing named to the extent that one knows the meaning of a name, since he sometimes seems to have used the terms 'notion' and 'definition' synonymously, and since he claimed that one can know what some things are, and thereby determine the meaning of a word, on the basis of a relation, I believe it is reasonable to turn to an account of definitions that was certainly familiar to Berkeley in attempting to elucidate the epistemic content of the doctrine of notions.[10]

Among the most influential logical works of the seventeenth century was Antoine Arnauld's *The Art of Thinking: Port-Royal Logic*. Arnauld's discussions of definitions concern two kinds of definitions: nominal definitions and real definitions. Nominal definitions reflect either the common usage of words in a society (lexical definitions) or they are used to introduce a technical term or a specific sense of a commonly used term in a specific discourse (stipulative definitions).[11] Real definitions, on the other hand, are intended to reflect the nature of the definiendum.[12] Since Berkeley's objective in elucidating the meaning of a term (*PHK*, 49) was to provide a list of all and only those classes of objects in which the objects in the extension of a term are to be found, that is, a description of the objects in the extension of a term, we will do well to focus on real definitions.

According to Arnauld, most real definitions proceed *per genus et differentia*, although this is not the only means of providing a real definition of a word. He also allowed that one can define a word on the basis of the relations in which the thing denoted by the word stands to other known things. Of this he wrote: 'Sometimes we define a word by identifying the cause, or the matter, or the purpose of the referent of the defined word. For example, we define 'clock' as 'an iron machine composed of various wheels, and whose regulated movements are used to tell time.'[13] Since such a relative definition corresponds to the general pattern in Berkeley's theory of relative notions, that is, to Berkeley's claim that some words are meaningful only due to the relation the referent holds to a known idea, Arnauld's criteria for the adequacy of a real definition might prove instructive. He proposed three criteria:

(1) A definition must be exhaustive, that is, the defined words must refer to all those things to which the defining words refer.
(2) A definition must be proper, that is, the defining words must refer to only those things to which the defined word can refer.
(3) A definition must be informative — that is, the defining words must express a clearer, more distinct idea than does the defined word.[14]

An adequate real definition must pick out all and only those things in the extension of a term: it must be neither too broad nor too narrow. Further, the definiens must be more clear and determinate than the definiendum.

These criteria for the adequacy of a real definition can be reformulated to cover the notional situation. If there is something corresponding to one's notion of x, to have a notion of x, x and only x must stand in a determinate relation to some idea a. Just as an adequate real definition must be exhaustive and proper, that is, the definiens must pick out all and only those things the definiendum denotes, so one's notion of x must single out one thing (as type or token) that stands in a determinate relation to some idea a. Further, just as the definiens of an adequate real definition must be more clear and distinct than the definiendum, so Berkeley contended that one must have a clear notion of the relation and one relatum if one is to claim to have a relative notion of an object. If there were no clear notion of the relation, a putative relative notion could not single out a particular object (cf. *DHP*, I, 197-9 and III, 223).[15] Hence, one can linguistically express the intent of Berkeley's doctrine of relative notions (although not describe a relative notion itself) by a definite description of the following form: 'the x that is related to a by R', where a is a particular idea and *R* is a determinate relation. A relative notion will succeed in singling out an actual object just in case the contextual definition of the definite description corresponding to a given relative notion is true, that is, just in case $(\exists x)(xRa \,\&\, (y)[yRa \to (x=y)])$. If the contextual definition is false but consistent, it will single out a *de dicto* possible object. I shall call this 'the describing model of relative notions', and we shall see that it will allow us to account for relative notions of substance (mind), relations among ideas and actions of the mind.[16]

Now someone might object to the use of the Russellian analysis of definite descriptions as a model for understanding relative notions, holding that since the logic of the definite article was only worked out in the early twentieth century, it would be an anachronism to suggest that Berkeley had a basic understanding of this logic by suggesting that it is operative in his doctrine of relative notions. In reply to this objection, two points should be taken into consideration. First, my concern is with the uniqueness claim that seems to be implicit in Berkeley's doctrine of relative notions. If one accepts an extensional theory of meaning, it is incumbent upon one to be able to single out objects in the extension of a given term. Further, if one is to ground the meaning of a term on the basis of a relation, the criteria for the adequacy of a real definition together with Berkeley's claim that notions are particulars (Intro., 15), which seems to indicate that the object of a relative notion must itself be a particular (distinct) object, suggest that a relative notion must pick out precisely one thing. To understand relative notions on the model of definite descriptions will account for this uniqueness requirement.

Second, discussions of determinations in the seventeenth century indicate that there was a general awareness of the uniqueness claims made by a definite description. A determination is a complex linguistic expression whose extension is less than the extension of the principal word in that expression.[17] Arnauld indicated that one type of determination is what we now call a definite description, that is, a complex linguistic expression that can function as a logically proper name. Thus, Arnauld wrote the following:

> Some determinations are proper names: A general word may be joined with other words in such a way that the idea expressed has in its extension but a single individual. When, for example, I

form the complex expression 'the present Pope,' I have determined the general word 'pope' in such a way that the complex expression applies to no other person than to Alexander VII.[18]

Further, this understanding of the function of the definite article was not peculiar to Arnauld, and it seems to have been quite generally recognized by the logicians in the early eighteenth century. For example, one finds the same point made by Isaac Watts in his *Logick* of 1724:

> *Note* in the *third* place, That any *common* name whatsoever is made *proper* by terms of particularity added to it, as the common words *pope, king, horse, garden, book, knife*, &c. are designed to signify a singular idea, when we say the *present pope*; *the king of Great Britain*; *the horse that won the last plate at Newmarket*; *the royal garden at Kensington*; *this book, that knife*, &c.[19]

Now, given that there was a general understanding of the uniqueness claims made by a definite description and that a definition can single out a class of entities on the basis of a relation, it is at least plausible to suggest that Berkeleian relative notions should be understood on the model of a definite description. To show that this is not merely a plausible model for understanding relative notions but a reasonable model as well, we must now turn to Berkeley's discussions of our notions of material and immaterial substance.

Notions of Substance

Berkeley claimed one has a notion of immaterial substance, while one has no notion of material substance (*PHK*, 16-22, 27, 89, and 142; *DHP*, I, 197-200, and III, 232-3). In applying the describing model of relative notions to Berkeley's discussions of material and immaterial substance, we shall find that it is impossible to have a notion of material substance due to the inappropriateness or vagueness of the candidates for the term standing for the relation in a definite description that corresponds to the supposed relative notion of material substance, while no such problems are confronted regarding the notion of immaterial substance.

Before turning to Berkeley's discussions of one's relative notions of substance, however, a point of clarification should be made. The expression 'relative term' is multiply ambiguous in the parlance of the eighteenth century. In some cases, it referred to a word denoting a relation without reference to its relata. In other cases, it referred to a word denoting a relation together with its relata. In still other cases, it referred to a word denoting a relatum.[20] To avoid such ambiguity, I shall avoid the expression 'relative term' and shall use the expression 'relational term' to refer to a word denoting a relation without reference to its relata.

According to my view, if one has a relative notion of matter, there must be a corresponding definite description that singles out a material substance as material, that is, as categorially distinct from both ideas and spirits. As will be seen, Berkeley considered two possible ways of singling out a material object and rejected both. In the first case, Berkeley argued that the relational term is improperly applied; in the second case, he argued that it is impossible to provide an explicit sense for the relational term. Let us examine these alternative gambits.

Berkeley's attack on the putative notion of material substance begins with a consideration of the representational model of perception. According to this hypothesis, material objects are distinct from but resemble ideas, that is, given a particular idea *a*, the corresponding material object would be singled out by a relative notion corresponding to the definite description, 'the entity that resembles *a* and is not itself an idea'. In criticizing his hypothesis, Berkeley argued that no such resemblance relation can obtain. He wrote:

> But say you, though the ideas themselves do not exist without the mind, yet there are things like them whereof they are copies or resemblances, which things exist without the mind, in an unthinking substance. I answer, an idea can be like nothing but an idea; a colour or figure can be like nothing but another colour or figure. If we look but ever so little into our thoughts, we shall find it impossible for us to conceive a likeness except only between our ideas. Again, I ask whether those supposed originals or external things, of which our ideas are the pictures or representations, be themselves perceivable or no? If they are, then they are ideas, and we have gained our point; but if you say they are not, I appeal to anyone whether it be sense, to

assert a colour is like something which is invisible; hard or soft, like something which is intangible, and so of the rest. (*PHK*, 8; cf. *PC*, 51, *PHK*, 57 and *DHP*, II, 189-90 and 206)

If one can single out a material object on the basis of a definite description including resemblance as its relational term, it must be proper to employ resemblance in a transcategorical context. Berkeley did not allow this. He claimed that the employment of the relation of resemblance between an idea and something that is not an idea is improper, although his evidence came to showing that it is merely suspect (cf. *PC*, 51). His likeness principle, the claim that only an idea can resemble an idea, precludes the propriety of claiming to single out a material object on the basis of the relation of resemblance. If one is willing to accept this move, it follows that one cannot single out a particular material object on the basis of a relative notion corresponding to the definite description, 'the entity that resembles *a* and is not itself an idea'. Hence, such a phrase cannot correspond to a relative notion of a material object.[21]

Berkeley expands upon this theme in his initial criticisms of the primary/secondary qualities distinction. Notice what he wrote in Section 9 of the *Principles*:

> Some there are who make a distinction betwixt *primary* and *secondary* qualities. By the former they mean extension, figure, motion, rest, solidity or impenetrability, and number; by the latter they denote all other sensible qualities, as colours, sounds, tastes, and so forth. The ideas we have of these last they acknowledge not to be the resemblances of anything existing without the mind, or unperceived; but they will have our ideas of the *primary qualities* to be patterns or images of things which exist without the mind, in an unthinking substance which they call Matter. By Matter, therefore, we are to understand an inert, senseless substance, in which extension, figure, and motion do actually subsist. But it is evident, from what we have already shewn, that extension, figure and motion are only ideas existing in the mind, and that an idea can be like nothing but another idea; and that consequently neither they nor their archetypes can exist in an unperceiving substance. Hence, it is plain that the very notion of what is called *Matter* or *corporeal substance*, involves a contradiction in it. (*PHK*, 9)

Berkeley's contention that one cannot have a notion of extension as a property of matter is based upon two kinds of considerations. Either the extension of a material object is something distinct from the extension of an idea or it is not. If it is something distinct from the extension of an idea, then the extension of a material object can be represented by an idea only if there is a resemblance relation between the extension of the idea and the extension of the object. But given his likeness principle, nothing can be like an idea except an idea. Thus, one cannot single out the extension of a material object as something categorially distinct from the extension of an idea on the basis of a relative notion involving resemblance. Hence, if there is a resemblance relation between the extension of one of one's ideas and something else, it is a relation that can only obtain between one's idea and some other idea, that is, the extension of a material object must itself be an idea. But ideas exist only as perceived by a mind (*PHK*, 3). Material objects are said to be able to exist unperceived. Thus, if the extension of a particular material object is identical with the extension of a particular idea, that is, if one's relative notion of the extension of a material object is said to correspond to the definite description, 'the extension that is identical with the extension of the idea *a* but does not exist in the mind', then one's putative notion is inconsistent, that is, it is impossible that there be such a notion (cf. *DHP*, III, 232-3). Since on Berkeleian principles a material object cannot be consistently described, Berkeley held that it is impossible that there be any material objects, and since notions single out objects, it is impossible that there is a notion of such an object.

A second supposed relative notion of a material substance corresponds either to the phrase 'the entity that supports extension' (cf. *PHK*, 16), or to the phrase 'the entity that supports modes or qualities' (*DHP*, I, 197). This alleged notion of material substance is drawn from Locke's discussion of one's notions of substance in general. In the *Essay*, Locke had written:

> We have no such *clear Idea* at all, and therefore signify nothing by the word *Substance*, but only an uncertain supposition of we know not what; (*i.e.* of something whereof we have no particular distinct positive) *Idea*, which we take to be the *substratum*, or support, of those *Ideas* we do know.[22]
> So that of *Substance*, we have no *Idea* of what it is, but only a confused obscure one of what it does.[23]

Thus, according to Locke, one has only 'An obscure and relative *Idea* of Substance in general'.[24] Now in the *Essay* Locke did little to elucidate his claim that one has only a relative idea of substance in general, but in responding to Edward Stillingfleet's charge that he had 'almost discarded substance out of the reasonable part of the world',[25] Locke provided an account of the origin of one's relative idea of substance in general. He wrote:

> To explain myself, and clear my meaning in this matter: all the ideas of all the sensible qualities of a cherry come into my mind by sensation; the ideas of perceiving, thinking, reasoning, knowing, &c. come into my mind by reflection: the ideas of these qualities and actions, or powers, are perceived by the mind to be by themselves inconsistent with existence; or, as your lordship well expresses it, 'we find that we have no true conception of any modes or accidents, but we must conceive a substratum or subject, wherein they are;' i.e., that they cannot exist or subsist of themselves. Hence the mind perceives their necessary connexion with inherence or being supported; which being a relative idea superadded to the red colour in a cherry, or to thinking in a man, the mind frames the correlative idea of a support. For I never denied, that the mind could frame to itself ideas of relation, but have showed the quite contrary in my chapters about relation. But because a relation cannot be founded on nothing, or be the relation of nothing, the thing here related as a supporter or support is not represented to the mind by any clear and distinct idea; therefore, the obscure, indistinct, vague idea of thing or something, is all that is left to be the positive idea, which has the relation of support or substratum to modes or accidents; and that general indetermined idea of something, is, by the abstraction of the mind, derived also from the simple ideas of sensation and reflection: and thus the mind, from the positive, simple ideas got by sensation and reflection, comes to the general relative idea of substance; which, without positive ideas, it would never have.[26]

The reader should notice that the account Locke here provides of one's relative ideas of substance corresponds exactly to the describing model of Berkeleian relative notions. In claiming to have a relative idea of substance, Locke is contending that one is able to single out a substance on the basis of a positive idea and the relation of inherence or support. Insofar as it is a relative idea, this account is consistent with the passages we noted from the *Essay*, for although a relative idea will allow one to single out a particular object or, if it is based upon a general positive idea, a kind of object, it does not provide one with any positive understanding of the nature of that thing of which one has a relative idea. Thus, although Locke claimed that one has a relative idea of substance, he could consistently claim that 'we have no *Idea* of what it is, but only a confused obscure one of what it does'.[27]

There can be little doubt that it was with an eye to Locke's account of the relative idea of substance that Berkeley wrote in Section 16 of the *Principles*:

> It is said extension is a *mode* or *accident* of Matter, and that Matter is the *substratum* that supports it. Now I desire that you would explain to me what is meant by Matter's *supporting* extension. Say you, I have no idea of Matter; and therefore cannot explain it. I answer, though you have no positive, yet if you have any meaning at all, you must at least have a relative idea of Matter; though you know not what it is, yet you must be supposed to know what relation it bears to accidents, and what is meant by its supporting them. It is evident *support* cannot here be taken in its usual or literal sense, as when we say the pillars support a building. In what sense therefore must it be taken? (*PHK*, 16; cf. *PHK*, 17 and 68, and *DHP*, I, 197-9)

If the criteria I have suggested Berkeley employed in judging the adequacy of a relative notion are correct, the criticism Berkeley advances here are just what one would expect. If a relative notion (in Locke's parlance, a relative idea) is to single out exactly one object (or kind of object), one must have a clear idea of one of the relata and a determinate notion of the relation involved. Assuming for the sake of the argument that one can have an idea of extension as a mode or accident of matter — a position that is properly inconsistent with the principle that only an idea can be like an idea — Berkeley asks whether one has a determinate notion of the relation denoted by the term 'supports'. In examining this question, he notes that one is using the relational term 'supports' literally when one refers to the pillars of a building supporting a building or one's legs supporting one's body (*DHP*, I, 199). In the *Dialogues*, Hylas concedes that it is not the literal sense in which proponents of a

Lockean relative idea would have one understand the term 'supports' (*DHP*, I, 199), and Philonous replies:

> **Philonous.** Pray let me know any sense, literal or not literal, that you understand it in. —— How long must I wait for an answer, Hylas?
> **Hylas.** I declare I know not what to say. I once thought I understood well enough what was meant by matter's supporting accidents. But now the more I think on it, the less I can comprehend it; in short, I find that I know nothing of it.
> **Philonous.** It seems then you have no idea at all, neither relative nor positive of matter; you know neither what it is in itself, nor what relation it bears to accidents.
>
> (*DHP*, I, 199)

If the sense of the term 'supports' in either the definite description 'the entity that supports extension' or the definite description 'the entity that supports modes and qualities' is not the literal sense, and one is incapable of specifying a technical sense of that term, Berkeley takes this to be sufficient to establish that the relational term is meaningless, and therefore one cannot have a relative notion of matter that corresponds to either of these descriptions.

In reading both these sections from the *Principles* and the passage from the *First Dialogue*, the reader is apt to suggest that Berkeley moves to his conclusion a bit too rapidly. After all, we have seen that he was willing to allow that one can have metaphorical knowledge of relations (assign a metaphorical meaning to a relational term). Why could one not do the same thing in the case of the relational term 'supports'? Since one can assign a metaphorical meaning to the relational term 'higher than' when used in visual contexts on the basis of an analogy to its use in tangible contexts, is Berkeley's contention that one cannot provide a metaphorical meaning of the relational term 'supports' a defensible claim? Or is Berkeley's contention that one cannot provide a metaphorical meaning of the term 'support' that would be germane to the Lockean account of one's idea of substance merely a convenient subterfuge?

To answer these questions, we should consider again the metaphorical uses of a relational term such as 'higher than'. The head of the elephant is visibly higher than the foot of the elephant. The head of the elephant is tangibly higher than the foot of the elephant. The tone represented by the note on the second line of the treble clef is higher than the tone represented by the note on the first line below the treble clef. According to Berkeley, in each of these sentences the relational term 'higher than' denotes a different specific kind of relation, although the relations are said to be similar. What are the aspects of each of these experiential situations that are similar? First, it should be noticed that in each of these situations one is (or can be) sensibly aware of both of the relata in the relation: both of the relata are ideas. It is on the basis of the kinds of relatum involved that Berkeley classifies relations into kinds. Second, as we shall see shortly, Berkeley appears to reduce relations among ideas to acts of judgment (volitions), and since he held that there are ideas of reflection that are concomitant with the operations of the mind (cf. *PC*, 661a), in claiming that these several 'higher than' relations are analogous, it is reasonable to assume that there is a similarity among the kinds of ideas of reflection that are concomitant with those actions of the mind that constitute the several 'higher than' relations, and therefore, that there is also a similarity among those several kinds of actions of the mind.[28] Given this, we should be able to reconstruct the reasoning that led Berkeley to contend that one cannot supply so much as a metaphorical meaning to the term 'supports' when used in the context of the theory of material substance.

Berkeley's paradigms of the relation of support are the relations between a building and its pillars (*PHK*, 16) and the relation between a person's legs and his or her torso (*DHP*, I, 199). In both of these cases one is concerned with relations among ideas, and, following his suggestions in Section 46 of the *Theory of Vision, Vindicated*, in both of these cases one might claim that there are two distinct kinds of relations of support that obtain between the relata, these being visible and tangible relations of support. Now remember, in so far as one is concerned with relations among ideas, in these cases one is immediately acquainted with the relata in each of the support relations. In this respect, the case is dissimilar to that which obtains in the case of the putative relation of support that holds between a material substance and its modes or accidents: in the latter case one is immediately acquainted with neither of the relata and, as I mentioned above, to suggest one is mediately aware of the modes of a material substance would violate Berkeley's likeness principle. Since in one of his early allusions to his likeness principle Berkeley claimed that 'A man cannot compare 2 things together without perceiving each of them, ergo he cannot say any thing wch is not an idea is like or unlike an idea' (*PC*, 51), he appears to have been committed to the claim that one must be aware of both relata in a relation if one is to make any claims of similarity between the relations themselves. Nor will it help to suggest that in so far as Berkeley is able to explicate the meaning of 'support' in the case of immaterial substance that he could have a metaphorical notion of the relation of support in the case of material substance. Berkeley explicates the relational term 'supports' in the case of immaterial substance in terms of the relations of perception and causation. On his own principles, the relation of perception can obtain only between an immaterial substance and an idea, and only immaterial substances can be efficient causes (cf. *PC*, 850; *PHK*, 26; *DHP*, III, 239; Cor., 2, 2). But why could one not claim that there is a relation that is similar to one or both of these relations that obtains between a material substance and its modes? The difficulty is in spelling out the sense in which they are similar. Remember, in this case, unlike the case of analogous relations among ideas, one is not aware of both relata in both relations: properly, one has no immediate awareness of either the mode of a presumptive material substance nor of the substance itself. Even if one were to suggest, as I shall do below, that one also does not have direct awareness of an immaterial substance, that is, one has only a relative notion of an immaterial substance that is grounded upon an idea and a positive notion of causality and perception, the case is in no way analogous in the case of material substance. In the latter case, one has no ideational ground for one's relative notion, and apart from at least such a ground, there is no basis whatsoever for spelling out the sense in which a putative relation between a material substance and its mode is similar to that between an immaterial substance and an idea: the relation(s) involved cannot be a relation or perception or causation, and there is no basis for holding that they are similar to such relations. Thus, there are no grounds for claiming that one can know the meaning of 'support' in the description 'the entity that supports extension' on the basis of an analogy to immaterial substance, and Berkeley has won his point that one has no notion of a material substance and, therefore, there are no grounds for claiming the existence of a material substance.[29]

Although Berkeley repeatedly claimed that one has neither a

positive nor a relative notion of material substance, he also claimed that one has a notion of immaterial substance or spirit. One should ask, then, is one's notion of immaterial substance a positive notion or a relative notion? While Berkeley never explicitly addressed this issue in his printed works, some of the things he claims imply that he could only have taken it to be a relative notion. As early as the *Philosophical Commentaries*, for example, several entries suggest that Berkeley, like the Cartesians, considered thought to be essential to the mind (*PC*, 650 and 704), and his principle that the *esse* of a sensible object is *percipi* is intended to mark a necessary connection between an idea and the mind that perceives it (*PHK*, 3-5, and 90; cf. *PC*, 429 and 429a). Now, in so far as Berkeley, like the Cartesians, contended that the mind is distinct from its modes and ideas, while ideas are dependent upon a mind, it would be reasonable to suggest that he also agreed with them regarding how the mind was known. It is clear that Berkeley understood Descartes to have only mediate knowledge of the mind. As he wrote: 'M.S. Descartes owns we know not a substance immediately by it self but by this alone that it is the subject of several acts. Answer to 2nd objection of Hobbs' (*PC*, 795; cf. 752 and 798). In so far as Berkeley accepts a Cartesian account of the mind and acknowledges that Descartes took one's knowledge of mind to be relative to one's knowledge of its acts, it is at least plausible to suggest that Berkeley held the same view.

While the evidence from the *Philosophical Commentaries* is circumstantial at best, stronger evidence that he considered notions of the mind to be relative is to be found in the *Principles*. Within the context of arguing that it is impossible to have an *idea* of the mind in Section 27 of the *Principles* (both editions), Berkeley wrote, 'Such is the nature of Spirit, or that which acts, that it cannot be of itself perceived, but only by the effects which it produceth.' If one can only know one's mind on the basis of 'the effects which it produceth', one does not know the nature of the mind (one has no positive notion of the mind): one is capable of doing no more than singling out one's mind on the basis of those effects: one's notion of one's mind is relative. This passage suggests that one's relative notion of one's own mind corresponds to the definite description, 'the thing that caused *a*', where *a* is a positive idea of reflection. Nor is this the only passage in the *Principles* that suggests that one has a relative notion of mind. In Section 138, Berkeley suggests that one has a relative notion of one's own mind that corresponds to the definite description, 'the thing that thinks, wills, and perceives'. In his words:

> Do but leave out the power of willing, thinking, and perceiving ideas, and there remains nothing else wherein the idea can be like a spirit. For by the word *spirit* we mean only that which thinks, wills, and perceives: this, and this alone, constitutes the signification of the term. (*PHK*, 138; cf. *PC*, 829)

This passage also suggests that one has a relative notion of mind, that is, that one does not know what a mind is in itself, but that one can single out a mind as that which thinks, wills and perceives, where thinking, willing and perceiving are taken to be either relations between minds and ideas or properties of the mind. Since Berkeley, like Reid, held that the notion of a property or quality is inherently relative, even if one would contend that Berkeley took the words 'willing', 'thinking' and 'perceiving' to name properties of the mind, one's notion of the mind would still be relative: it would pick out that thing that has those properties.

But here someone is certain to raise an objection.[30] Citing passages from the *Third Dialogue* where Berkeley wrote, 'I know what I mean by the terms *I* and *myself*, and I know this immediately, or intuitively, though I do not perceive it as I perceive a triangle, a colour, or a sound' (*DHP*, III, 231), and that you know 'your self by a reflex act' (*DHP*, III, 232), the critic would contend that Berkeley is here claiming that one has a positive notion (a direct conception) of one's own mind, that is, a notion of the mind as it is in itself. Hence, it would be claimed, to contend that one has merely a relative notion of one's own mind and its acts is false.

There are two things to notice in reply. First, to claim that one knows the meaning of the words 'mind' or 'self' immediately does *not* imply one knows what the mind is in itself. As was noted above, in *De Motu* Berkeley claimed 'that all things we designate by names are known by qualities or relations' (*DeM*, 54), and since the notion of a quality *qua* quality is inherently relative, a notion of the mind based upon the qualities of the mind would be a relative notion. I am willing to grant that Berkeley held that one has *positive notions* of willing and perceiving (as relations or qualities) on the basis of a reflex act, but this does not entail that one has a positive notion of the mind itself on the basis of such an act. Indeed, in so far as Berkeley took will and perception to be relations between a mind and an idea, he was committed on pain of inconsistency to maintaining that they are categorially distinct from relations among ideas. Since Berkeley contended that being perceived and being caused by a mind (being willed)[31] are essential to ideas (*PHK*, 3-5 and 90; *DHP*, III, 239; cf. *PC*, 429 and 429a), it follows that the relations between minds and ideas are to be construed as internal relations. On the other hand, his comment in the *Philosophical Commentaries* that 'the connexion of no two Ideas is necessary' (*PC*, 884) indicates that relations among ideas are external relations. If there is not an internal/external relations distinction implicit in Berkeley's philosophical system, his work ultimately must be judged incoherent, for while he claimed that the mind is passive in perception (*DHP*, I, 196-7), he contended in Section 142 of the *Principles* that all relations involve actions of the mind. If he held that perception is an internal relation, while those relations that involve actions of the mind are solely external relations, that is, relations among ideas, there would be no inconsistency in Berkeley's position on relations. But if perception and causation (will) are internal relations, then, since minds and ideas are necessarily connected, one knows that there is a mind in knowing that there is an idea. Further, within its context, this is perfectly consistent with Berkeley's claim that he knows his own mind 'immediately, or intuitively, though I do not perceive it as I perceive a triangle, a colour, or a sound' (*DHP*, III, 231), for in the sentence immediately before that he claimed, 'I do nevertheless know, that I who am a spirit or thinking substance, exist as certainly, as I know my ideas exist' (*DHP*, III, 213). Since ideas are internally related to immaterial substances, in so far as one knows that there is an idea, one knows that there is a thing that perceives that idea. Hence, to claim that there is a relative idea of the mind seems to be consistent with Berkeley's claim that one knows the mind intuitively.

Second, although Berkeley claimed that one knows one's own mind 'immediately, or intuitively', this does not entail that one knows the inherent nature of the mind. In the sentence following that in which Berkeley claims immediate and intuitive knowledge of his own mind, he stated what this mind or spirit is: 'The mind, spirit, or soul, is that indivisible unextended thing, which thinks, acts, and perceives' (*DHP*, III, 231). He then proceeded to argue that the mind is indivisible because it is unextended, and that it is unextended because it is not an idea and only ideas can be extended (*DHP*, III, 231). There are two things we should notice here. First, Berkeley's characterization of the mind is what one would expect if one claimed to have a relative notion of the mind and, second, it seems that it is only on the basis of a process of reasoning that one can claim to know the nature of the mind, the reasoning being that it is indivisible and unextended. To suggest that there is a process of reasoning involved in determining the nature of the mind seems contrary to the claim that one's knowledge of one's own mind is immediate and intuitive. So if one's immediate knowledge of one's own mind is limited to the meaning of the word 'I' or 'myself', this would seem to restrict one's immediate knowledge to the mind's essential properties or relations to ideas, and it is consistent with that contention to hold that one has merely a relative notion of one's own mind.

Hence, it seems reasonable to contend that a Berkeleian notion of one's own mind is a relative notion, which is the notion corresponding to the definite description, 'the thing that perceives and wills'. But if the describing model of relative notions is to prove adequate, it should allow one to provide an account of one's notions of such mental acts as loving and hating and the relations among ideas. It is to this task that we shall now turn.

Notions of Actions and Relations

So far I have shown that Berkeley drew a distinction between positive and relative notions. If one has a positive notion of a thing, one knows the nature of that thing. Knowledge based upon positive notions is analogous to what Bertrand Russell called knowledge by acquaintance. If one has a relative notion of a thing, one does *not* know the inherent nature of that thing, although one is able to single out that thing on the basis of an idea and a relation. I have argued knowledge based upon relative notions is analogous to Russell's knowledge by description. I have shown that my describing model of relative notions is consistent with Berkeley's criticisms of the doctrine of material substance and his discussions of one's notions of immaterial substance.

I also *suggested* Berkeley held that one's notions of perception and causation are positive. My evidence for this is quite limited and primarily based upon philosophical considerations. Berkeley took perception and causation to be necessary connections between minds and ideas (cf. *PHK*, 3, 6, and 25-6). In this respect they differ from relations among ideas, all of which are contingent (*PC*, 884). Since one's relative notions of immaterial substance presuppose a determinate notion of either the relation of causation or the relation of perception, this suggests that one's notions of causation and perception are positive notions. Further, we shall see that all notions of operations of the mind and of relations among ideas reasonably can be construed as relative notions. If one's notions of *all* relations were relative notions, one would be caught in an infinite regress: there would never be a conceptual foundation for one's relative notions. Since Berkeley took the relations of perception and causation to be necessary, while he took the relations among ideas to be contingent, and since the contention that one's notions of perception and causation are positive is a necessary presupposition if one is to intelligibly claim that one has relative notions of immaterial substance, operations of the mind, and relations among ideas, I consider it reasonable to conclude that one's notions of perception and causation are positive notions. But my argument for the positivity of one's notions of perception and causation itself rests upon the unestablished presumption that one's notions of the operations of the mind and of relations among ideas are relative notions. I now shall show that that presumption is reasonable.

Although Berkeley provided several brief discussions of one's notions of spirit, he did little more than indicate that one has notions of the actions of minds and of relations among ideas: he provided an account of neither the nature of these notions nor of the nature of actions and relations (see *PHK*, 27, 89, and 142). Consequently, anything one says about notions of actions of the mind and relations must be somewhat speculative. None the less, I hope to show that such evidence as there is suggests that one has relative notions of the actions of the mind and relations among ideas. I shall begin by considering some of Berkeley's remarks on one's knowledge of mind and the distinction between ideas of sense and reflection. Turning to relations, I shall take seriously Berkeley's claim that all relations among ideas involve actions of the mind (*PHK*, 142), and that will provide evidence that my account of notions of actions of the mind can be extended to cover notions of relations among ideas as well.

If I am correct in suggesting Berkeley held one has a positive notion of will (cause) as either a property of the mind or a relation between a mind and ideas, this need not entail that one has positive notions of such types of actions as loving and hating. The relativity of one's notions of actions of the mind is suggested by Berkeley's statement that 'Such is the nature of *spirit* or that which acts, that it cannot be of it self perceived, but only by the effects which it produceth' (*PHK*, 27), and one of his comments in the *Philosophical Commentaries* can leave little doubt that he took one's notions of the several kinds of actions of the mind to be relative. There he wrote:

S   We see no variety or difference between the Volitions, only between their effects. Tis One Will one Act distinguish'd by the effects. This will, this Act is the Spirit, operative Principle, Soul, etc (*PC*, 788; cf. *PC*, 661a)

Berkeley's claim that 'we see no variety or difference between the Volitions' indicates that there is no variety among one's notions of volitions *qua* volitions. This is consistent with my contention that one has a positive notion of volition (causality), for to have a positive notion of volition is to conceive of the nature of volition directly (to conceive of what volition itself is), and this would be common to all kinds of volitions. Although there are no differences among volitions *qua* volitions, there are differences among the effects produced by the various operations of the mind and one classifies such actions into kinds on the basis of their effects, that is, the ideas that are produced by those actions of the mind. For example, an act of loving produces an idea that differs in kind from that produced by either an act of hating or an act of willing to move one's arm. One's notion of such an action of the mind is the relative notion corresponding to the definite description 'the act of mind that caused a', where a is a particular idea produced by that act. It is clear, however, that if actions of the mind are known and differentiated on the basis of their effects (the ideas they produce), not all the ideas produced are ideas of the senses. The reason is that if the only effects of the actions of the mind were ideas of sense, without any ideas of reflection, one could not differentiate kinds of mental act, for it is possible that qualitatively identical ideas of sense could be involved in such diverse mental acts as hating the mouse that inhabits my kitchen, loving to set mouse traps and imagining myself setting mouse traps in my kitchen. Consequently, while the ideas of sense must play some role in providing an account of Berkeleian actions of the mind, they cannot be the only kinds of ideas to which one would appeal in giving an analysis of such actions of the mind, and they can play little or no role in giving an account of one's notions of such actions. Different kinds of mental acts provide different kinds of 'feelings' or ideas of reflection, that is, such ideas 'as are perceived by attending to the passions and operations of the mind' (*PHK*, 1).[32] It is on the basis of similarities and differences among ideas of reflection that one can classify and differentiate kinds of action of the mind. Since Berkeley held that ideas are particulars (Intro., 12), the particularity of the idea of reflection that is found in the relative notion corresponding to the definite description 'the act of mind that causes a', where a is a particular idea of reflection, will succeed in singling out a particular mental act.[33]

Turning to notions of relations among ideas, we must begin by examining those clues Berkeley provided regarding the nature of relations among ideas. I hope to show that those relations are to be analyzed as actions of the mind, that is, 'relatings',[34] and if this is correct, that one can have notions of relations among ideas (*qua* actions) along the lines I have defended above. So let us turn to Berkeley's remarks on the nature of relations.

Berkeley's writings provide four clues to the nature of relations among ideas. First, Berkeley suggested that the relata of a relation are epistemically prior to the relation itself and, second, therefore we have no ideas of relations. He wrote, 'In like manner [to our notions of spirit] we know or have a notion of relations among ideas, which relations are distinct from the ideas of things related, inasmuch as the latter may be perceived by us without our perceiving the former' (*PHK*, 89). In claiming that one has no ideas of relations and that ideas can be known apart from relations, Berkeley at least suggested that relations cannot be known apart from their relata. Third, Berkeley suggested that actions of the mind are inherent to relations. In his words, 'It is also to be remarked, that all relations including an act of the mind, we cannot properly be said to have an idea, but rather a notion of the relations or habitudes between things' (*PHK*, 142). In so far as relations among ideas involve actions of the mind, this passage suggests that relations are to be identified with certain types of mental acts, that is, relations are to be understood as 'relatings' of ideas.[35] Fourth, in the *Theory of Vision, Vindicated*, Berkeley suggested that relations either are acts of judgment or come to be known on the basis of acts of judgment. As he wrote:

> Though I may have an erroneous notion of the cause, or though I may be utterly ignorant of its nature; yet this doth not hinder my making true and certain judgments about my ideas: my knowing which are the same and which different: wherein they agree, and wherein they disagree: which are connected together, and wherein this connexion consists: whether it be found in likeness of nature, or merely experience. (*TVV*, 20)

Notice that Berkeley is concerned here with judgments of similarity and difference. Judgments are clearly actions of the mind, while similarity and difference are clearly relations. What is involved in making a judgment of similarity or difference? Presumably the mind perceives two or more objects and reacts in a particular way. If the objects are similar, the mind reacts in one way; if the objects are different, the mind reacts in a different way. These judgments of similarity and difference, as acts of the mind, can be distinguished on the basis of Berkeleian ideas of reflection. But is the *relation* of similarity and the *relation* of difference anything over and above such an act of judgment? It would seem not. What more could it be? Remember, a relation *cannot* be part of an idea, for then it would itself be an idea — but since relations among ideas include actions of the mind, they neither are nor can be ideas (*PHK*, 142; cf. *PHK*, 27). Further, since Berkeley deemed relations among ideas 'connexions', and since only a mind could connect ideas, this also suggests that a mental act of connecting or relating is the essential element of a relation. But to see that this act of 'connecting' might reasonably be identified with a relation, that is, that Berkeley held that relations are relatings by the mind, we should look more closely at the passage from the *Theory of Vision, Vindicated* and consider some examples.

Notice also that Berkeley indicates that there are at least two, perhaps three, kinds of judgments of similarity and difference: there is the initial judgment that two things are similar or different; there is the judgment regarding the respect in which these things are similar or different; and there is the judgment of connections among ideas. As we shall see, there is at least some evidence that the judgments of the respect in which things are the same or different and judgments of connections are not obviously distinct (inde-

The Epistemic Intent of Berkeleian Notions 159

pendent): one judges sameness and difference, at least in part, on the basis of judgments of connections.

To see how this might fit into Berkeley's theory of relations, consider the two following ideas, a and b:

a △ ☐
b ☐ △

If one were to perceive these ideas, one might judge that they are different from each other. Were this to occur, and if our earlier analysis of Berkeleian mental acts is adequate, an act of judgment of difference would be distinguished from other types of mental acts on the basis of an idea of reflection. This is a first-level judgment. A second-level judgment concerns the respects in which the two ideas are similar or different. The similarity is, of course, in the objects composing the ideas, and the difference is in the spatial relations obtaining between the triangle and the square in the two ideas. But what is involved in the judgment that there is a difference in spatial relations? It must be a difference in the locating of the triangle with respect to the square in a and comparing it with the locating of the triangle with respect to the square in b. Locatings are acts. Since they are acts, and since the locating of the triangle with respect to the square in a (a locating of the triangle to the left of the square) is a different type of locating from the locating of the triangle with respect to the square in b (a locating of the triangle to the right of the square), they would reasonably be expected to yield different types of ideas of reflection, and these different types of ideas of reflection differentiate the relations insofar as the relations are acts of locating.

The plausibility of taking Berkeley's relations among ideas to be acts of mind is that it complies with his contentions that we have no ideas of relations and that all relations include an act of the mind — the other things included are the ideas upon which the mind acts. As acts of mind, relations (relatings) can be differentiated on the basis of the ideas of reflection they produce. These relatings can be singled out on the basis of relative notions corresponding to a definite description of the following general form: 'the act of mind that relates $n_1, n_2, n_3 \ldots, n_m$ in complex idea a and causes a particular idea of reflection i^r', where n_1 through n_m are component ideas of sense or reflection (according to the case) in the complex idea a. The number of ideas being related by an act will depend upon the species of the act. In cases of locating, for example, there would be only two ideas.[36] In cases of numerical relations, the mind will 'number', that is, count, the things of a particular sort in a complex idea, and the number of relata in the relation will depend upon the number of objects in the complex idea. Although the number of ideas will vary with the types of relatings and, at least in the case of number, the number of objects, it would seem that each type of relating produces a distinct idea of reflection and the relatings are differentiated on the basis of the ideas of reflection they produce. Hence, I take it to be reasonable to contend that Berkeley held that relations among ideas can be reduced to actions of mind, and that one can have relative notions of these actions in accordance with the describing model of relative notions.

If my account of Berkeleian relations is correct, then relations as acts of judgment are subjective in the sense that individual human beings make judgments and on the basis of these judgments impose a certain structure on the perceptually given. But here some commentators might object on either of two grounds. First, they might maintain that if Berkeley held that relations are subjective in this sense, it is difficult, if not impossible, to account for the general agreement among human beings regarding the kinds of relations that obtain among ideas. Surely Berkeley would have been aware of this problem and it is, therefore, unreasonable to saddle him with so unreasonable an account of relations. Second, one might develop a criticism on the basis of a passage in the *Third Dialogue*. There Berkeley wrote, '[T]hings, with regard to us, may properly be said to begin their existence, or be created, when God decreed they should become perceptible to intelligent creatures *in that order and manner which He then established* ...' (*DHP*, III, 253, emphasis added). This passage might suggest that the ideas of which we are aware are related when we become aware of them, that is, they are related by the activities of God's mind. Regarding this passage, Gotterbarn has recently commented:

> It is God who establishes the sensible order or the relations of ideas for us. Sensible relations, such as 'above', are established by the activity of some mind, namely GOD'S MIND, and it is not in our power to alter these relations. If these relations could be altered by some other mind, then Berkeley's inductive justification of prediction would fail. We could not even predict with

any certainty that 'onions are more aromatic than celery.' Sensible relations involve a mental activity which is not an activity of the perceiver of these sensible ideas. Thus an appeal to notions [our notions] cannot be used to explain our knowledge of such relations. They come to us related. If this is so, then either we do not know this sort of sensible relation (I certainly do not know God's relating activity) or there are relations which obtain only if it is perceived that they obtain without any dependency on my relating activity. I do know this sort of relation! Consequently, there are relations which obtain only if it is perceived that they obtain.[37]

If Gotterbarn is correct in suggesting that the passage from the *Third Dialogue* indicates that some ideas come to us related, then it would seem that it cannot be the activities of the perceiver that are responsible for imposing a relational structure on the world, and my account of relations must be rejected.

Is either of these objections decisive? I think not. To see why neither is decisive, I shall examine the second objection in detail, and by so doing, we shall also see why there is no force in the first objection.

The second objection rests upon considerations of the creative activity of God. In creating the world, 'God decreed they [ideas] should become perceptible to intelligent creatures in that order and manner which he then established and we now call laws of nature' (*DHP*, III, 253). In the *Philosophical Commentaries* Berkeley made much the same point in writing:

N   I think not that things fall out of necessity, the connexion of no two Ideas is necessary. 'tis all the result of freedom, i.e., tis all Voluntary. (*PC*, 884)

As in the *Third Dialogue*, Berkeley's point here is that uniform relations among ideas (laws of nature) are based upon the voluntary acts of God. This theme arises again and again throughout Berkeley's works. In the *New Theory of Vision*, the *Alciphron* and the *Theory of Vision, Vindicated*, Berkeley expressed this in terms of an analogy to the arbitrary use of words to represent objects: by an arbitrary 'decree of God' human beings take visible objects to be signs of tangible objects just as they take words to be signs of objects (see *NTV*, 51, 66, 73, 140, 143-4, 147; *A*, 4, 7 and 4, 10-

12; *TVV*, 7, 9, 39, 40, 45; cf. *PHK*, 43-4). The issue, then, is how does God 'decree' that one kind of object is to be a sign of another kind of object, or, to follow Gotterbarn's suggestion, how is it that 'Sensible relations, such as "above", are established by the activity of some mind, namely GOD'S MIND'?[38]

God's creative activity occurs on two planes: not only does God create sensible ideas and decree that they be perceptible to intelligent creatures (minds) he also creates those creatures (*PHK*, 141; cf. *DHP*, III, 250-1). Now, in so far as God creates both the sensible objects and the spirits that perceive them, God might instill order on sensible ideas in either of two ways. God might, as Gotterbarn suggests, 'order' the ideas themselves. If God did this, it might be reasonable to suggest that, contrary to Berkeley, relations are to be found 'in' complex ideas or that one would have to know the actions of God's mind that are involved in ordering the ideas. As Gotterbarn indicates, neither alternative is defensible on Berkeleian principles.[39] On the other hand, since God creates spirits as well as ideas, God might create all human spirits 'from the same mold', as it were, that is, all human spirits might be created with the same sorts of dispositional properties. If this were the case, then the types of judgments human beings would make would be relatively uniform and, in so far as there would be a uniformity of judgment among human beings, it would be reasonable to construe relations among ideas in terms of human acts of judgment. The issue, then, is whether Berkeley held that there is a uniformity among human spirits and whether, therefore, it is plausible to contend that God's ordering of ideas is to be construed in terms of the individual acts of ordering (judging) by human minds.

There can be little question that Berkeley presumed that there is a general uniformity with respect to the abilities and dispositions of human minds. Some evidence for this can be drawn from the *Alciphron*, for there Alciphron was made to say, 'And, as I am apt to think men's minds and faculties are made much alike, I suspect that other men, if they examined what they call grace with the same exactness and indifference, would agree with me that there is nothing in it but an empty phrase' (*A*, 7, 4). While Euphranor argues that one has a notion of grace, he does not challenge the assumption that 'men's minds and faculties are made much alike' (cf. *A*, 7, 5). Similarly, earlier in the same work Euphranor objected to Alciphron's criticisms of the theory of innate ideas by arguing it is not the ideas that are innate, but the natural dispositions to have ideas of certain kinds under certain conditions that is innate (*A*, 1, 14). Both of these passages from the *Alciphron* tend to support my contention that Berkeley held that there is a great deal of uniformity among human minds, and the latter also tends to support my contention that Berkeley analyzed relations among ideas as dispositions to make judgments of certain kinds.

Further, it is clear that the presumption that there is a great deal of similarity among human minds is operative in some of the arguments that are central to his defense of immaterialism, for many of these arguments make an appeal to introspection and such an appeal could show nothing if it were not *presumed* that there is a great deal of similarity among human minds. As we saw in Chapter 1, one of the arguments Berkeley presents against abstract ideas in Section 10 of the Introduction to the *Principles* is based upon considerations of what he is, in fact, capable of and incapable of conceiving. While I have argued that this is the weakest of the arguments he advances, it can have no persuasive force apart from the presumption that human minds are uniform in their abilities. Similarly, in his defense of the likeness principle in Section 8 of the *Principles*, Berkeley makes another appeal to introspection. There he wrote, 'If we look but ever so little into our thoughts, we shall find it impossible for us to conceive a likeness except only between our ideas' (*PHK*, 8).[40] Again, there is an introspective appeal in his criticisms of the primary/secondary qualities distinction. There he wrote, 'For my own part, I see evidently that it is not in my power to frame an idea of a body extended and moved, but I must withal give it some color or other sensible quality which is acknowledged to exist only in the mind' (*PHK*, 10), and again, 'Unity I know some will have to be a simple or uncompounded idea accompanying all other ideas into the mind. That I have any such an idea answering the word *unity* I do not find' (*PHK*, 13). The persuasive force of each of these arguments rests upon the presumption that there is a great deal of similarity among human minds. Hence, Berkeley seems to have accepted the uniformity of the mental abilities of human beings as an operative assumption, and it is, therefore, reasonable to suggest that God introduced relations into the world by structuring human minds in such a way that there is general uniformity with respect to the judgments human beings make, that is, that Berkeley reduced relations among ideas to the judgments of human minds.

But some readers might find Berkeley's critical appeals to introspection to provide little or no evidence that he himself accepted a principle of psychological uniformity. After all, psychological uniformity was assumed by all the proponents of these doctrines, and it is plausible to suggest that in these cases Berkeley himself only accepted the assumption of psychological uniformity for the sake of the argument. Given that his arguments are purely negative, they can provide little evidence with regard to Berkeley's positive views.

I shall grant that Berkeley's arguments from introspection taken by themselves provide only limited evidence that he himself assumed that human minds are (relatively) uniform. None the less, the fact that the presumption of such uniformity was part of the intellectual milieu in which Berkeley wrote provides some evidence that Berkeley was himself caught up in this milieu. It was not only the proponents of the primary/secondary qualities distinction who made this assumption, it was shared by the moral-sense theorists of the early eighteenth century. But there is additional evidence that Berkeley held that human minds are psychologically uniform. Remember, Berkeley classified objects into kinds on the basis of their similarities. In so far as a mind 'cannot be of itself perceived, but only by the effects which it produceth' (*PHK*, 27), Berkeley would classify things as human minds on the basis of their effects (ideas of reflection) or reports of these effects. Given his principles of classification, this alone indicates that there must be a fair amount of uniformity (although certainly not perfect uniformity) among the observable effects of those objects Berkeley would classify as human minds, and he recognized that there actually are such uniformities. In the *New Theory of Vision*, for example, he recognized that, as a matter of fact, virtually all human beings take visible objects to signify tangible objects (*NTV*, 140). Further, there is some evidence that relations also are simply what virtually everyone says they are, that is, they rest upon a uniformity of judgment. In the *Third Dialogue* Philonous discusses the 'vulgar acceptation' of the notion of identity. There Philonous is made to say:

> If the term *same* be taken in the vulgar acceptation, it is certain (and not at all repugnant to the principles I maintain) that different persons may perceive the same thing; or the same thing

or idea may exist in different minds. Words are of arbitrary imposition; and, since men are used to apply the word *same* where no distinction or variety is perceived, and I do not pretend to alter their perceptions, it follows that, as men have said before, *several saw the same thing,* so they may, upon like occasions, still continue to use the same phrase, without any deviation from either propriety of language, or the truth of things. But, if the term *same* be used in the acceptation of philosophers, who pretend to an abstracted notion of identity, then, according to their sundry definitions of this notion (for it is not yet agreed wherein that philosophic identity consists), it may or may not be possible for diverse persons to perceive the same thing. But whether philosophers shall think fit to *call* a thing the *same* or no, is, I conceive, of small importance. *Let us suppose several men together, all endued with the same faculties, and consequently affected in like sort by their senses, and who had yet never known the use of language; they would, without question, agree in their perceptions* [my emphasis]. (*DHP*, III, 247)

Notice that Berkeley here is concerned, at least in part, with the use of the word 'same' or 'identical'. Human beings who have not been tainted by philosophy generally agree that they see the same objects. If you and I were having supper together, for example, we would claim to see the same bowl of potatoes. Which objects count as being identical depends upon what the majority of human beings judge to be identical: considerations of identity are based upon conventions. But notice that in the last sentence of the section quoted above, Berkeley again introduces the assumption that all human beings have the same faculties and suggests that it is because they have the same faculties that there will be a uniformity of judgments of identity. If relations among ideas are reducible to judgments, and human minds are psychologically uniform, it is reasonable to suggest that God introduced relations into the world on the basis of the structure of the human mind: objects are identical because virtually all human beings judge them to be identical, and virtually all human beings judge them to be identical because all human minds have basically the same psychological structure.[41]

Although I believe these considerations are sufficient to show that Berkeley held that human minds are psychologically uniform and that God introduced relations into the world on the basis of the common structure of human minds, there is one more point we might consider in support of this. In Section 141 of the *Principles*, Berkeley argued for the natural immortality of the soul. The soul is immortal because it is incapable of corruption (change). Now traditionally, to claim that the soul is immortal is to claim that it will exist at all times in the future, that is, it will exist eternally. In traditional Christian theology, while both God and souls exist eternally, there is a difference between the eternal existence of a human mind and the eternal existence of God: while claiming that a human mind will exist eternally one means that it will exist at all future times, to claim that God exists eternally is to claim that God exists outside of time. In Berkeley's case, however, there is a difference: human minds do not properly exist 'in time', rather, since time is analyzed in terms of a succession of ideas (*PHK*, 98), time is in minds. Hence, to claim that once a human mind is created it exists eternally is to claim that there will be a continual succession of ideas even after the 'death' of one's body (cf. Cor. 2, 6). On the other hand, to claim that God exists eternally is to assert 'that all things past and to come are actually present to the mind of God, and that there is in him no change, variation, or succession [of ideas]' (Cor. 4, 2; cf. *DHP* III, 252). Since there is no succession of ideas, there is no time in God. Although divine ideas are ordered, they do not succeed one another: God is 'always' aware of all his ideas. God causes human beings to be aware of ideas,[42] and, in the case of human beings, one is aware of these ideas successively. To claim that idea *b* is successive to idea *a* is to claim that *b* occurs after *a*, and 'after' is a relational term. Does this not mean that temporal relations are also created by God? Perhaps, but this need not entail that they are anything more than created dispositions of the mind to judge that *a* occurs after *b*.

Consider an example. I am now perceiving a copy of Berkeley's *Principles*. I am now perceiving the keyboard of my typewriter. I might now judge that I perceived my copy of the *Principles* before I perceived the keyboard of my typewriter, or I might not make this judgment. One can be aware of two (successive) ideas without being aware that they are successive. I consider it quite plausible to suggest that Berkeley would claim that in God's creative activity he created human minds in such a way that they are disposed to judge that ideas are successive, and that to claim that ideas in the mind are successive is to claim nothing more than that human beings have a disposition to judge them, and actually do judge them, to be successive. Given that human psychology is basically uniform, this would be sufficient to account for temporal relations: temporal relations, like all other relations among ideas, are nothing other than individual acts of judgment.

If my argument is cogent, then neither of the objections we considered above has any force against my account of Berkeleian notions of relations. Recall that the first objection was that if, as I suggested, relations are subjective acts of judgment, it would be difficult to account for the general agreement regarding the relations that obtain among ideas. The second objection was that it is God's activity that is involved in relating ideas and, therefore, either it is impossible to have notions of relations or, contrary to Berkeley's stated position, relations among ideas are perceived 'in' complex ideas. In showing that Berkeley held that all human minds are 'made from the same mold', that is, that he presumed it to be given that all human minds have the same dispositional properties, I have shown that neither objection has any force against my account of Berkeley's position. The first objection is side-stepped, for, in so far as Berkeley takes it to be given that all human minds are psychologically similar, he need not explain why there is a uniformity of judgment, or rather, this provides the explanation. The second objection carries no weight since, although there is a sense in which God's activity establishes relations among ideas, it does so only in so far as God creates minds that uniformly make judgments of certain kinds. Thus, the actual relating of ideas occurs at the level of individual human minds. If a particular relation is a particular act of judgment, I am capable of distinguishing one such act from others on the basis of the ideas of reflection that are concomitant with those actions of my mind, that is, I am able to single out my own relating activities on the basis of a relative notion corresponding to the definite description, 'the action of the mind that causes (some particular idea of reflection) a'. Since Berkeley reduced relations among ideas to actions of the mind, the set of one's notions of relations is merely a subset of the set of one's notions of actions of the mind.

Conclusions

Thus we have seen that Berkeley drew a distinction between positive and relative notions, a distinction that was anticipated by Locke's distinction between positive and relative ideas. Berkeley held that one has positive notions of causality and perception, that is, one is directly aware of the nature of these relations and relative notions of immaterial substances, actions of the mind and relations among ideas. These relative notions are comparable to definite descriptions: they allow one to indirectly single out a particular mind, action of the mind, or relation on the basis of its causal or perceptual relations to a particular idea. Since one's relative notions are based upon relations of causality or perceptions, my account of relative notions meets Berkeley's challenge in the *Second Dialogue* — that if one claims to have a notion of a thing that is not perceived, 'reason or revelation [must] induce us to believe in the existence of [that] thing' (*DHP*, II, 223), for the relations of causality and perception are internal to ideas. Hence, having a relative notion based upon an idea provides a sufficient reason for claiming the existence of such objects or actions of mind. We also should notice that my account of one's relative notions of substance and actions of the mind is consistent with Berkeley's claim that one has a notion of a mind or its actions in so far as one knows the meaning of the words denoting them, for, consistent with an extensional theory of meaning, Berkeleian relative notions single out particular minds and their actions.

Thus, if my arguments in this chapter have been successful, part of the shroud of mystery surrounding Berkeley's doctrine of notions has been lifted. One has positive notions of the relations of causality and perception: one knows their nature directly. One has relative notions of minds, their actions, and relations among ideas: one knows they exist, but not their nature, if and only if the contextual definition of the definite description corresponding to one's relative notion is true. While this removes the epistemic shroud surrounding the doctrine of notions, two important questions remain to be answered. First, what is the *nature*, as distinct from the epistemic function, of Berkeleian notions? Second, did Berkeley draw an ontological distinction between notions and ideas, and if he did, what is the nature of that distinction? It is to these questions we shall turn in the next chapter.

Notes

1. Cummins is one of the few commentators to acknowledge that Berkeley drew such a distinction. See Phillip D. Cummins, 'Hylas' Parity Argument', in

Berkeley: Critical and Interpretive Essays (ed. Colin Murray Turbayne) (University of Minnesota Press, Minneapolis, 1982) pp. 288-9 and p. 293, note 9.
   2. John Locke, *An Essay concerning Human Understanding* (ed. P.H. Nidditch) (Clarendon Press, Oxford, 1975), 2.23.3; cf. Locke's *Letter to the Bishop of Worcester, Works of John Locke*, 10 vols. (London, 1823), 3:21-2. I have discussed Locke's positive/relative ideas distinction in 'Locke's Relative Ideas', *Theoria*, 47 (1981), pp. 142-59.
   3. Hume, *A Treatise of Human Nature* (ed. L.A. Selby-Bigge, 2nd edn rev. by P.H. Nidditch) (Clarendon Press, Oxford, 1978), I.ii.6, p. 68; cf. *Treatise*, I.iv.5, p. 241 and *An Enquiry concerning Human Understanding*, p. 77n. I have discussed Hume's account of relative ideas in 'Hume's Relative Ideas', *Hume Studies*, 7 (1981), pp. 55-73, and 'Relative Ideas Revisited: A Reply to Thomas', *Hume Studies*, 8 (1982) pp. 158-71.
   4. Thomas Reid, *Essays on the Active Powers of the Human Mind* (ed. Baruch Brody) (M.I.T. Press, Cambridge, 1969), p. 7.
   5. Reid, *Active Powers*, pp. 7-10; cf. Thomas Reid, *Essays on the Intellectual Powers of Man* (ed. Baruch Brody) (M.I.T. Press, Cambridge, 1969), pp. 252-6, 273, 277, 381, and 473.
   6. Reid, *Active Powers*, p. 7.
   7. Ibid., p. 9.
   8. It is also clear that there is at least one sense in which those who claim that the doctrine of notions was an *ad hoc* addition to Berkeley's system are in error. (See, for example, James W. Cornman, 'Theoretical Terms, Berkeleian Notions, and Minds', in *Berkeley, Principles of Human Knowledge: Text and Critical Essays* (ed. Colin Murray Turbayne) (Bobbs-Merrill, Indianapolis, Indiana, 1970), pp. 166-7.) As I have suggested above, a distinction between positive and relative ideas was current throughout the eighteenth century. Indeed, as we shall see, Berkeley's criticisms of claims to have a notion of material substance follow Locke's discussion of the relative idea of substance in general so closely that one might believe that Berkeley had Locke's *Letter to the Bishop of Worcester* on the table before him as he wrote sections 16 and 17 of the *Principles* and the parts of the *Dialogues* we have been considering. Since this type of distinction was current at the time Berkeley wrote, he should certainly have been free to employ it.
   9. It should be noted that earlier in the same section Berkeley wrote, 'Such is the nature of Spirit, or that which acts, that it cannot be of itself perceived, but only by the effects which it produceth.'
   10. In his recent book *Berkeley* (Routledge & Kegan Paul, London, 1977), George Pitcher has presented an alternative account of the intent of Berkeleian relative notions. Pitcher claimed that 'we have a relative notion of x just in case we have reason to believe that $(\exists x)(xRy)$, where y is directly perceived' (*Berkeley*, p. 120). There are several reasons to believe that, while it takes a step in the right direction, this is not an adequate account of Berkeley doctrine of relative notions, for it is both too broad and too narrow. First, Pitcher proposed this model of notions explicitly for one's notions of substance. Anything that is to count as a general model of Berkeleian notions, however, must apply to one's notions of relations as well, and it is at best doubtful that this is an adequate model for one's notions of relations. Suppose one claims to have a notion of something being to the left of something else on the basis of a complex idea, an idea of something y being to the left of something z. Assuming that the relations in Pitcher's model could be triadic as well as diadic, one might be inclined to characterize one's notion of 'to the left of' as $(\exists x)(xByz)$, i.e., there is something x between y and z. This cannot be correct. It is inconsistent with Berkeley's criterion of ontological commitment to claim that a relation is an existent *in* a complex idea, that is, a relation is not perceived (an idea). Secondly, if one has merely relative notions of *all* relations, Pitcher's position would involve one in a vicious infinite regress: apart from a

positive notion of at least one relation, there would be no way to stop a conceptual regress. Hence, his position is too narrow. Finally, it is not at all clear that Pitcher's model is even adequate for notions of substance. In his discussion of abstract ideas, Berkeley indicated that notions are 'in their own nature *particular*' (Intro., 15), by which he presumably means that they are notions of particular objects: only such a view is consistent with his extensional theory of meaning. But if this is correct, Pitcher's characterization of the intent of relative notions in terms of the existential operator cannot carry the burden of uniqueness that is required of a relative notion, and consequently, his model is too broad. Perhaps, however, I have misrepresented the intent of Pitcher's model, since in the sentence immediately preceding the sentence quoted above he wrote, 'We have a relative notion of an entity, x, just in case there are good grounds for supposing that x is the entity that bears a certain relation R to something else, y, where y is directly perceived by us' (*Berkeley*, p. 120). The 'the' in the sentence just quoted suggests the uniqueness of the s of which one has a relative notion — which is the position I consider correct — although apart from a discussion of the nature of relations, there is still a possibility of an infinite regress in attempting to apply this model to notions of relations.

11. Arnauld, *The Art of Thinking: Port-Royal Logic* (trans. James Dickoff and Patricia James) (Bobbs-Merrill, Library of Liberal Arts, Indianapolis, 1964), pp. 82-3 and 86-95.

12. Ibid., pp. 82 and 165-6. Cf. Isaac Watts, *Logick, or the Right Use of Reason, in the Inquiry After Truth*, 3rd American edn (Ranlett and Norris, Boston, 1806), pp. 68-88. Watts's *Logick* was originally published in 1724.

13. Arnauld, *The Art of Thinking*, p. 165.

14. Ibid., pp. 165-6. Watts provided basically the same criteria plus two more (see Watts, *Logick*, pp. 85-8). Notice also that Arnauld's first two criteria for the adequacy of a real definition comply almost exactly with Russell's criteria for the adequacy of a definite description. (See Bertrand Russell, 'The Philosophy of Logical Atomism', in his *Logic and Knowledge* (ed. Robert Charles Marsh) (Capricorn Books, New York, 1971), p. 249.)

15. Someone might object that it is too strong to claim that the clarity of one's notion of the relevant relation is a necessary condition for claiming to have a relative notion, that, at most, Berkeley might be able to claim that the clarity of one's notion of the relation is a necessary condition for having an *adequate* relative notion. After all, the objection would continue, Berkeley proposed a theory of metaphorical meaning, and if one holds that the relation of support between a building and its pillars is analogous to that between a substance and its modes, one might claim to have a relative notion of matter. There are two things to notice in reply. First, if one would allow that one could have a relative notion of an object without a clear notion of the relation involved, one would allow that one could meaningfully use a term without being able to precisely single out any actual or possible object in the extension of a particular term. To allow this would be incompatible with an extensional theory of meaning. Secondly, as we shall see shortly, within the constraints of Berkeley's theory of metaphorical meaning, it is impossible to metaphorically specify a sense of 'supports' that could provide the basis for a notion of material substance.

16. As we shall see in the fourth part of this chapter, apart from a consideration of the nature of Berkeleian relations, the doctrine of relative notions cannot commit one to a claim of real existence.

17. Arnauld, *The Art of Thinking*, p. 60.

18. Ibid.

19. Watts, *Logick*, p. 50, Watt's emphasis.

20. Locke, *Essay*, 2.25.2-3.

21. For a detailed discussion of Berkeley's likeness principle, see Phillip D.

Cummins, 'Berkeley's Likeness Principle', in C.B. Martin and D.M. Armstrong (eds), *Locke and Berkeley: A Collection of Critical Essays* (Doubleday Anchor Books, Garden City, New York 1968), pp. 353-63.
22. Locke, *Essay*, 1.4.18.
23. Ibid., 2.13.19.
24. Ibid., 2.23.3.
25. Quoted in Locke, *A Letter to the Bishop of Worcester, Works of John Locke*, 2:5.
26. Locke, *Letter to the Bishop of Worcester, Works of John Locke* 2:21-2.
27. Locke, *Essay*, 2.13.19. For a detailed discussion of this, see my 'Locke's Relative Ideas'.
28. Even if the reader will ultimately judge that my argument that Berkeley reduced relations among ideas to actions of the mind fails, there remains at least this much similarity: people judge that various kinds of 'higher than' relation obtain among pairs of objects of many distinct kinds (cf. *TVV*, 46). It is at least reasonable to suggest that there is a similarity among these several kinds of judgments.
29. Notice that Berkeley's claim in Sections 16-17 of the *Principles* is merely that one has no notion of a material substance, and therefore, one has no grounds for claiming the existence of a material substance. He does *not* there claim that the existence of a material substance is impossible. His claim to the impossibility of the existence of a material substance is based upon the inconsistency of one's alleged descriptions of a material substance. See *PHK*, 23 and *DHP*, III, 232-3.
30. Tipton and Park would be among these critics, for they hold that notions are identical with minds, relations, or actions of minds. See I.C. Tipton, *Berkeley: The Philosophy of Immaterialism* (Methuen & Co. Ltd., 1974), p. 270: Desiree Park, *Complementary Notions: A Central Study of Berkeley's Theory of Concepts* (Martinus Nijhoff, The Hague, 1972), especially pp. 15-16; and Desiree Park, '*Notions*: The Counter-Poise of Berkeleyan *Ideas*', *Giornale di Metafisica* (New Series), 3 (1981), pp. 243-66.
31. Berkeley clearly took spirit to be the only properly efficient cause, i.e., there can be no efficient cause except where there is will. Cf. *PHK*, 26; Cor. 2, 2.
32. While I shall grant, as Luce and Jessop contend, that the expression 'such as' in Section 1 of the *Principles* is ambiguous between 'such ideas' and 'such objects' (*Works* 2:25, note 1), the fact that the thing to which Berkeley referred was *perceived* would seem to indicate that he was referring to ideas. Further, since Berkeley claimed to be a defender of common sense, and since there are different feelings that accompany different mental states — the feeling of jealousy is different from the feeling of pride, for example — it would seem Berkeley must grant that one is aware of such ideas of reflection.
33. While this might show that one has relative notions of individual actions or operations of the mind, this account is not intended to provide analysis of the nature of Berkeleian actions of the mind. For the present, suffice it to say that it appears that Berkeleian actions of the mind are intentional, for such actions as loving and hating must be directed toward some object. We shall examine this in greater detail in Chapter 5.

In an earlier discussion of Berkeleian notions I claimed that one's relative notion of an action of the mind is based upon both ideas of reflection and ideas of sense. I had written, 'Recognizing that an action of the mind will cause *both* a particular idea of sense (i_s) and a particular idea of reflection (i_r), one's relative notion of a particular action of the mind will correspond to the definite description, "the act of mind that causes i_s and i_r"' ('Berkeley's Notions', *Philosophy and Phenomenological Research*, 45 (1985), p. 422). This is certainly wrong, for it assumes that all actions of the mind produce both an idea of sense and an idea of reflection. While it might be true that some actions of the mind produce both kinds of ideas, e.g., acts of imagination, it cannot hold for such actions as loving and hating. If I see a mouse scurry across my kitchen floor, my subsequent hatred will be directed at the real mouse that inhabits my kitchen. Seeing or thinking about the mouse might be the occasion upon which I actively hate the mouse, but the mouse-related ideas I might have are not *caused* by the act of hatred, rather, they are part of the content of my conception of the mouse: they are what is involved in having an object of hatred.

34. Leibniz also seems to have had such a position on relations (see his Letter to Des Bosses, 21 April 1714, in his *Philosophical Papers and Letters*, 2nd edn (ed. Leroy E. Loemker) (D. Reidel Publishing Company, Dordrecht, Holland, 1976), p. 609), and such a position might be attributable to Locke (cf. *Essay*, 2.25.1 and 2.25.5).

35. Luce and Jessop have acknowledged this (*Works* 2:106, note 1). Cf. Don Gotterbarn, 'Berkeley's Mistaken Notion about Relations', a paper presented at the Berkeley Tercentenary Conference, Newport, Rhode Island, 10 March 1985, manuscript p. 6.

36. In spite of the fact that a relation such as 'to the left of' is a triadic relation, i.e., x is to the left of y from the perspective of z, I have claimed that there are only two ideas involved in the act of locating, since perspective is built into Berkeleian ideas.

37. Gotterbarn, 'Berkeley's Mistaken Notion about Relations', pp. 6-7.

38. Ibid., p. 6.

39. See ibid., pp. 7-12.

40. Given Berkeley's contention that ideas are the only immediate objects of knowledge (*PHK*, 1) and that ideas can exist only within the mind (*PHK*, 3), principles that were widely accepted within the way of ideas, Berkeley's argument for the likeness principle is not merely an argument from introspection. His argument is intended to show that on the principles accepted by the proponents of the way of ideas, they are implicitly committed to the contention that the only likenesses they can know are likenesses among ideas, and, therefore, to contend that there is a similarity between an idea and anything that is not an idea is, at best, unjustified. None the less, the appeal to introspection adds persuasive force to the argument.

41. The reader should also notice that the force of Berkeley's objection to Locke's account of personal identity also rests upon one's natural proclivity to deem identity transitive. See *A*, 7, 8.

42. It may seem paradoxical to claim that God can cause events, since God is atemporal and one's notion of a cause seems to be rooted in a temporal matrix. If this is a paradox, it is not one that is peculiar to Berkeley's God, for in the human case, Berkeley held that time, as a succession of ideas, is properly 'in' the mind — the mind is not properly 'in' time — and as a consequence, even in the human case one cannot properly talk of causes occurring 'in time'.

5 THE NATURE OF NOTIONS

In the last chapter we examined the questions concerning the epistemic intent of Berkeleian notions and the nature of Berkeleian relations. We noticed that Berkeley distinguished between positive and relative notions, and we saw that Berkeley held that while one has positive notions of causality and perception, one has relative notions of substances, particular actions of the mind and relations among ideas. I argued that relative notions provide one with knowledge by description and that one's relative notion of a mind, of an operation of a mind, or of a relation among ideas succeeds in singling out a mind, an act, or a relation just in case the contextual definition of its corresponding definite description is true. Given Berkeley's extensional theory of linguistic meaning and the corresponding need to be able to single out objects of various kinds, this account of the epistemic intent of the doctrine of notions is consistent with Berkeley's claim to have 'some notion of soul, spirit, and the operations of the mind, such as willing, loving, hating, in as much as we know or understand the meaning of those words' (*PHK*, 27; cf. *PHK* 140, 142; *DHP*, III, 233; *A*, 7, 5). Although one might not know what the inherent nature of a mind, an operation of a mind, or a relation is on the basis of a relative notion, these things can be singled out on the basis of such a relative notion and, given Berkeley's extensional theory of meaning, this is sufficient to allow one to claim to know the meaning of a term.

In this chapter we shall be concerned with the ontological question of the analysis of Berkeleian notions, that is, given that the only entities in Berkeley's ontological inventory are minds, operations of the mind and ideas, we shall ask in which of these categories notions are to be placed. I hope to show that Berkeleian notions are to be construed as intentional acts.[1] I shall begin my discussion by critically examining an alternative account of Berkeleian notions that attempts to relate Berkeleian notions to considerations of linguistic meaning — the contention that notions are concepts. Focusing primarily upon Bracken's several defenses of this thesis,[2] I shall argue that to construe a notion as a concept is either inconsistent with his ontological presuppositions or uninformative. Second, I shall examine the positive evidence for contending that a notion is an intentional act. If I am correct in contending that Berkeley held that notions are intentional acts, then, given the historical context, this will also explain why Berkeley was apparently hesitant to introduce a technical sense of the term 'notion' into his works. Finally, I shall examine the relationship between Berkeley's doctrine of notions and his theory of ideas.

Notions and Meanings: The Sergeant Connection

Some scholars have looked beyond the Berkeleian corpus in their attempts to elucidate Berkeley's doctrine of notions. Several have argued that since Berkeley was known to have at least a passing acquaintance with a doctrine of notions developed by the seventeenth-century scholastic John Sergeant (cf. *PC,* 840), and since there are a number of similarities between Berkeley's views and Sergeant's, an examination of Sergeant's doctrine will allow one to draw some significant conclusions regarding the content of Berkeley's doctrine of notions.[3] While I shall argue that ultimately the disanalogies outweigh the analogies, I shall grant that a Sergeantian interpretation of Berkeley's doctrine of notions has some plausibility. To grasp the *prima facie* plausibility of such an interpretation, we shall briefly examine some of Sergeant's discussions of notions before turning to Bracken's arguments that an analogous view is found in Berkeley.

Sergeant developed his doctrine of notions in both his *Method to Science* (1696) and his *Solid Philosophy Asserted* (1697), the latter being primarily a scholastic critique of Locke's *Essay.* Like Berkeley, Sergeant held that notions are to be contrasted with ideas and that there is a close relationship between his doctrine of notions and his theory of linguistic meaning. The following passage is sometimes cited as providing evidence for these similarities between Sergeant and Berkeley. Sergeant wrote:

> *We find we have in us* Meanings; *now the* Meanings *of Words, or (which is the same, taking the word* objectively, *what's meant by those Words,) are most evidently the same Spiritual Objects as are our Notions, and 'tis Impossible those* Meanings *should be the same with* Ideas *or Similitudes, but of a quite different Nature. Let it be as* Like *the thing as 'tis possible, 'tis not the*

Likeness of which we aim in our Language: For we do not intend *or* mean *when we speak of any thing, to talk or discourse of* what's Like *that* Thing, *but of what the same with it, or rather* what that thing it self is: *which the mere Similitude of a thing cannot possibly be. For a* Similitude *being* Related *to the Thing, in so far from being* that *Thing, or the* Same *as It is, that it is relatively* Opposite *to it; that is, quite Distinct from it. Now, what's essentially and formally* Distinct *from a Thing, nay* Opposite *to it, should of it self, and by it self alone, give us the First Knowledge of It, (as they put their Ideas to do;) or that the Meaning of the one should be the Meaning of the* other, *is utterly Unintelligible, and against Common Sense. Wherefore the* Meaning, *which is the Immediate and Proper Object of the* Mind, and which *gives us,* or rather *is* the First Notice of the Thing, must be a quite different Nature from an *Idea* or *Likeness* of it; and since there can be no Middle between *Like* and the *Same*; nor any nearer Approach or Step, proceeding from *Likeness,* towards *Unity* with the Thing, but it falls into *Identity,* it must necessarily be *more than Like it*; that is, the *Same with it*; which an *Idea* or *Likeness* cannot possibly be, as was proved lately.[4]

Notice that in this passage Sergeant contrasts notions with ideas. While ideas represent things by resemblance, there is no presumption of resemblance between one's notion of a thing and the thing of which one has a notion. This is a theme that he had also sounded in his *Method to Science*. There he wrote, '*Notions* are the very *Natures* of the *Thing,* or the *Thing* it self existing in us *intellectually,* and not a bare *Idea* or Similitude of it.'[5] Sergeant's contrast between notions and ideas, and his contention that there is no resemblance between one's notion of a thing and the thing of which one has a notion, is reminiscent of Berkeley, for Berkeley held that it is impossible for an idea to resemble anything other than an idea (*PHK*, 8), and, in particular, it is impossible for an idea to represent active beings (spirits), operations of minds, and relations (*PHK*, 27, 89, 140, 142). This is the first point of similarity between Sergeant's doctrine of notions and Berkeley's doctrine.

A second point of similarity concerns the relationship between their doctrines of notions and their theories of linguistic meaning. While Berkeley's claim to have a notion of mind in so far as one knows the meaning of the word 'mind' (*PHK*, 27) might leave ambiguous whether the notion *is* the meaning of those terms or whether knowing the meaning of such a term is merely a necessary condition for having a notion of those things,[6] Sergeant's notions are clearly intended to be the meanings of terms. This was suggested in the passages we examined above, and Sergeant stated this explicitly at another point in *Solid Philosophy Asserted*. There he wrote: 'Notions are the *Meanings*, or (to speak more properly) *what is meant* by the words we use: But *what's meant* by the words is the *Thing it self*; therefore the *Thing it self* is in the Meaning; and consequently in the *Mind*; only which can *mean*.'[7] Apparently consistent with Berkeley's extensional theory of meaning, Sergeant identifies the notion *qua* meaning with the thing itself. It is the thing itself which is meant by a name of categorematic term; the notion is the object meant. As he noted at another point: 'I do not here take the word [NOTION] for my *Act* of Simply Apprehending; but the *Object* in my mind which *informs* my understanding power, and about which that Power is Employed; in which *Objective* meaning I perceive Mr. *Locke* does also generally take the word [Idea].'[8] If it is the object itself that is meant by a term, then given that Berkeley also held that it is objects themselves that provide the meanings of terms, one might suggest that Berkeleian notions are to be construed along the same lines as Sergeant's.

Indeed, one might cite a third similarity between Berkeley and Sergeant. As we saw in last chapter, Berkeley contended that one's notions of substance are relative, they are not direct and positive. Sergeant made the same claim. He wrote:

> As for the Knowledge we have of *Spiritual* Natures, my Principles oblige me to discourse it thus: We can have no Proper or Direct Notions of Spiritual Natures, because they can make no Impressions on our Senses; yet, (as was shewn above,) our Reflexion on the Operations, and Modes which are in our Soul make us acknowledge that those *Modes* are not *Corporal*; and therefore, that the Immediate Subject of those Modes (our Soul) is not a *Body*, but of another nature, vastly different, which we call *Spiritual*.[9]

Thus, given that, like Berkeley, Sergeant drew a distinction between notions and ideas, he held that notions are the things

The Nature of Notions 177

themselves (as they exist in the soul), and he held that one does not have a positive notion of soul or spirit, one might well contend that in so far as a Sergeantian notion is to be construed as a concept, it seems *prima facie* reasonable to claim that Berkeley held the same view.

Harry Bracken is one commentator who has drawn this conclusion. As he wrote:

> As the earlier citations from John Sergeant show, *notion* was used in talking about the *meaning* of a thing. There is an imprecisely defined tradition running back to the scholastics and probably to the Stoics in which having a concept or notion of a thing is to understand the thing. This concept or notion is also the bearer of linguistic meaning. Hence one finds these concepts or notions also spoken of as *natural signs* as distinguished from linguistic markers (conventional signs). Having the concept or notion of a thing is not to have an image of it. It is to know something of it *as a substance*, i.e., as an active thing. It is to know something of its capacities and dispositions. This is part of what Sergeant is trying to do in contrasting notions with ideas. There are echoes of it in Leibniz's comments on the usefulness of individual concepts and among the earlier scholastics. Thus Berkeley's divine language talk is a straightforward variation on the sort of thing said within the scholastic tradition from the thirteenth to the seventeenth century.[10]

And again:

> Substances are active. Activity can only be known notionally. Notions or concepts are natural signs of substances. In Berkeley, however, the only substances are minds. This may be a factor in his preferring to talk of *notions* rather than concepts. Descartes, for example, speaks of innate notions. La Forge speaks (in his chapter xx) of innate notions of substances.[11]

In both of these passages Bracken draws upon the several traditions in which philosophers spoke of notions. In each of these traditions, notions are taken to be 'concepts' in the mind, although there is some difference among these traditions regarding the ontological status of these 'concepts'. Since we have seen that there are several respects in which at least Sergeant's account of notions is similar to Berkeley's, it is at least *prima facie* plausible to suggest that, like Sergeant, Berkeley held that '*A Notion is the very thing itself existing in my understanding.*'[12]

While there are similarities among the several accounts of notions that were current in the latter part of the seventeenth century, there are also several respects in which these accounts differ from one another. Since Bracken has suggested that there are similarities not merely between Berkeley's doctrine of notions and Sergeant's doctrine, but between Berkeley's doctrine of notions and the Cartesian doctrine of innate ideas (notions), we might do well to begin by considering the similarities and differences between Sergeant's doctrine of notions and the Cartesian doctrine of innate ideas and then ask to what extent either of these doctrines is similar to Berkeley's.

Sergeant was a scholastic. Within the scholastic tradition, what Sergeant called a 'notion' is also known as an intelligible form. An intelligible form is formally identical with the essential or accidental form of a substance, and it is to this formal identity that he referred when he claimed 'Notions are the very *Natures* of the Thing, or the *Thing* itself existing in us *intellectually.*'[13] None the less, while intelligible forms are formally identical with the essential or accidental forms of substances, they are numerically distinct from them. They are, in this respect similar to abstract ideas, and they would seem to be subject to Berkeley's criticisms of the doctrine of abstract ideas on the grounds of parsimony (cf. Intro., 11-12). Unlike abstract ideas, however, notions (intelligible forms) do not always require that the mind be active in forming them, for, as Sergeant noted, notions are 'Naturally wrought in the Soul by the strokes of occurring Objects, without any Industry or Active Concurrence on our part.'[14] Nonetheless, it seems that on some occasions the mind is active in forming a Sergeantian notion, for Sergeant also allowed that one can have notions of fictitious things.[15]

There are several respects in which Sergeantian notions are similar to what are known in the Cartesian tradition as innate ideas. Like Sergeant's notions, innate ideas are ideas of the essences of things. They are numerically distinct from the essences of existent objects and Descartes allowed that it is possible to have innate ideas of things that do not actually exist.[16] Further, as innate ideas, the formation of such ideas requires no activity on the part of the mind, although some activity is generally required to

Further, it is agreed that R is an asymmetrical relation: c is said to mean, or to be about, or to represent o, but o does not mean c. However, there is little agreement regarding the logical or metaphysical status of R, that is, whether R is a necessary[24] or a contingent[25] relation. In the twentieth century, many philosophers have held that the cognitive content of an intentional act is 'propositional' (descriptive), although there has been some disagreement regarding the ontological status of propositions. Whether or not it is possible to reduce the cognitive content of all intentional acts to propositional content, that is, to show that all intentional acts are descriptive,[26] it is clear that some earlier philosophers construed the cognitive content of an intentional act nonpropositionally, that is, they held that intentional acts are nondescriptive. Sergeant, for example, held that the cognitive content of an intentional act is an intelligible form (notion).[27] Finally, the ontological status of intentional objects is a matter of considerable disagreement. Some philosophers hold that only actual objects or states of affairs can be the objects of intentional acts.[28] Others hold that both actual objects and (*de dicto* or *de re*) possible objects or states of affairs can be intentional objects.[29] If one is sufficiently Meinongian one might suggest that impossible as well as actual and possible objects (or states of affairs) can be the objects of intentional acts.

If Berkeleian notions are to be construed as intentional acts, we must ask (1) whether the relation (R) between the cognitive content and the intentional object is necessary or contingent (2) whether the cognitive content of an Berkeleian intentional act is propositional or nonpropositional (whether it is a descriptive or a nondescriptive act); and (3) what the ontological status of Berkeleian intentional objects is. Since we have seen that there is a close analogy between both the structure of an intentional act and Berkeley's semantic theory — in both cases the mind directs itself at a particular object(s), relates a certain word or cognitive content to that object(s), and the relation involved is asymmetrical — it is reasonable to appeal to Berkeley's account of linguistic meaning to answer these questions regarding intentional acts.

(1) It is fairly clear that Berkeley deemed the relation between the cognitive content of an intentional act and its object contingent. This is consistent with both his account of meaning and his more general theory of signs. In the case of linguistic meaning, Berkeley held that the relation between a word and an object or objects is arbitrary both at the societal level and at the individual

level (cf. *NTV*, 143; *A*, 4, 6; *TVV*, 39). Meaning is arbitrary. It is merely a matter of fact that a certain word, that is, visible mark or sound, is used to pick out a certain object or objects. Nor is the situation significantly different in the case of 'natural signs' such as fire and smoke. As Berkeley noted in the *Theory of Vision, Vindicated*:

> A great number of arbitrary signs, various and apposite, do constitute a language. If such arbitrary connection be instituted by men, it is an artificial language; if by the Author of nature, it is a natural language. Infinitely various are the modifications of light and sound, whence they are each capable of supplying an endless variety of signs and, accordingly, have been each employed to form languages; the one by the arbitrary appointment of mankind, the other by that of God himself. (*TVV*, 40)

In both cases, the relation between the sign and the object meant is arbitrary and contingent; it is only the source of the convention that differs. In learning either an artificial (human) language or the divine language of nature, a human being learns to use one kind of idea to 'mean' or represent some other kind of idea or thing. The relation between either a 'natural sign' and its object or an artificial sign (word) and its object or objects is contingent. Hence, in so far as Berkeley's intentional relation is analogous to the meaning relation, it is contingent.

(2) It should also be clear that there are both descriptive and nondescriptive acts in Berkeley and, consequently, the cognitive content of some intentional acts is propositional, while that of other acts is nonpropositional. Let us consider the nondescriptive case first. In the case of natural signs one's intentional act is nondescriptive: the cognitive content of the act is an idea that is related to (taken as a sign of) another idea. If one claims, for example, that smoke is a natural sign of fire, there is a visual or olfactory idea of smoke that is related to (means or signifies) a visual idea of fire. (Of course, on one occasion or another, an olfactory idea of smoke might be taken as a sign of a visual idea of smoke or vice versa.) Although there is a lawful relation between these two kinds of ideas, it is only on the basis of experience that one learns of this lawful relation and, as one learns of this lawful relation, one kind of idea becomes a sign of another kind of idea. In so far as there is a signification relation between an olfactory

idea that is immediately conceived and a visual idea of fire that it is taken to signify, the olfactory idea constitutes the cognitive content of an act by which the mind intends the visual idea of fire.

Some Berkeleian intentional acts are descriptive, that is, their cognitive content is propositional, or, in Berkeley's case, more properly sentential: propositions do not constitute a separate category in Berkeley's ontology. As we saw in the last chapter, it is reasonable to claim that one's notions of minds, actions of minds and relations are analogous to definite descriptions, since, in so far as minds and their actions are 'simple', they can be known only by description. Given Berkeley's nominalism, 'what' a thing is — or, at least, one's understanding of what something is — is determined in part by its correlation to a system of linguistic signs. Hence, it is reasonable to suggest that those intentional acts by which one knows minds, actions of minds, and relations are descriptive acts, that is, they are acts whose cognitive content is sentential.

(3) Finally, it should be clear that Berkeley allowed that 'real' objects, *de re* possible objects and *de dicto* possible objects, but not impossible objects, can be intentional objects. This follows from the suggestion that there is a close analogy between notions (that is, intentional acts) and linguistic meaning. Only 'real' objects, *de re* possible objects (possible components of real objects, that is, ideas) and *de dicto* possible objects can be meant by sortal terms. Hence, one might plausibly assume that only such objects could be the objects of intentional acts. Further evidence for this might be drawn from the criteria of possibility and impossibility we considered in Chapter 2. Given that some of Berkeley's notions (intentional acts) are descriptive and that he accepted the principles that:

(49) $(\exists y)Dy(\exists x)\Phi x \leftrightarrow \Diamond(\exists x)\Phi x$ and

(53) $-(\exists y)Dy(\exists x)\Phi x \rightarrow -(\exists x)\Diamond\Phi x$,

it follows that with respect to descriptive acts there can be an intentional object if and only if the description in question is consistent. Hence, *de dicto* possible objects can be intentional objects. If one's description is not merely consistent but describes a 'real' object, 'real' objects can be intentional objects — *de re* impossible objects cannot be intentional objects. With respect to non-descriptive acts, one simply intends one kind of idea (*de re* possible object) by another, and the occurrence of such nondescriptive intentional acts depends upon the kinds of experience one has had. In the case of nondescriptive acts, both the cognitive content and the intentional object are ideas of which one has actually been aware. Hence, it appears that Berkeley would allow that only 'real' objects, *de dicto* possible objects and *de re* possible objects can be the objects of an intentional act.

So far we have considered the analogy Berkeley claimed to hold between notions and meaning, and we have seen that this analogy suggests that Berkeley held that notions are to be construed as intentional acts. Further, we have seen that some such intentional acts are descriptive, while others are nondescriptive, and that the intentional objects of such acts are limited to 'real' objects, *de dicto* possible objects and *de re* possible objects (ideas). None the less, the fact that there is a close analogy between Berkeley's theory of meaning and a doctrine of intentional acts is not sufficient to show that Berkeley himself held that notions are to be analyzed as intentional acts. To show that my interpretation is plausible, one can reasonably request some hard textual evidence. As I shall show, while Berkeley never provided an explicit discussion of intentionality and there are relatively few places where he discusses notions in terms of acts, such evidence as there is tends to support my interpretation. So let us turn to the textual evidence.

Early in the *Third Dialogue*, Hylas asks Philonous two questions regarding the ways in which one can conceive of God. First, if one cannot conceive of God by way of ideas, how is it possible to conceive of God at all? Second, if one can conceive of God without an idea, why cannot one be allowed to conceive of matter without an idea of it (*DHP*, III, 231)? In his reply to the first question, Berkeley claimed that one has a notion of God. In his reply to the second question one finds evidence that Berkeley construed notions as intentional acts. He wrote:

> For the second: I suppose by this time you can answer it your self. For you neither perceive matter objectively, as you do an inactive being or idea, nor know it, as you do yourself by a *reflex act* [my emphasis]: neither do you mediately apprehend it by similitude of the one or the other: nor yet collect it by reasoning from that which you know immediately. All which makes the case of *matter* widely different from that of the *Deity*. (*DHP*, III, 232; cf., *PHK*, 89)

The Nature of Notions   187

Notice that Berkeley here claims one knows oneself by means of a reflex *act*. A reflex act is an act of a mind by which that mind directs itself at itself, that is, it is an intentional act in at least the minimal sense that it is an act by which the mind directs itself at something. Simply to claim that the act of mind is a reflex act will not directly support my contention that relates a certain propositional content to an object. Indeed, since in *this* passage there is no concern with the question of the nature of the mind, one might suggest that even if a reflex act is in some sense intentional there is no reason to suggest that the act relates a *propositional content* to an object: one might suggest it is merely the mind's attending to the object itself. None the less, if one examines the passage within its context, one will notice that the passage cited above follows a discussion of how one comes to know the mind, a discussion in which Berkeley claimed that one knows the nature of one's mind immediately or intuitively (*DHP*, III, 231). Since we saw in the last chapter that this passage is consistent with my contention that the mind is known relatively, that is, that one's notion of the mind is relative, Berkeley's contention that one knows one's mind by a reflex act would seem to provide some support for my contention that an intentional act relates a certain propositional content to an object.

The passage we have been considering is found in all editions of the *Three Dialogues* and it provides at least circumstantial evidence for my contention that Berkeley held that notions are intentional acts. But the evidence is not conclusive and it leaves several questions open. First, is there any additional evidence that Berkeley analyzed notions as intentional acts? In particular, since the textual evidence from the *Three Dialogues* is from one of Berkeley's early works, is there any evidence in his later works that he construed notions as intentional acts? Second, if there is such evidence, does it support my contention that an intentional act relates a certain propositional content to an object or state of affairs? Finally, in recent discussions of intentionality, philosophers have distinguished among various species of intentional acts, for example, meaning, believing, knowing, loving, hating, and so on. If Berkeley held that notions are intentional acts, does he also distinguish among these several species of acts? In attempting to answer these questions we shall turn first to Berkeley's final work, the *Siris*.

In Section 308 of the *Siris* Berkeley suggests that some persons construe notions as actions or operations of the mind. In his words:

> That philosopher [Aristotle] held that the mind of man was a *tabula rasa*, and that there are no innate ideas. Plato, on the contrary, held original ideas in the mind, that is, notions which never were or can be in the sense, such as being, beauty, goodness, likeness, parity. Some, perhaps, may think the truth to be this — that there are properly no ideas, or passive objects, in the mind but were derived from sense: but that there are also besides these her own acts or operations; such are notions. (*S*, 308)

This passage is peculiar in several respects. Berkeley's putative topic of discussion is innate ideas. Berkeley might be taken to contend here that there are innate ideas and these innate ideas — however 'innate ideas' is to be construed — are to be identified with notions. Bracken has read the passage in this way.[30] But, as we have seen, to construe notions as innate ideas or concepts seems to be inconsistent with Berkeley's account of meaning. Further, the 'innate ideas' he lists are themselves somewhat peculiar. To claim that one has an 'idea' of being in any sense might be deemed inconsistent with his claim in *Principles*, Section 17 that 'The general idea of Being appeareth to me the most abstract and incomprehensible of all other.' 'Likeness', on the other hand, is a relational term and therefore it cannot properly denote an idea at all. If my arguments in the last chapter are sound, 'likeness' denotes a peculiar kind of judgment (act) of the mind, or, perhaps, the disposition of the mind to make certain kinds of judgments vis-à-vis ideas. Hence, if one were to identify Berkeleian notions with 'innate ideas', these would be 'properly no ideas, or passive objects, in the mind' (*S*, 308; cf. *PHK* 142), rather, they would be construed as actions of the mind or dispositions of the mind to act in certain ways. Notice, however, that if notions were to be identified with actions of the mind or dispositions to act, they would differ significantly from classical innate ideas, for unlike ideas, actions and operations *as such*, that is, apart from the ideas acted upon, have no positive content (cf. *PHK*, 89).

There is good reason to believe, however, that the final sentence from Section 308 of the *Siris* expresses Berkeley's own views regarding the nature of notions. First, the claim 'that there are properly no ideas, or passive objects, in the mind but what were derived from sense' seems to be consistent with the opening section of the *Principles*. There, he claimed that the objects of human knowledge 'are either ideas actually imprinted on the senses, or else such [ideas] as are perceived by attending to the passions and operations of the mind, or lastly ideas formed by help of memory and imagination' (*PHK*, 1).[31] It is only in the case of ideas of sense that the mind is purely passive, since it is certain activities of the mind that produce ideas of reflection (cf. *PC*, 661a) and ideas of memory and imagination presuppose certain activities of the mind, even though the mind might be passive in its awareness of the resultant ideas. It is in the last two phrases of the sentence that Berkeley seems to identify notions with acts or operations of the mind. In his words, '... there are also besides these [ideas] her own acts or operations; such are notions' (*S*, 308). Again, the distinction between ideas and a mind that 'knows or perceives them, and exercises diverse operations, as willing, imagining, remembering about them' (*PHK*, 2) is consistent with Berkeley's more general position. It is with acts or operations of the mind that Berkeley identifies notions. But this raises a significant question: is it with only some acts of the mind that Berkeley identifies notions, or with all acts? If it is with all acts, are all acts of the mind intentional, or are only some intentional? If he identifies notions with all acts or operations of the mind — as this passage suggests — but not all mental acts or operations are intentional, then my interpretation is too narrow. What is the evidence?

Since Berkeley does not provide an explicit discussion of intentionality, in attempting to determine whether or not he considered all acts or operations of the mind to be intentional, we must go beyond the explicit evidence available in the texts and consider the kinds of operations of the mind Berkeley lists. In Section 2 of the *Principles*, Berkeley lists willing, imagining and remembering as operations of the mind, and in Section 27 he lists willing, loving and hating as examples of operations of the mind. Are there any common characteristics of these several acts or operations of the mind?

Yes — in each of these kinds of act a mind directs itself particular objects or states of affairs, that is, each of these acts or operations quite plausibly can be construed as intentional acts. To see this clearly, let us consider two of these kinds of acts as test cases, and then ask whether similar considerations apply to the remaining cases.

Consider imagining: imagining involves the willful construction of complex ideas (cf. *PHK*, 30). Imagining, as such, is an act. Is it an intentional act? It would seem so. The mind directs itself at an object, in this case a complex idea and, as we saw in Chapter 2, such a complex idea is at least a possible component of a real object. But on the model of intentionality that I am using, to claim that a mental act is intentional it is not sufficient simply to claim that the mind directs itself at an object or state of affairs. While such an object or state of affairs might be the intentional object, in an intentional act there is a propositional content that the act relates to the object. The act itself relates the propositional content to the object in the same way that a meaning relation relates a word to an object. Is there any propositional content in an act of imagining? It would seem that there is. In a typical case, one does not simply imagine, one imagines what it would be like for a particular state of affairs to obtain. On the side of the object, Berkeley's principles require that the object imagined be quantitatively and qualitatively determinate. But Berkeley's nominalism, that is, his rejection of theories of natural kinds, indicates that what a thing is is a function of the words used to classify it. Thus, if I were to imagine what it would be like for my car to be black, the mental image I would produce would be an image of the appropriate kind only in virtue of its relation to a certain propositional content; the propositional content 'what it would be like for my car to be black'. These same kinds of considerations would seem to hold for other kinds of imaginings, states of reverie or dreaming, for example. In a dream, one is aware of various mental images (ideas), but in so far as one claims that one's dream has a certain content, this occurs only on the basis of the classification of the objects in one's dream and such a classification proceeds along semantic lines. Thus, states of imagining seem to be intentional states having an intentional object (an idea or ideas), a certain propositional content and an act that relates the content to the object.

One finds the same kind of relationship in acts of loving or hating. Let us say that I hate the mouse that inhabits my kitchen. According to Berkeley, hating is a mental act. If I hate the mouse that inhabits my kitchen, my act must pick out that particular mouse: my psychological attitude is directed at a particular real object and it is insufficient to simply form various mouse-like ideas and deem them the object of my hatred.[32] Again, my act is intentional in so far as my mind is directed at a particular object. The thing at which my hatred is directed is what it is in virtue of the propositional content of my act — 'the mouse that inhabits my kitchen' — and hatred is a particular species of intentional act.

It should be clear that the same kinds of considerations apply, *mutatis mutandis*, to willing and remembering. If I will to move my arm, for example, there is a particular possible state of affairs at which I direct my mind and, in the case of willing, attempt to realize, a certain propositional content that classifies that state of affairs and an act of mind that relates the state of affairs to the propositional content.

If Berkeley identified notions with intentional acts and I am correct in contending that all Berkeleian mental acts are intentional, this tends to explain why he apparently was hesitant to use the word 'notion' in a technical sense. As several scholars have noticed,[33] in an early draft of Section 140 of the *Principles*, he inserted the expression 'or notion', only to delete it from the manuscript before publication and to add 'or rather a notion' in the 1734 edition of the *Principles*. Placing the addition in square brackets, the early manuscript version of the section reads: 'In a large sense, indeed we may be said to have an Idea [or notion] of *Spirit*, that is, we understand the meaning of the Word, otherwise we cou'd not affirm or deny any thing of it.'[34] In the First edition of the *Principles* (1710) the section reads: '140 In a large sense indeed, we may be said to have an idea of *spirit* that is, we understand the meaning of the word, otherwise we could not affirm or deny any thing of it.' In the Second edition of the *Principles* (1734) the section reads: '140 In a large sense, indeed, we may be said to have an idea, or rather a notion of *spirit*, that is, we understand the meaning of the word, otherwise we could not affirm or deny any thing of it.'

If Berkeleian notions are intentional acts, one can understand his hesitance to use to the term 'notion', for virtually all his contemporaries took notions to be intentional objects, ideas, or 'concepts'. Although Locke's usage of the term 'notion' is anything but consistent, he used it technically to stand for an idea of a mixed mode. As he wrote:

But if we attentively consider those *Ideas* I call *mixed Modes*, we are now speaking of, we shall find their Original quite different. *The Mind* often *exercises an active Power in making these* several *Combinations.* For it being once furnished with simple *Ideas*, without examining whether they exist so together in Nature. And hence, I think, it is, that these *Ideas* are called *Notions*: as if they had their Original, and constant Existence, more in the Thoughts of Men, than in the reality of things; ...[35]

Sergeant used 'notion' as a technical term, and he explicitly claimed that notions are intentional objects, *not* intentional acts. In his words:

To clear then the meaning of the word [*Notion*,] as 'tis used here from this *Slight*, and (in our case) *Unconcerning* Ambiguity, I declare, that, there are two Considerations in *Knowledge*, viz. the *Act* of my Knowing Power, and the *Object* of that Act, which, as a kind of *Form*, actuates and determines the Indifferency of my Power, and thence specifies my Act; I do not here take the word [*Notion*] for my *Act* of Simply Apprehending; but that that *Object* in my mind which *informs* my Understanding Power, and about which that Power is Employed; in which *Objective* meaning I perceive Mr. *Locke* does also generally take the word [*IDEA.*][36]

Even those who were not concerned with a technical sense of the term 'notion' tended to use that word as a synonym of 'concept' or 'purely conceptual entity'. Thus, Robert Boyle contrasted real entities with mere 'notional entities',[37] and Joseph Butler tended to use the terms 'notion' and 'conception' interchangeably.[38] Hence, given Berkeley's identification of notions with intentional acts, rather than with intentional objects, one can understand why he apparently was hesitant to use the term 'notion'.

Notions and Ordinary Objects

So far I have shown that Berkeley identified notions with actions of the mind and I have argued that it is reasonable to contend that these are intentional acts that relate a certain cognitive content to a certain object or state of affairs. I have shown that this reconstruction is consistent with this repeated contention that there is a close relationship between notions and linguistic meaning, and I have shown that there are several texts in which Berkeley appears to identify notions with mental acts. If my reconstruction is correct, the doctrine of notions fits well in an ontology that recognizes only minds, ideas, and actions of minds.

The issue to which we shall now turn concerns the relationship between notions, ideas and ordinary objects. If notions are actions of the mind, Berkeley's repeated contention that ideas are passive (*PHK*, 25, 27; *DHP*, III, 231; *S*, 292) implies that the distinction between ideas and notions is exclusive and exhaustive — no notions are ideas and no ideas are notions — a point that also is suggested by Berkeley's repeated claims that one can have a notion, but not an idea, of minds, relations and actions of minds (*PHK*, 27, 89, 140, 142; *DHP*, III, 231-3). The fact that my reconstruction is consistent with the notions/ideas distinction and explains why the distinction is exclusive and exhaustive tends to support my interpretation.

But the fact that ideas and notions are distinct does not entail that they are utterly unrelated to one another. In the last section I argued that it is consistent with both the intentionality model of notions and the Berkeleian texts to suggest that ideas can be intentional objects. In this section I hope to show that it is by an intentional act that diverse kinds of ideas are 'bundled' together to form such ordinary objects as flowers, tables and pieces of gold. If I am correct, this also will resolve the apparent inconsistencies in Berkeley's discussions of perception, that is, it will explain why he could claim at some points that the mind is passive in perception (*DHP*, I, 196-7; Cf. Cor. III, 3 and IV, 3; *PC*, 301), while suggesting at other points that the mind is active in perception (*PHK*, 27; *PC* 791, 821, 833, 848; *S*, 253-4).[39] To see that this is plausible, let us begin by examining those passages in which Berkeley claims that the mind is passive in perception.

In the *First Dialogue*, Berkeley has Philonous argue that the mind is passive in perception. There one finds this:

Philonous. When is the mind said to be active?
Hylas. When it produces, puts an end to, or changes any thing.
Philonous. Can the mind produce, discontinue, or change any thing but by an act of the will?
Hylas. It cannot.

Philonous. The mind, therefore is to be accounted active in its perceptions, so far forth as volition is included in them.
Hylas. It is.
Philonous. In plucking this flower, I am active, because I do it by the motion of my hand, which was consequent upon my volition; so likewise in applying it to my nose. But is either of these smelling?
Hylas. No.
Philonous. I act too in drawing the air through my nose; because my breathing so rather than otherwise, is the effect of my volition. But neither can be called *smelling*: for if it were, I should smell every time I breathed in that manner.
Hylas. True.
Philonous. Smelling then is somewhat consequent to all this.
Hylas. It is.
Philonous. But I do not find my will concerned any farther. Whatever more there is, as that I perceive such a particular smell or any smell at all, this is independent of my will, and therein I am altogether passive. Do you find it otherwise with you, Hylas?
Hylas. No, the very same.
Philonous. Then as to seeing, is it not in your power to open your eyes, or keep them shut; to turn them this way or that way?
Hylas. Without doubt.
Philonous. But doth it in like manner depend upon your will, that in looking on this flower, you perceive *white* rather than any other colour? Or directing your open eyes toward yonder part of the heaven, can you avoid seeing the sun? Or is light or darkness the effect of your volition?
Hylas. No certainly.
Philonous. You are then in these respects altogether passive.
Hylas. I am.
Philonous. Tell me now, whether *seeing* consists in perceiving light and colors, or in opening and turning your eyes.
Hylas. Without doubt, in the former.
Philonous. Since therefore you are in the very perception of light and colours altogether passive, what is become of that action you were speaking of, as an ingredient of every sensation? And doth it not follow from your own concessions, that the perception of light and colours, including no action

in it, may exist in an unperceiving substance? And is that not a plain contradiction?

(*DHP*, I, 196-7)

In this passage, Berkeley suggests that the mind is passive in its perception of ideas. If my suggestion in the last chapter is correct that perception is a necessary connection between a mind and an idea, one should not find this surprising: being perceived by a mind is part of what it is to be an idea. Further, the thesis that the mind is passive in perception was a fairly common theme in the writings of Berkeley's predecessors,[40] and Berkeley himself seems to have been strongly committed to the passivity thesis. In the *Philosophical Commentaries*, one finds this:

> M[1] Whatsoever has any of our ideas in it must perceive, it being that very having, that passive reception of ideas that denominates the mind perceiving. that being the very essence of perception, or that wherein perception consists. (*PC*, 301).

Similarly, when Samuel Johnson raised the question of the passivity of the mind in his correspondence with Berkeley, Berkeley replied, 'That the soul of man is passive as well as active I make no doubt' (Cor. IV, 3), although Berkeley follows this claim with little more than a discussion of abstraction.[41] The issue we must consider is what is involved in claiming that the mind is passive in perception.

If one looks closely at the passage from the *First Dialogue*, one will notice that most of Berkeley's examples concern the perception of simple qualities, for example, light and color or aroma. If I open my eyes, I cannot help being aware of (perceiving) light and color. My mind need engage in no activity to do so; indeed, the only way in which the mind can prevent its perceiving of light and colors is by causing one's eyes to close. But what, exactly, is involved in this passive perception of light and colors? One is aware of light and colors *simpliciter*; one is not aware of light and colors *as* light and colors, that is, one does not classify the objects of one's awareness as light and colors. It is in the classification of objects — the relating of objects to words — that the mind is active. Even in the case of seeing the sun, it is one thing to be aware of the sun — here one is passively aware of light, color and shape — it is something else to be aware of the sun as the sun, that is, to classify the complex idea of one's awareness as a particular kind of object. While the mind might be passive in simply perceiving ideas (simple perception), it is active in perceiving ideas as objects of a certain kind, that is, in perceiving *and classifying* objects. To understand this more clearly, it might be helpful to consider an analogy.

Assume you are visiting an exhibition of Paul Cezanne's paintings. As persons familiar with Cezanne's works will grant, many of his paintings are relatively abstract: to the untutored eye, some of them might appear to be little more than indiscriminate patches of color. As you stare at one of these paintings, you remember that a teacher in an art history class once informed you that Cezanne's paintings were intended to be abstract representations of ordinary things. You continue to stare at the blotches of paint on the canvas, asking yourself what, if anything, the painting might be intended to represent. Finally you look at the brass plate stating the picture's title: 'Landscape'. Upon reading the title you 'see' that the painting depicts a landscape, that is, you begin to notice several features of the painting and notice their similarities to other landscapes with which you have been familiar: the view out of your back door and other paintings with the same name. Now notice that in one sense what you are seeing is the same before and after you 'saw' that it is a landscape: you are fundamentally aware of light and colors. In 'seeing that' the painting is a landscape, there are various kinds of mental activities involved. Initially, one simply might be aware of light and colors without an awareness that it is light and colors of which one is aware, that is, without classifying the objects of one's awareness as light and colors. Next, one might be aware that one is aware of the colors red, blue, yellow and green, that is, one might so classify the objects of one's awareness. One might next be aware that the combination colors is a painting and, finally, that the painting is a landscape. In each case the objects of one's awareness are classified in accordance with a scheme of categories, and even though in simple perception — awareness without classification — one's mind might be passive, the mind is certainly active in its several classifications of the objects of its awareness.

Recognizing this distinction between simple perception and perception with classification will resolve the apparent inconsistencies in Berkeley's discussions of the passivity or activity of perception. Among the passages commentators have cited to support the claim that the mind is active in perception are the following:

S   Understanding is in some sort an Action. (*PC*, 821)

S   It seems there can be no perception, no Idea without Will, being there are no Ideas indifferent but one had rather Have them than annihilation, or annihilation than them. (*PC*, 833)

S   I must not Mention the Understanding as a faculty or part of the Mind, I must include Understanding & Will etc in the word Spirit by wch I mean all that is active. (*PC*, 848)

A Spirit is one simple, undivided, active being — as it perceives ideas it is called the *understanding*, and as it produces or otherwise operates about them it is called the *will*. (*PHK*, 27)

We know a thing when we understand it; and we understand it when we can interpret or tell what it signifies. Strictly, the sense knows nothing. We perceive indeed sounds by hearing, and characters by sight. But we are not therefore said to understand them. After the same manner, the phaenomena of nature are alike visible to all: but all have not alike learned the connexion of natural things, to understand what they signify, or know how to vaticinate by them. There is no question, saith Socrates *to Theaeteto*, concerning that which is agreeable to each person; but concerning what will in time to come be agreeable, of which all men are not equally judges. He who foreknoweth what will be in every kind is the wisest. According to Socrates, you and the cook may judge of a dish on the table equally well; but while the dish is making, the cook can better foretell what will ensure from this or that manner of composing it. Nor is this manner of reasoning confined only to morals or politics, but extends also to natural science. (*S*, 253; cf. *S*, 254)

Notice that in these passages Berkeley is primarily concerned with *understanding*. To understand something is to know what it is. But what something is is relatively arbitrary: remember, Berkeley denied that there are universals or Aristotelian forms. A thing's being a thing of a kind is merely a matter of the imposition of arbitrary linguistic conventions upon objects. Further, as we saw in

Chapter 3, not all things classified by the same categorematic term resemble one another, for example, there is no resemblance between visual and tangible extension — they are distinct kinds of objects — although because they are constantly conjoined in experience, only the most careful observer will notice that they are distinct. Thus, in using the word 'extension' generally, one is picking out objects of more than one kind.

Consider a typical case of being aware of an object, for example, a flower. In being aware of a flower one is immediately aware of certain colors, shapes, aromas, and so on. These ideas are the objects immediately available to the senses. But to be barely aware of these sensible objects is neither to understand what each sensible idea is individually nor to understand what a flower is. Understanding would seem to involve the imposition of a categorial (semantic) schema upon one's ideas and, in so far as one is concerned with qualitatively complex objects, a recognition that certain kinds of ideas are constantly conjoined with other kinds of ideas in 'forming' the complex object. Thus, if one might speak of 'perception with understanding', to perceive with understanding involves not only the perception or basic awareness of objects, but the awareness that those objects are objects of a certain kind. It is in this awareness *that* those objects are objects of a certain kind that the mind is active: the mind is classifying the objects of one's awareness in terms of a certain semantic schema. This act of classification is an intentional act: the mind focuses on an object or state of affairs (several distinct objects, ideas) and relates it to a certain propositional content, for example, the mind focuses upon a number of distinct ideas and indicates that this is the meaning of the expression 'flower'.

A little more should be said about understanding before we turn to a consideration of the relationship between notions, ideas and ordinary objects. Typically, when one claims to understand what something is, one claims something more than the ability to apply the proper word to a particular object or state of affairs. If one considers various philosophers before Berkeley, for example, Locke, to understand what a thing is is to have an idea of the essence of that thing. While such ideas are abstract and are, therefore, not to be found in Berkeley's ontological schema, considerations of 'essences' raise an important issue even in the case of Berkeley. If, as Berkeley suggests, ordinary objects are nothing but 'collections of ideas' (*PHK*, 1), it is reasonable to claim that one has a more complete understanding of what it is to be a flower, for example, if one can provide an enumeration of the various kinds of ideas that constitute a flower than if one merely associates the term 'flower' with a certain visible idea. Nor would Berkeley deny this. In Section 49 of the *Principles* he wrote:

> As to what philosophers say of subject and mode, that seems very groundless and unintelligible. For instance, in this proposition, a die hard, extended, and square, they have it that the word *die* denotes a subject or substance, distinct from the hardness, extension and figure, which are predicates of it, and in which they exist. This I cannot comprehend: to me a die seems to be nothing distinct from those things which are termed its modes or accidents. And to say a die is hard, extended and square, is not to attribute those qualities to a subject distinct from and supporting them, but only an explication of the meaning of the word *die*. (*PHK*, 49)

Consider the relationship between a term and its (connotative) definition. If one knows the definition of a term, one might claim to have a better understanding of the meaning of a term than if one merely can point to one particular object that the term denotes. In knowing the connotative definition of a term, one might claim to know the essence or constitutive properties of a thing of a certain kind — certainly such claims were common in Berkeley's day. However, as we noted in Chapter 3, given Berkeley's extensional theory of meaning, to be able to provide a connotative definition or 'an explication of the meaning of [a] word' is to do no more than to list the several classes of objects into which objects of the kind in question fall. In the case of a *conventional* definition, this comes to no more than an elucidation of the convention, that is, listing the several classes into which most members of a linguistic group place the objects in question.

But there are explications and there are explications. One of the virtues of Locke's discussion of nominal essences is the recognition that as one's experience increases, the number and kinds of distinct properties one considers constitutive of a thing of a kind also increases. Notice what Locke wrote in this regard:

> But however, these *Species* of Substances pass well enough in ordinary Conversation, it is plain, that this complex *Idea*,

wherein they observe several Individuals to agree, is, by different Men, made very differently; some more, and others less accurately. In some, this complex *Idea* contains a greater, and in others a smaller number of Qualities; and so is apparently such as the Mind makes it. The yellow shining Colour, Makes *Gold* to Children; others add Weight, Malleableness, and Fusibility; and others yet other Qualities, which they find joined with that yellow Colour, as constantly as its Weight and Fusibility: For in all these, and the like Qualities, one has as good a right to be put into the complex *Idea* of that Substance, wherein they are all join'd, as another. And therefore *different Men* leaving out, or putting in several simple *Ideas*, which others do not, according to their various Examination, Skill, or Observation of that subject, *have different Essences of Gold*; which must therefore be of their own, and not Nature's making.[42]

As one's experience with things of a kind increases, one notices that a greater number of properties are found together in a thing of that kind and, consequently, the number and kind of properties one considers constitutive of a thing of a certain kind increases. Linguistically, this increased understanding of the complexity of a particular kind of thing is expressed in more complex connotative definition (the explication of the meaning of a term). A child's explication of the meaning of the sortal term 'gold' will differ significantly from a chemist's explication of the meaning of the same term, since the chemist has had a greater amount of experience with respect to the properties that are constantly conjoined in a piece of gold, particularly experience with repect to the dispositional properties of gold (laws specifying the correlation of properties or ideas). Thus, when a chemist uses the word 'gold', the 'ordinary objects' he or she picks out are qualitatively richer than those picked out by the child: the chemist intends various properties with which the child has had no experience. None the less, for purposes of communication, there is a sufficient similarity in qualitative content — enumerations of the classes onto which gold things fall — that communication is possible, that is, that the majority of objects both would include in the class of gold things will be the same.

Given these considerations of meaning, I believe we are in a position to examine the relationship between notions (intentional acts), ideas and ordinary objects. Berkeley held that ordinary objects are 'collections' of ideas (sensible qualities). As Berkeley indicates in the *New Theory of Vision* (*NTV*, 46), ideas are divided into kinds, at least in part, on the basis of the sensible modality from which they are derived. Thus, visual ideas are distinct kinds of objects from tactile ideas or auditory ideas. None the less, ordinary objects are generally collections of ideas of several different kinds. A flower, for example, is a collection of ideas of touch, sight, smell and, perhaps, taste. One should remember that ideas are one of Berkeley's classes of fundamental existents. As collections of ideas, ordinary objects do not constitute a separate category in Berkeley's ontological inventory: they are derivative entities. But, as we saw in Chapter 4, Berkeley held that human minds are uniform in terms of their dispositions. One such disposition is to take visual extension as a sign of tangible extension and, in general, to take ideas that are constantly conjoined in experience to be signs of one another. If my observations above regarding nondescriptive intentional acts are correct, to claim that a mind takes one idea to be a sign of another is to claim that there is a nondescriptive intentional act whose cognitive content consists of an idea of one sensible mode which is related to an intentional object consisting of an idea (or ideas) of (an) other sensible mode(s). This is the relation of natural signs, and, at one level, to understand is merely to take one object to be a sign of another object (cf. *PHK*, 65). Even in a world without words, for example, that of Berkeley's solitary philosopher (cf. *Works* 2:141), one's survival would depend upon one's ability to intend one kind of object by another. The solitary philosopher would not long survive if he did not recognize that certain sounds were constantly conjoined with certain visual objects, for example, if a visible bear were not the intentional object of an act in which a certain sound is the cognitive content.[43] None the less, to intend one idea by another idea is to recognize no more than *that* there is a correlation between two kinds of ideas; it is not to understand *what* a thing is. Given Berkeley's nominalism, to understand *what* a thing is is to intend an object (a simple idea or a collection of ideas) by a word or a descriptive phrase: to understand *what* a thing is involves a descriptive act.

As we saw above, there is a close analogy between Berkeley's theory of meaning and the doctrine of intentional acts and, since Berkeley drew no distinction between propositions and declarative sentences, the analogy is even closer in the case of descriptive acts than it is in the case of nondescriptive acts. This indicates that in so far as one knows *what* a thing is, a word or descriptive phrase is related to an intentional object. But what, exactly, is the nature of the intentional object to which the word or descriptive phrase is related? Is it a 'real' object, or merely a (complex) *de re* possible object (a possible component of a real object)? It would seem to be the latter. Remember, 'real' objects are composed of an indefinitely large number of lawfully related ideas. In so far as one can claim to have knowledge of 'real' objects, one's knowledge is generally, if not always, incomplete. Berkeley held that it is only on the basis of experience that one can come to know which distinct kinds of ideas are lawfully related (constantly conjoined) in forming an object. Now if one takes literally Berkeley's contention that an ordinary object is a 'collection' of ideas (*PHK*, 1), one would suggest that there must be something or someone who collects these ideas together to form ordinary objects. On the basis of a consideration of this need for a 'collector' together with his language metaphor, I shall argue that, for Berkeley, ideas are collected together to form ordinary objects by the intentional acts of individual human beings.[44]

In examining the common sense core of Locke's theory of nominal essences — that is, considering the doctrine of nominal essences apart from a theory of abstract ideas — we noted that as one's experience increases, one's connotative definition of a sortal terms becomes more complex. Given his concern with one's discovery of the lawful relationship between various kinds of ideas together with his concerns with the explication of the meaning of a term (*PHK*, 49), Berkeley would certainly grant this. But in that discussion we also noticed that there is a clear sense in which the 'ordinary objects' picked out by the term 'gold' when used by a chemist are qualitatively more complex than those picked out by a child or a layman. Since Berkeley's theory of meaning entails that in using the word 'gold' both the child and the chemist *mean* gold things, there is a clear sense in which the objects intended by the chemist are different from those intended by the child: the chemist collects together a greater number of distinct kinds of ideas in using the term 'gold' than does the child, simply because he or she has had far more experience with things that are gold than has the child. On the side of linguistic meaning, this indicates that there is a correlation between the object meant and the explication of the term 'gold'. On the side of intentionality, it indicates that there is a correlation between the various ideas that are collected together in the intentional object and the propositional content of the intentional act. The propositional content is a description of the intentional object, and there is a one-to-one correlation between the ideas (qualities) in the intentional object that are considered 'essential' to a thing of that kind and sortal terms in the description.[45] But since the description involves not only sortal (categorematic) terms but also syncategorematic terms, and since we saw in Chapter 3 that syncategorematic terms denote acts of the mind, there is also a correlation between acts of the mind and the syncategorematic terms in the description. Just as the grammatical particles 'tie together' the several categorematic terms in a sentence, these acts of the mind 'tie together' the several distinct sensible ideas that are collected together into an intentional object.

Now the perceptive reader will notice that in the last paragraph there was a shift from 'ordinary objects' to intentional objects. My contention is that, for Berkeley, it is the intentional relation that ties together distinct ideas into ordinary objects, that is, that ordinary objects are intentional constructs,[46] but at the individual level there is no distinction between the intentional object and what we commonly call an ordinary object. This entails that since there is a difference in the experience of various people and, therefore, there is a difference among the intentional objects of various people even when they claim to see or think about the 'same thing'. Thus, my intended identification of intentional objects and ordinary objects yields the seemingly noncommonsensical claim that the things each individual thinks about are numerically distinct from those thought about by any other individual, and some might consider this to provide grounds for rejecting my contention that 'ordinary objects' are to be identified with the intentional objects constructed by individual minds.

Interestingly, Hylas raised the same kind of objection to Philonous. By considering their exchange in the light of Berkeley's more general contention that the language model is an appropriate model for understanding the world, we shall see that it is quite plausible to claim that, for Berkeley, 'ordinary objects' are to be identified with intentional objects. Notice what one finds in the *Third Dialogue*:

> **Hylas.** Is it not your opinion that by our senses we perceive only ideas existing in our minds?

Philonous. It is.

Hylas. But the same idea which is in my mind, cannot be in yours, or in any other mind. Doth it not therefore follow from your principles, that no two can see the same thing? And is not this highly absurd?

Philonous. If the term *same* be taken in the vulgar acceptation, it is certain (and not at all repugnant to the principles I maintain) that different persons may perceive the same thing; or the same thing or idea exist in different minds. Words are of arbitrary imposition; and since men are used to apply the word *same* where no distinction or variety is perceived, and I do not pretend to alter their perceptions, it follows, that as men have said before, *several saw the same thing*, so they may upon like occasions still continue to use the same phrase, without any deviation from either propriety of language, or the truth of things.

(*DHP*, III, 247)

In this interchange Hylas raises the objection that if ordinary objects are composed of the ideas in one's mind, and the ideas in my mind are numerically distinct from the ideas in your mind, it follows that no two persons can see (or even think about) the same thing. Philonous' reply to this objection consists of little more than denying that it is a problem. He does nothing more than appeal to the ordinary usage of the expression 'same thing', and suggests that his principles are consistent with ordinary usage. How can this be? There seem to be two considerations underlying Philonous' tendency to dismiss Hylas' objection. First, as Hume was later to argue at length, among the vulgar the distinction between numerical and specific identity (identity of kind) is often overlooked.[47] Given this conflation of two senses of 'identity', it is consistent with ordinary usage to claim that two people see 'the same thing' — things identical in kind (specifically identical) — even though the ideas of which they are composed are numerically distinct. Philonous goes on to argue that questions regarding identity are basically verbal. In attempting to convince Hylas that questions of identity are verbal, he provides an analogy to a house whose interior is entirely refurbished. Philonous is made to say:

> Or suppose a house, whose walls or outward shell remaining unaltered, the chambers are all pulled down, and new ones built

in their place; and that you should call this the *same*, and I should say it was not the *same* house: would we not for all this perfectly agree in our thoughts of the house, considered in it self? and would not all the difference consist in a sound? (*DPH*, III, 248)

Philonous' analogy here is far from perfect. In Philonous' example, the issue is how much change an object can undergo while retaining its numerical identity. In the case of ideas in the minds of different people, the *numerical difference* of the ideas is given. The most one could claim is that the ideas in the two minds are identical in kind (specifically identical), and to suggest that there is merely a verbal difference between numerical and specific identity is shocking. In the case of ideas in the minds of different people the *numerical* difference is absolute, even if some observer could look into both minds and notice that the ideas are identical in kind (resembling). None the less, there is a second consideration to which Philonous might have appealed to bolster his argument.

This second consideration concerns Berkeley's use of the linguistic model for understanding the world. Let us assume, as a working hypothesis, that both Smith and Jones are thinking about my car and that the ideas in Smith's mind are numerically distinct from the ideas in Jones's mind. Let us assume, further, that the intentional object Smith calls 'Flage's car' is qualitatively far richer than that Jones calls 'Flage's car'. Even if this were the case, Smith and Jones could carry on an intelligible conversation regarding my car. If Smith and Jones were each to provide a description of my car, there would be a certain amount of qualitative correlation between their two descriptions. Now given Berkeley's account of language, one must grant (1) that a person 'knows the meaning of a word' if and only if the objects included in that person's subjective extension of a term resemble objects that the majority of persons in a society include in the extension of the same term — basically, if one's use of a word is neither corrected by others nor results in unexpected behavior on the part of others; and (2) that given variations in the amount and kinds of experience speakers of a language will have, there will be some differences — occasionally very significant differences — in the explications (connotative definitions) of the meaning of a term among speakers of a language. Nonetheless, speakers of a particular language can generally communicate quite well. In so far as Berkeley intended the language model to help us understand the nature of the phenomenal world, it seems reasonable to suggest that just as speakers of a language might 'define' a particular word in different ways while still being able to communicate, so individuals might construct 'the same' ordinary objects in significantly different ways: there is a limited overlap among the kinds of qualities that persons include in their intentional objects because there is a certain amount of common experience of the constant conjunctions of ideas.

Thus, it appears to be consistent with Berkeley's language model to contend that notions (intentional acts) 'collect' distinct ideas together to form ordinary objects. Although there are significant differences among the intentional objects *cum* ordinary objects of different individuals, there is a sufficient commonality of experience to account for the fact that virtually all persons intend some of the same kinds of ideas in ordinary objects of a certain kind. But before we leave this topic, there is a possible objection that should be considered.

The objection might be put this way. In Chapter 2 it was argued that God creates real objects. If the contention is correct that it is merely the intentional acts (notions) of individual human beings that tie together diverse ideas to form ordinary objects and, therefore, that there is a sense in which ordinary objects are whatever we say they are, it seems to follow that (1) God does not create real objects such as trees and mountains, rather, there is a clear sense in which they are created by individual acts of human minds; and (2) that if God does create real objects, mere mortals can never know them. In reply to this objection, one must first consider what is involved in claiming that God creates real objects. Remember, to claim that God creates a real object is to claim that God creates lawfully ordered sequences of ideas. The ideas God creates are identical with those ideas human beings perceive by the senses. Hence, there is no ontological distinction between the components of 'real objects' and the immediate objects of perception. As Berkeley put this in the *Philosophical Commentaries*:

> P. The Philosophers Talk much of a distinction twixt absolute & relative things, or twixt things consider'd in their own nature & the same things considered with respect to us. I know not w^t they mean by things consider'd in themselves. This is nonsense, Jargon. (*PC*, 832)

If the objects God creates are nothing but lawfully ordered sequences of ideas and ideas are the immediate objects of our perception, there is no hard and fast distinction between ideas and objects. Because there is no such distinction, Berkeley maintains it is possible to come to know more and more about the nature of the real objects God created. Such knowledge consists of no more than a knowledge of correlations among ideas. Berkeley clearly made this point in his discussion of the 'microscopic examination of objects.' As he made Philonous say:

> And, when I look through a microscope, it is not that I may perceive more clearly what I perceived already with my bare eyes; the object perceived by the glass being quite different from the former. But in both cases, my aim is only to know what ideas are connected together; *and the more a man knows of the connexion of ideas, the more he is said to know of the nature of things.* (*DHP*, III, 245, emphasis added)

The non-Berkeleian scientist might claim that as one examines an ordinary object or ordinary objects of a certain kind, one discovers more and more of the properties of the object. On the basis of a microscopic examination of an object, one discovers properties of the object that are not available to the naked eye, and the more powerful the microscope one uses, the more such properties one discovers. Of course, while in principle there might be an upper limit to the properties one can discover with respect to an object, that is, in principle there might be a complete enumeration of the properties and of the laws governing the properties of an object or an object of a kind, it is a working hypothesis of scientific inquiry that such a complete description has not yet been obtained. *All of this is consistent with Berkeley's philosophy.* Since 'real' objects are nothing other than lawfully ordered sequences of ideas, what we discover in discovering the properties of 'real' objects is nothing more than correlations among distinct kinds of ideas. The intentional objects we 'create' (tie together) by our acts (notions), reflect an increased understanding of the distinct ideas of sense that God has lawfully correlated. Thus, Berkeley's account of one's knowledge of real objects allows one to claim at least as much knowledge of real objects as one finds on any other account and, in so far as he held that the components of such objects are ideas immediately present to the mind, Berkeley avoids the scepticism implicit in a representational view such as Locke's.

Conclusions

In this chapter I have attempted to provide an account of Berkeley's ontological analysis of the nature of notions. Beginning with a fairly common account of the nature of notions — the claim that notions are concepts — I argued that as an ontological account, this is either inconsistent with Berkeley's rejection of 'abstract ideas' or uninformative. I then argued that both the analogy between notions and meaning and the positive textual evidence suggest that notions are to be construed as intentional acts. I concluded by examining the relationship between notions as intentional acts and both ideas and ordinary objects. I argued that in nondescriptive intentional acts, ideas function as both the cognitive content of the act and the intentional object although, in such a case, the idea that is the intentional content is numerically and specifically distinct from the idea that is the intentional object. Descriptive intentional acts, on the other hand, tie together diverse kinds of ideas to form 'ordinary objects'. Such 'ordinary objects' are the intentional objects of descriptive intentional acts. I concluded by showing that even though this entails that there are vast differences among the intentional objects of various individuals, this is consistent with both Berkeley's discussions of 'real' objects and a common sense view of one's acquisition of knowledge of ordinary objects.

Notes

1. I am not the first to make this suggestion (see Sidney C. Rome, 'Berkeley's Conceptualism', *Philosophical Review*, 55 (1946), p. 686; John W. Davis, 'Berkeley's Doctrine of the Notion', *Review of Metaphysics*, 12 (1959), pp. 384-5; Sami M. Najm, 'Knowledge of the Self in Berkeley's Philosophy', *International Philosophical Quarterly*, 6 (1966), pp. 248-69), although the grounds I shall provide in support of this claim differ somewhat from that of earlier commentators.

2. Harry M. Bracken, 'Berkeley and Mental Acts', *Theoria*, 26 (1960), pp. 140-6; Harry M. Bracken, *Berkeley* (St. Martin's Press, New York, 1974), pp. 82-5 and 135-48; cf. Joseph W. Browne, *Berkeley's Intellectualism* (St. John's University Press, New York, 1975), p. 100; G.A. Johnston, *The Development of Berkeley's Philosophy* (Macmillan and Co., Limited, London, 1923), pp. 158-69;

The Nature of Notions 209

I.C. Tipton, *Berkeley: The Philosophy of Immaterialism* (Methuen and Co. Ltd., London, 1974), p. 270; Desiree Park, *Complementary Notions: A Critical Study of Berkeley's Theory of Concepts* (Martinus Nijhoff, The hague, 1972), p. 15, cf. p. 101.

  3. Johnston, *The Development of Berkeley's Philosophy*, pp. 158-69; Bracken, *Berkeley*, pp. 82-4 and 135-48; but cf. John Wild, *George Berkeley: A Study of His Life and Philosophy* (Russell and Russell, Inc., New York 1962), pp. 77-80.

  4. John Sergeant, *Solid Philosophy Asserted, Against the Fancies of the Ideists: Or, the Method to Science Farther Illustrated* (London, 1697), Preface, Section 21; quoted, in part, in Bracken, *Berkeley*, p. 83.

  5. Sergeant, *Method to Science*, p. 2.

  6. Cf. M.W. Beal, 'Berkeley's Linguistic Criterion', *Personalist*, 52 (1971), p. 503.

  7. Sergeant, *Solid Philosophy Asserted*, p. 26; quoted in Bracken, *Berkeley*, p. 83.

  8. Sergeant, *Solid Philosophy Asserted*, p. 26; quoted in Bracken, *Berkeley*, p. 82.

  9. Sergeant, *Solid Philosophy Asserted*, p. 250; this is *not* quoted in Bracken's *Berkeley*.

  10. Bracken, *Berkeley*, p. 137.

  11. Ibid., p. 139; cf. Bracken, 'Berkeley and Mental Acts', pp. 145-6.

  12. Sergeant, *Solid Philosophy Asserted*, p. 27.

  13. Sergeant, *Method to Science*, p. 2.

  14. Ibid.

  15. Ibid., pp. 3-4, 5.

  16. Descartes, *Meditation V*, HR, I: 179-80.

  17. Descartes's several discussions of innate ideas leave it unclear how much activity is involved, or indeed, what kinds of ideas are innate. While in his *Conversation with Burman*, Descartes seems to suggest that it is only the most general ideas that are innate, viz., 'ideas' of eternal truths (see *The Conversation with Burman* (trans. John Cottingham) (Clarendon Press, Oxford, 1976), p. 31, in the *Notes against a Programme* he suggests that *all* ideas, even adventitious or factitious ideas, are innate (see HR, I: 442). If there is a sense in which adventitious ideas are innate, then sense experience can be a cause of at least one's awareness of innate adventitious ideas, and in such cases the mind would seem to be passive. A thorough examination of the nature of innate ideas in Descartes, however, is beyond the scope of this work.

  18. Sergeant, *Solid Philosophy Asserted*, Preface, Section 21 and p. 33.

  19. It might be suggested that I might have misconstrued Bracken's account of Berkeleian notions. In his book *Berkeley*, Bracken suggests that notions and archetypes are to be conflated. This *suggests* that notions are to be construed as ideas in the mind of God (cf. *Berkeley*, pp. 139-48), and in another context Bracken came very close to claiming that Berkeleian notions are to be construed as Malebranchean Ideas, i.e., ideas in the mind of God (Bracken, 'Berkeley and Mental Acts', pp. 145-6). I take this to be an implausible account of Berkeleian notions. As we saw in Chapter 3, it is things themselves that provide the meaning of sortal terms: Berkeley's theory of meaning is extensional. While he includes *de dicto* and *de re* possible objects in the extension of a term, he also includes 'real' objects. If notions were identified with ideas in the mind of God, these would be only *de dicto* possible objects. Hence, it appears to be inconsistent with Berkeley's account of meaning.

  20. Tipton and Park seem to identify notions with those elements of Berkeley's ontology that neither are ideas nor can be analyzed in terms of ideas. See Tipton, *Berkeley*, p. 270; Park, *Complementary Notions*, p. 15; Desiree Park, '*Notions*:

The Counter-Poise of the Berkeleian *Ideas*', *Giornale di Metafisica* (New Series), 3 (1981), p. 250.

21. As we saw in Chapter 3, this seems to be consistent with considerations of the ways in which one actually learns the meaning of a word.

22. In so far as I have been concerned with Berkeley's psychology of meaning, my account goes beyond what is available in the texts. None the less, in so far as there are significant similarities in the general theories of linguistic meaning advanced by Berkeley and Hume, viz. that they were extensional, and Hume provides a psychological explanation of how one can use general terms meaningfully if an extensional theory is adequate (cf. David Hume, *A Treatise of Human Nature* (ed. L.A. Selby-Bigge, 2nd edn. rev. by P.N. Nidditch) (Clarendon Press, Oxford, 1978), I.i.7, pp. 17-24), I believe it is plausible to reconstruct the psychological theory underlying Berkeley's theory of meaning along Humean lines. This is what I have done here.

23. Indeed, whether intentionality is to be construed as an *act* or a *state* is itself a matter of some contention, since to deem it an 'act' suggests that it is irreducibly mental and that the mental is categorically fundamental. See John R. Searle, *Intentionality* (Cambridge University Press, Cambridge, 1983), pp. vii-x. For our purposes, we need not worry about this issue. If Berkeley held that there are intentional acts or states, these would be mental acts. Hence, I shall use the word 'act' throughout my discussion, noting only here that, in general, some philosophers would contend that this begs a fundamental question.

24. See Gustav Bergmann, 'Intentionality', *Archivo di Filosofia*, 1955; reprinted in his *Meaning and Existence* (University of Wisconsin Press, Madison, 1959), pp. 3-38; Gustav Bergmann, 'Acts', *Rivista di Filosofia*, 51 (1960), pp. 3-51; reprinted in his *Logic and Reality* (University of Wisconsin Press, Madison, 1964), pp. 3-44, especially p. 33; Gustav Bergmann, *Realism* (University of Wisconsin Press, Madison, 1967), pp. 125-9; cf. Sergeant, *Solid Philosophy Asserted*, p. 26.

25. Cf. Searle, *Intentionality*, p. 11.

26. Cf. Bergmann, 'Intentionality' and Bergmann, 'Acts'.

27. See Sergeant, *Solid Philosophy Asserted*, p. 26. If Yolton's recent interpretation of Locke is correct, then one also finds intentional acts in Locke, and Locke held that ideas are the cognitive content of such acts (see John W. Yolton, *Perceptual Acquaintance From Descartes to Reid* (University of Minnesota Press, Minneapolis, 1984), pp. 88-104). Similarly, the case can be made that nondescriptive intentional acts are found in Malebranche (see Bracken, 'Berkeley and Mental Acts', pp. 143-4; Thomas Lennon, 'Philosophical Commentary', in Malebranche, *The Search After Truth* (trans. Lennon and Olscamp) (The Ohio State University Press, Columbus, 1980), pp. 794ff.).

28. Cf. Searle, *Intentionality*, pp. 16-17.

29. Cf. Bergmann, *Realism*, pp. 125-9.

30. Bracken, *Berkeley*, p. 139; cf. Ian T. Ramsey, 'Berkeley and the Possibility of an Empirical Metaphysics', in Warren E. Steinkraus (ed.) *New Studies in Berkeley's Philosophy* (Holt, Rinehart, Winston, New York, 1966), p. 20.

31. I argued in Chapter 4 that the 'such as' in Section 1 of the *Principles* refers to such *ideas* and suggested that Berkeley, like Locke, recognized a distinction between ideas of sensation and ideas of reflection.

32. This assumes, of course, that there is a mouse that inhabits my kitchen. Even if I am deluded, that is, even if I believe that a mouse inhabits my kitchen but my belief is false, there would still be an intentional object, viz., a *de dicto* possible object in the mind of God.

33. T.E. Jessop, 'Editor's Introduction' to the *Principles*, Berkeley's *Works*, II: 53n; Davis, 'Berkeley's Doctrine of the Notion', p. 381; Park, *Complementary Notions*, p. 56; A.D. Woozley, 'The Doctrine of Notions and Theory of Meaning',

Journal of the History of Philosophy, 14 (1976), p. 428.
34. Quoted in Park, *Complementary Notions*, p. 56.
35. John Locke, *An Essay concerning Human Understanding* (ed. D.N. Nidditch) (Clarendon Press, Oxford, 1975), 2.22.2.
36. Sergeant, *Solid Philosophy Asserted*, pp. 26-7.
37. Robert Boyle, 'A Free Inquiry into the Vulgarly Received Notion of Nature', in *Selected Philosophical Papers of Robert Boyle* (ed. M.A. Stewart) (University of Manchester Press, Manchester, 1979), pp. 183 and 184.
38. Joseph Butler, *The Analogy of Religion* (ed. E.C. Mossner) (Frederick Unger Publishing Co., 1961), pp. 7, 33, 226.
39. Noticing these passages, several commentators have distinguished between sensation and perception in Berkeley's works, suggesting that the mind is passive in sensation while it is active in perception (see Reinhardt Grossmann, 'Digby and Berkeley on Notions', *Theoria*, 26 (1960), pp. 17-30; Bracken, 'Berkeley and Mental Acts'. Other commentators have maintained that Berkeley held that the mind is *active* in perception. See Tipton, *Berkeley*, pp. 268-9; E.J. Furlong, 'Berkeley on Relations, Spirits and Notions', *Hermathena*, 106 (1968), p. 65.
40. See Descartes, *Meditations*, HR I: 188; Locke, *Essay*, 2.9.1; cf., Malebranche, *The Search After Truth*, p. 2.
41. For a discussion of Berkeley's views on the passivity of the mind in his *Philosophical Correspondence with Samuel Johnson*, see Adams, 'Berkeley's "Notion" of Spiritual Substance', *Archiv für Geschichte der Philosophie*, 55 (1973), p. 51.
42. Locke, *Essay*, 3.4.31; cf. 4.12.9.
43. Hume would claim after observing a limited conjunction of auditory and visual impressions, the sound causes one to think of a certain visual idea. Given Berkeley's contention that only mental substances can be causes (*PHK*, 26), such a move is not open to him. None the less, if my suggestion that there are nondescriptive intentional acts in Berkeley is correct, it is reasonable to construe the relation of natural signification as a nondescriptive intentional act.
44. We shall consider below the contention that it is God who does this collecting.
45. Remember, in the Introduction to the *Principles* Berkeley indicated that, for example, color and shape are inseparable (Intro., 7). Hence, the intentional object will have a specific shape and, although reference to a specific shape will not be included in the description, if the description is complete, it would indicate that all things that are gold have some shape or other.
46. Cf. George J. Stack, *Berkeley's Analysis of perception* 2nd printing (Morton Press, The Hague, 1972), p. 155; Harry M. Bracken, 'Substance in Berkeley', in Warren E. Steinkraus (ed.) *New Studies in Berkeley's Philosophy* (Holt, Reinehart, Winston, New York, 1966), pp. 88-91.
47. Cf. Hume, *Treatise*, I.iv.2 and I.iv.6.

tive notion is inconsistent that nothing is singled out (cf. *DHP*, III, 232). None the less, the constraints Berkeley placed on the adequacy of a relative notions suggest the one must have a *positive* notion of the relation upon which one's relative notion is based and, consequently, one's relative notion would never single out a merely possible object. Secondly, in the case of one's notions of the mind, its operations and relations among ideas, the relations in one's relative notions, these being perception or causation, are necessary connections between a mind and an idea, and since one's relative notion is grounded upon an idea and a positive notion of the relation, to have such a relative notion provides conclusive evidence that the thing of which one has a notion exists. Hence, if one has a relative notion of a mind, an operation of a mind, or a relation among ideas, one can know that an actual mind, operation of a mind, or idea is singled out by one's relative notion.

In Chapter 5 I turned to the ontological issues. I argued that notions are to be analyzed as intentional acts. I argued, first, that it is implausible to contend that a notion is a concept, in any ontologically significant sense of that term. My arguments were based upon considerations of Berkeley's analogy between the doctrine of notions and his theory of linguistic meaning. If notions were identified with concepts in an ontologically significant sense of the term, this would be inconsistent both with his contention that the world is composed solely of minds, operations of minds and ideas, and with his arguments against abstract ideas based upon the principle of parsimony (Intro., 12-13). Focusing on the analogy between notions and Berkeley's extensional theory of linguistic meaning, I argued that notions are either analogous to the objects meant or to the meaning relation. If they are analogous to the objects meant, the relationship between the doctrine of notions and his theory of linguistic meaning is merely tangential. If notions are analogous to the meaning relation itself, it is reasonable to suggest that notions are to be analyzed as intentional acts. I showed that the issues germane to the analysis of intentional acts are the same as the issues germane to an extensional theory of linguistic meaning. I then examined the textual evidence and showed that such evidence as Berkeley provided tends to support my contention that notions are to be analyzed as intentional acts. Finally, I examined the relationship between notions and ideas. I argued that it is consistent with Berkeley's account of notions to contend that ideas can be the cognitive content of nondescriptive intentional acts and they can be the intentional objects of either descriptive or nondescriptive intentional acts. Given this, I argued that since Berkeley analyzed ordinary objects in terms of ideas, there is no distinction between an ordinary object and an intentional object.

Since my reconstruction of the doctrine of notions is now complete, I believe we can profitably raise the question of when Berkeley developed his doctrine of notions, that is, having shown that one can reasonably claim that there is a doctrine implicit in the 1734 editions of the *Principles* and the *Dialogues*, is the same doctrine implicit in the first editions of these works? To answer this question we must focus on passages that are common to both editions of the works as well as the *Philosophical Commentaries* and the First Draft of the Introduction to the *Principles*. These considerations will tend to show that Berkeley's doctrine of notions was implicit in the first editions of these works.

Given our considerations in Chapter 4, it should be clear that Berkeley had thought through many of the epistemic issues germane to the doctrine of notions prior to 1710. Already in the *Philosophical Commentaries* Berkeley had alluded to Descartes's account of one's knowledge of substance, commenting that 'Descartes owns we know not a substance immediately by itself but by this alone that it is the subject of several acts' (*PC*, 795). Further, the positive/relative notions distinction is already found in the first edition of the *Principles* (cf. *PHK*, 16, 17, 68; *DHP*, I, 197-9; *DHP*, II, 223). Nor should one find this surprising. Most of the discussions in which Berkeley was concerned with a positive/relative notions distinction focus on the doctrine of material substance. As we saw in Chapter 4, Locke drew an analogous distinction between positive and relative ideas and his discussions of one's ideas of substance are couched in terms of relative ideas. Berkeley used the term 'idea' more narrowly than Locke — limiting ideas to sensible qualities and the feelings of reflection — and couched his criticisms of Locke's position in terms of relative notions. For epistemic purposes, this difference is purely verbal. Berkeley's criticisms focused upon the contention that it is possible to have a relative idea (relative notion) of material substance, arguing (1) that one has no positive notion of a material substance; and (2) because one has no positive notion of the relation of support, it is impossible to have a relative notion of a material substance. Hence, by focusing on the epistemic issues implicit in

Locke's account of one's relative ideas of substance, Berkeley argued that it is impossible to have a relative idea (relative notion) of substance. Thus, it is reasonable to contend that the epistemology of positive and relative notions was already implicit in the first edition of the *Principles*.

Whether or not Berkeley had already developed his ontology of notions by 1710 is somewhat more difficult to determine. Remember, although in some of his published works Berkeley suggested that notions are to be construed as *acts* (cf. *DHP*, III, 232, *S*, 308), he never explicitly claimed that they are to be analyzed as intentional acts and he provided no analysis of the nature of an intentional act. None the less, there are three pieces of evidence that suggest the ontology of notions is also implicit in the first edition of the *Principles* and *Dialogues*. First, throughout his philosophical career Berkeley held (1) that the world is composed solely of minds (spirits), ideas and operations of minds; and (2) that it is impossible to have ideas of minds and their operations (cf. *PHK*, 27, first edition). This entails that one's knowledge of minds must rest upon something other than ideas, that is to say, notions. But if there are only minds and their operations in addition to ideas, it must be in terms of either minds or their operations that notions are to be analyzed. Given that Berkeley had already developed his theory of signs in the *New Theory of Vision*, it is reasonable to suggest that he recognized that the mind engages in at least nondescriptive intentional acts. Given also that both the epistemology of positive and relative notions and his defense of nominalism are found in the first edition of the *Principles*, it seems reasonable to conclude that he also recognized that one's knowledge of mind is based upon descriptive intentional acts, that is, that the ontology of notions is also implicit in the first edition of the *Principles*.

Secondly, as we saw in the last chapter, one of the pieces of textual evidence supporting an analysis of notions as intentional acts is based upon Berkeley's discussions of one's knowledge of God and oneself in the *Third Dialogue* (*DHP*, III, 231-2). Recall that Berkeley there claimed that one knows oneself by a 'reflex act' (*DHP*, III, 232). The passage in which he makes this claim is common to all editions of the *Dialogues* and, if my reconstruction of the ontology of notions is correct, this implies that his ontological doctrine was implicit in the first edition of the *Dialogues*. Furthermore, it is in the same passage that Berkeley first introduces the analogy between the doctrine of notions and his theory of meaning. As he wrote, 'I know what I mean by the terms *I* and *myself*; and I know this immediately or intuitively, though I do not perceive it as I perceive a triangle, a colour, or a sound', that is, 'I have properly no idea, either of God or any other spirit' (*DHP*, III, 231). Again, this passage is common to all editions of the *Dialogues*. This provides further evidence that if my reconstruction of Berkeley's doctrine of notions is plausible, it was found in at least embryonic form in the first edition of the *Dialogues*. Thus, one can trace the doctrine of notions back at least as far as 1713.

Finally, given the relationship between Berkeley's extensional theory of meaning and his doctrine of notions, there is one further bit of evidence that Berkeley had developed his ontological account of notions prior to 1710. Remember, we have seen that the same issues are germane to an extensional theory of meaning and a theory of intentional acts. Further, if a word means an object rather than a concept or some other intermediary entity, when one uses a word one means, that is, intends, a certain object or objects. Now our consideration of Berkeley's theory of meaning focused solely upon the meaning of terms when used for purposes of communication, but it easily can be extended to cover the use of terms for 'the raising of some passion, the exciting to, or deterring from an action, the putting the mind in some disposition' (Intro., 20), issues Berkeley considered in the later sections of the Introduction. Here it is an individual's use of a term that is the issue in question. It is still a state of affairs that the speaker means or intends by the use of a particular word or phrase. As Berkeley notes, 'For example, when a Schoolman tells me *Aristotle hath said it*, all I consider he means by it, is to dispose me to embrace his opinion with the deference and submission which custom has annexed to that name' (Intro., 20). That is, when a scholastic claims that Aristotle has said that x, he intends the state of affairs in which I believe that x. If one examines the published version of the Introduction to the *Principles*, one will notice that Berkeley never used the word 'intends'. However, in an earlier version of Section 20, Berkeley makes clear that his use of words for purposes of influencing one's passions and beliefs is to be construed in terms of the intentions of the speaker or writer. In one of the early versions of Section 20 of the Introduction, he wrote:

What is it that hinders why a man may not be stirr'd up to diligence and zeal in his duty by being told he shall have a good thing for his reward, tho' at the same time there be excited in his mind no other idea than barely those sounds or characters? (7) When he was a child he had frequently heard those words used to him to create in him an obedience to the commands of those that spoke them, and as he grew up he found by experience that upon the mentioning of those words by an honest man it has been his interest to have doubled his zeal and activity for the service of that person. Thus there having grown up in his mind a customary connexion betwixt the hearing that proposition and being dispos'd to obey with chearfulness the injunctions that introduce into his mind any idea marked by the words 'good thing' yet to excite in him a willingness to perform that which is requir'd of him. And this seems to me all that is design'd by the speaker except only w^n he *intends* those words shall signify the idea of some particular thing, e.g. in the case I mentioned 'tis evident the Apostle never *intended* the words 'good things' should mark out to our understandings the ideas of those particular things our fancies never attain'd to. And yet I cannot think he used them at random and without design. On the contrary it is my opinion that he used them to very good purpose namely to beget in us a chearfulness and zeal and perseverance in the well doing, without any thought of introducing in to our minds the abstract idea of good thing. If any one will joyn so little reflexion of his own to what has been said I doubt not, it will evidently appear to him that general names are often used in the propriety of language without the speaker designing them for marks of ideas in his own which he would have them raise in the understanding of the speaker. (*Works*, 2: 138, emphasis added)

In a later passage from the First Draft, Berkeley makes much the same point. In his words:

I ask any man whether when he tells another that such an action is honourable and vertuous he has in that instant the abstract ideas of honour and vertue in his view; and whether in reality his *intention* be to raise those abstract ideas together with their agreement to the particular idea of that action in the understanding of him he speaks to. Or rather whether this be not his full purpose namely that those words should excite in the mind of the hearer an esteem of that particular action and stirr him up to the performance of it? (*Works*, 2: 139, emphasis added)

In both of these passages Berkeley is concerned with situations in which one uses a word to influence emotions or beliefs, and in both passages Berkeley is concerned with what the speaker *intends*. Perhaps one cannot put a great deal of weight on the simple use of a word; in particular, perhaps the fact that Berkeley used the word 'intend' is insufficient to establish that there is a doctrine of intentionality implicit in Berkeley's philosophy prior to 1710. None the less, both the wording and topic under consideration are consistent with the account of intentionality I have attributed to Berkeley. In the first passage, Berkeley mentions that the Apostle uses the term 'good thing' to evoke approval of various particular objects. The object of the Apostle's intention is neither particular objects nor goodness in the abstract, rather, the term 'good thing' is used to evoke a sense of approval of various kinds of object. A very natural way to read this is that there is a descriptive intentional act in which the cognitive content is the proposition 'I wish everyone to approve of things of kind x' and the intentional object is a possible state of affairs. Much the same can be said with respect to the second passage. This reading gains further plausibility if one recognizes that discussions of intentional acts were fairly common among Berkeley's scholastic predecessors,[2] and Berkeley respected the scholastics (cf. *PC*, 449, 779). None the less, although this is a plausible reading of these passages, it does not positively show that there is an implicit doctrine of intentionality in the First Draft of the Introduction. As readers of the later Wittgenstein will acknowledge, it is plausible to make claims similar to those in the First Draft without presupposing a doctrine of intentionality, or even if one assumes a doctrine of intentionality, one need not analyze intentionality in terms of mental acts.[3]

So can one conclude that there is an ontological doctrine of notions implicit in the first edition of the *Principles*? We have seen that there is some reason to believe there is, simply on the grounds that the epistemology of notions was already in place and, given the limits of Berkeley's ontological inventory, the most plausible analysis of notions is in terms of operations of the mind, that is, intentional acts. None the less, the answer to our question must be a *guarded* affirmative, for, even if Berkeley's position implies that notions must be analyzed in terms of intentional acts, this does not entail that Berkeley was aware of this implication. Hence, perhaps the most we can conclude is that whether or not the ontology of notions was implicit in the first edition of the *Principles*, it was at least implicit in the first edition of the *Three Dialogues*.

Notes

1. Bertrand Russell, *The Problems of Philosophy* (Oxford University Press, New York, 1912), pp. 46-59.

2. Cf. Timothy J. Cronin, S.J., *Objective Being In Descartes and Suarez* (Gregorian University Press, Rome, 1966), p. 83; Reinhardt Grossmann, 'Digby and Berkeley on Notions', *Theoria*, 26 (1960), pp. 17-30; Harry M. Bracken, 'Substance in Berkeley', in Warren E. Steinkraus (ed) *New Studies in Berkeley's Philosophy* (Holt, Rinehart, Winston, New York, 1966), pp. 89-90.

3. Cf. John Searle, *Intentionality* (Cambridge University Press, Cambridge, 1983).

BIBLIOGRAPHY

Adams, Robert Merrihew 'Berkeley's "Notion" of Spiritual Substance', *Archiv für Geschichte der Philosophie*, 55 (1973), pp. 47-69

Allaire, Edwin B. 'Berkeley's Idealism', *Theoria*, 1963, reprinted in *Essays in Ontology*, Iowa Publications in Philosophy (Martinus Nijhoff, The Hague, 1963), vol. 1, pp. 92-105

Ammerman, Robert 'Our Knowledge of Substance according to Locke', *Theoria*, 31 (1965), pp. 1-8

Aquinas, Thomas *Introduction to St. Thomas Aquinas* (ed. by Anton C. Pegis) (Modern Library, New York, 1948)

—— *On Being and Essence* (trans. by A.A. Maurer) (Toronto, 1949)

—— *Truth* 3 vols., (trans. Robert W. Mulligan) (Henry Regnery Company, Chicago, 1952-4)

—— *On the Truth of the Catholic Faith: Summa Contra Gentiles*, 5 vols. (trans. Anton C. Pegis) (Doubleday Image Books, New York, 1955-7)

Aristotle *The Basic Works of Aristotle* (ed. by Richard McKeon) (The Random House Lifetime Library, Random House, New York, 1941)

Arnauld, Antoine *The Art of Thinking: Port-Royal Logic* (trans. James Dickoff and Patricia James) (Bobbs-Merrill, Library of Liberal Arts, Indianapolis, 1964)

Atherton, Margaret 'The Inessentiality of Lockean Essences', *Canadian Journal of Philosophy*, 14 (1984), pp. 277-93

Beal, M.W. 'Berkeley's Linguistic Criterion', *Personalist*, 52 (1971), pp. 499-514

Bennett, Jonathan *Locke, Berkeley, Hume: Central Themes* (Clarendon Press, Oxford, 1971)

Bergmann, Gustav. 'Acts', *Rivista di Filosofia*, 51 (1960), pp. 3-51. Reprinted in his *Logic and Reality* (University of Wisconsin Press, Madison, 1964), pp. 3-44

—— 'Intentionality', *Archivo di Filosofia*, 1955. Reprinted in his *Meaning and Existence* (University of Wisconsin Press, Madison, 1959), pp. 3-38

—— *Realism* (University of Wisconsin Press, Madison, 1967)

Berkeley, George, *Principles of Human Knowledge: Text and Critical Essays* (ed. by Colin Murray Turbayne) (Bobbs-Merrill, Indianapolis, Indiana, 1970)

—— *A Treatise Concerning the Principles of Human Knowledge* (ed. by Kenneth Winkler) (Hackett Publishing Company, Indianapolis, 1982)

—— *The Works of George Berkeley, Bishop of Cloyne*, 9 vols. (ed. by A.A. Luce and T.E. Jessop) (Thomas Nelson and Sons, Ltd., London, 1948-1957)

Blanshard, Brand 'Forward' to *New Studies in Berkeley's Philosophy* (ed. Warren E. Steinkraus) (Holt, Rinehart, Winston, New York, 1966)

Blundevile, Thomas *The Art of Logike* (London, 1599); reprint edn Theatrum Obis Terrarum, Ltd. and De Capo Press, Amsterdam and New York, 1969

Boyle, Robert *Selected Philosophical Papers of Robert Boyle* (ed. by M.A. Stewart), *Philosophical Classics* (University of Manchester Press, Manchester, 1979)

Bracken, Harry M. *Berkeley*, Philosophers in Perspective (St. Martin's Press, New York, 1974)

—— 'Berkeley and Mental Acts', *Theoria*, 26 (1960), pp. 140-6

—— 'Hume on the "Distinction of Reason"', *Hume Studies*, 10 (1984), pp. 89-108

—— 'Berkeley on Substance', in *New Studies in Berkeley's Philosophy* (ed. Warren E. Steinkraus) (Holt, Rinehart, Winston, New York, 1966), pp. 85-97

Brown, S.C. 'Berkeley on the Unity of the Self', in *Royal Institute of Philosophy, Lectures V* (Macmillan, London, 1972), pp. 69-72
Browne, Joseph W. *Berkeley's Intellectualism* (St. John's University Press, New York, 1975)
Butler, Joseph *The Analogy of Religion* (ed. by E.C. Mossner) (Frederick Unger Publishing Co., New York, 1961)
Copleston, Frederick *Modern Philosophy: The British Philosophers: Berkeley to Hume*, vol. 5, pt. 2 of his *A History of Philosophy*, 9 vols. (Doubleday Image Books, New York, 1964)
Cornman, James W. 'A Reconstruction of Berkeley: Minds and Physical Objects as Theoretical Entities', *Ratio*, 13 (1971), pp. 76-87
—— 'Theoretical Terms, Berkeleian Notions, and Minds', in *Berkeley, Principles of Human Knowledge: Text and Critical Essays* (ed. by Colin Murray Turbayne) (Bobbs-Merrill, Indianapolis, Indiana, 1970), pp. 161-81
Craig, E.J. 'Berkeley's Attack on Abstract Ideas', *Philosophical Review*, 77 (1968), pp. 425-33
Cronin, Timothy J., S.J. *Objective Being in Descartes and Suarez* (Gregorian University Press, Rome, 1966)
Cummins, Phillip D. 'Berkeley's Likeness Principle', in *Locke and Berkeley: A Collection of Critical Essays* (ed. by C.B. Martin and D.M. Armstrong) (Doubleday Anchor Books, Garden City, New York, 1968), pp. 353-63
—— 'Hylas' Parity Argument', in *Berkeley: Critical and Interpretive Essays* (ed. Colin Murray Turbayne) (University of Minnesota Press, Minneapolis, 1982), pp. 283-94
—— 'Reid on Abstract General Ideas', in *Thomas Reid: Critical Interpretations* (ed. by Stephen F. Barker and Tom L. Beauchamp) (Philosophical Monographs, Philadelphia, 1976), pp. 62-76
Davis, John W. 'Berkeley's Doctrine of the Notion', *Review of Metaphysics*, 12 (1959), pp. 378-89
Davis, Lawrence H. *Theory of Action*, Foundations of Philosophy (Prentice-Hall, Englewood Cliffs, New Jersey, 1979)
Descartes, Rene. *The Conversation with Burman* (trans. by John Cottingham) (Clarendon Press, Oxford, 1976)
—— *Philosophical Letters* (ed. and trans. by Anthony Kenny) (University of Minnesota Press, Minneapolis, 1970)
—— *The Philosophical Works of Descartes* 2 vols. (trans. and ed. by Elizabeth S. Haldane and G.R.T. Ross) (Cambridge University Press, London, 1911)
de Wulf, Maurice *An Introduction to Scholastic Philosophy, Medieval and Modern* (trans. by P. Coffey) (Dover Publications, New York, 1956)
Doney, Willis 'Berkeley's Argument Against Abstract Ideas', in *Midwest Studies in Philosophy VIII, 1983: Contemporary Perspectives on the History of Philosophy*, pp. 295-308 (ed. by Peter A. French, Theodore E. Uehling, Jr, and Howard K. Wettstein) (University of Minnesota Press, Minneapolis, 1983)
—— 'Is Berkeley's a Cartesian Mind?' in *Berkeley: Critical and Interpretive Essays* (ed. by Colin Murray Turbayne) (University of Minnesota Press, Minneapolis, 1982), pp. 273-82
Flage, Daniel E. 'Berkeley's Notions', *Philosophy and Phenomenological Research*, 45 (1985), pp. 407-25
—— 'Hume's Relative Ideas', *Hume Studies*, 7 (1981), pp. 55-73
—— 'Locke's Relative Ideas', *Theoria*, 47 (1981), pp. 142-59
—— 'Relative Ideas Revisited: A Reply to Thomas', *Hume Studies*, 8 (1982), pp. 158-71
Furlong, E.J. 'Berkeley on Relations, Spirits, and Notions', *Hermathena*, 106 (1968), pp. 60-6
Gotterbarn, Don 'Berkeley's Mistaken Notion about Relations'. A paper presented

at the Berkeley Tercentenary Conference, Newport, Rhode Island, 10 March 1985

Grossmann, Reinhardt 'Digby and Berkeley on Notions', *Theoria*, 26 (1960), pp. 17-30

Hume, David *Enquiries concerning the Human Understanding and concerning the Principles of Morals* (ed. by L.A. Selby-Bigge; 3rd edn rev. by P.H. Nidditch) (Clarendon Press, Oxford, 1975)

— *A Treatise of Human Nature* (ed. by L.A. Selby-Bigge; 2nd edn rev. by P.H. Nidditch) (Clarendon Press, Oxford, 1978)

Jessop, T.E. 'Editor's Introduction' to the *Principles*, *Works*, 2:3-17

Johnston, G.A. *The Development of Berkeley's Philosophy* (Macmillan and Co., Limited, London, 1923)

Kretzmann, Norman 'The Main Thesis of Locke's Semantic Theory', *Philosophical Review*, 77 (1968), pp. 175-96

Kripke, Saul *Naming and Necessity* (Harvard University Press, Cambridge, 1980)

Leibniz, Gottfried Wilhelm *Philosophical Papers and Letters*, 2nd edn (ed. by Leroy E. Loemker) (D. Reidel Publishing Company, Dordrecht, Holland, 1976)

Leith John H. (ed.) *Creeds of the Churches: A Reader in Christian Doctrine from the Bible to the Present* (Doubleday Anchor Books, Garden City, New York, 1963)

Lennon, Thomas M. 'Philosophical Commentary', in the Lennon and Olscamp translation of Malebranche, *The Search After Truth and Elucidations of the Search After Truth*, pp. 759-848

Lewis, David K. *Convention: A Philosophical Study* (Harvard University Press, Cambridge, 1969)

Locke, John *An Essay concerning Human Understanding* (ed. by P.H. Nidditch) (Clarendon Press, Oxford, 1975)

— *The Works of John Locke*, 10 vols (London, 1823; reprint edn Scientia Verlag Aalen, Darmstadt, West Germany, 1963)

Luce, A.A. *Berkeley and Malebranche: A Study of the Origins of Berkeley's Thought* (Clarendon Press, Oxford, 1967)

— *Berkeley's Immaterialism* (Thomas Nelson and Sons Ltd., London, 1950)

— 'Editor's Notes on the Entries to the *Philosophical Commentaries*', in *Works*, 1: 107-139

Mackie, J.L. *Problems from Locke* (Clarendon Press, Oxford, 1976)

Malebranche, Nicholas *The Search After Truth and Elucidations of the Search After Truth* (trans. by Thomas M. Lennon and Paul J. Olscamp) (The Ohio State University Press, Columbus, 1980)

Najm, Sami M. 'Knowledge of the Self in Berkeley's Philosophy', *International Philosophical Quarterly*, 6 (1966), pp. 248-69

Park, Desiree *Complementary Notions: A Critical Study of Berkeley's Theory of Concepts* (Martinus Nijhoff, The Hague, 1972)

— '*Notions*: The Counter-Poise of Berkeleyan *Ideas*', *Giornale di Metafisica* (New Series), 3 (1981), pp. 243-66

Peifer, John Frederick *The Concept in Thomism* (Bookman Associates Inc., 1952)

Pitcher, George *Berkeley*, Arguments of the Philosophers (Routledge & Kegan Paul, London, 1977)

Prior, A.N. 'Logic, Modal', in *The Encyclopedia of Philosophy* 8 vols. (ed. by Paul Edwards) (Macmillan, New York, 1967) vol. 5, pp. 5-12

Quine, W.V. 'Two Dogmas of Empiricism', in his *From a Logical Point of View*, 2nd edn (Harper Torchbooks, New York, 1961), pp. 20-46

— *Word and Object* (M.I.T. Press, Cambridge, 1960)

Ramsey, Ian, T. 'Berkeley and the Possibility of an Empirical Metaphysics', in *New Studies in Berkeley's Philosophy* (ed. Warren E. Steinkraus) (Holt, Rinehart,

Winston, 1966) pp. 13-30
Raynor, David '"*Minima Sensibilia*" in Berkeley and Hume', *Dialogue*, 19 (1980) pp. 196-200
Reid, Thomas *Essays on the Active Powers of the Human Mind* (ed. by Baruch Brody) (M.I.T. Press, Cambridge, 1969)
—— *Essays on the Intellectual Powers of Man* (ed. by Baruch Brody) (M.I.T. Press, Cambridge, 1969)
Rome, Sidney C. 'Berkeley's Conceptualism', *Philosophical Review*, 55 (1946), pp 680-6
Russell, Bertrand 'The Philosophy of Logical Atomism', in his *Logic and Knowledge*, (ed. by Robert Charles Marsh) (Capricorn Books, New York, 1971), pp. 321-44
—— *The Problems of Philosophy* (Oxford University Press, New York, 1912)
Searle, John R. *Intentionality* (Cambridge University Press, Cambridge, 1983)
Sergeant, John (J.S.) *Method to Science* (W. Redamayne, London, 1696)
—— (J.S.) *Solid Philosophy Asserted, Against the Fancies of the Ideists: Or, The Method to Science Farther Illustrated* (Printed for Roger Clevil, London, 1697)
Stack, George J. *Berkeley's Analysis of Perception*, 2nd printing (Mouton, The Hague, 1972)
Steinkraus, Warren E. (ed.) *New Studies in Berkeley's Philosophy* (Holt, Rinehart, Winston, New York, 1966)
Taylor, C.C.W. 'Berkeley's Theory of Abstract Ideas', *Philosophical Quarterly*, 28 (1978), pp. 97-115
Tipton, I.C. *Berkeley: The Philosophy of Immaterialism* (Methuen & Co. Ltd, London, 1974)
Turbayne, Colin (ed.) *Berkeley: Critical and Interpretive Essays* (University of Minnesota Press, Minneapolis, 1982)
Turbayne, Colin Murray 'Lending a Hand to Philonous: The Berkeley, Plato, Aristotle Connection', in *Berkeley: Critical and Interpretive Essays* (ed. Colin Murray Turbayne) (University of Minnesota Press, Minneapolis, 1982), pp. 295-310
—— *The Myth of Metaphor*, rev. edn (Yale University Press, New Haven 1970)
Urmson, J.O. *Berkeley*, Past Masters (Clarendon Press, Oxford 1982)
Warnock, G.J. *Berkeley*, Pelican Philosophy Series (Pelican Books, Melbourne 1953)
Watts, Isaac *Logick, or the Right Use of Reason, in the Inquiry After Truth*, 3rd American edn (Ranlett and Norris, Boston, 1806)
Weinberg, Julius R. 'The Nominalism of Berkeley and Hume', in his *Abstraction, Relation, and Induction: Three Essays in the History of Thought* (The University of Wisconsin Press, Madison, 1965), pp. 3-32
Wild, John *George Berkeley: A Study of His Life and Philosophy* (Russell and Russell, Inc., New York 1962)
Winkler, Kenneth W. 'Berkeley on Abstract Ideas', *Archiv für Geschichte der Philosophie*, 63 (1983), pp. 63-80
—— 'Editor's Introduction', to the Hackett edition of Berkeley, *A Treatise Concerning the Principles of Human Knowledge*
Woozley, A.D. 'Berkeley's Doctrine of Notions and Theory of Meaning', *Journal of the History of Philosophy*, 14 (1976), pp. 427-34
Yolton, John W. *Perceptual Acquaintance From Descartes to Reid* (University of Minnesota Press, Minneapolis 1984)

INDEX

abstraction
  levels of 16-17
  linguistic meaning 36-41
  see also Arnauld; Berkeley;
    Cartesians; Descartes; Locke;
    Sergeant
Aquinas, Thomas 19, 33
archetypes 90-1n13, 209n19
Aristotle 18, 23, 28, 217
Arnauld, Antoine
  abstraction 21-2, 31
  conceivability criterion 34
  definition 139-40
  determinations 141-2

Bennett, Jonathan 15
Berkeley, George
  abstraction
    argument in the *Alciphron* 44-6
    arguments in the *Principles* 30-44
    mental images 46-7, 53n85
    scope of critique 23-30
  likeness principle 43, 143-5, 150
  linguistic meaning 36-41, 217-19
  and intentionality 180-6, 217-19
    categorematic terms 98-111
    metaphorical meaning 123-30, 147-50
    syncategorematic terms 111-15
  parsimony, principle of 36-41, 97
  possibility and impossibility, criteria of 74-89
  real objects 69-74, 206-8
  see also causation; *esse* is *percipi*;
    minimum sensibles; notions;
    perception; understanding
Boyle, Robert 192
Bracken, Harry M.
  archetypes 209n19
  innate ideas 177-8, 188
  minimum sensibles 91n18
  notions as concepts 177-8, 188
Butler, Joseph 192

Cartesians
  abstraction 19-22

innate ideas 178-80
  see also Arnauld; Descartes;
    Malebranche
causation 152-3, 154-5, 211n43

Descartes, Rene
  abstraction 20-1, 24
  conceivability criterion 34
  innate ideas 209n17
  mind 151
  substance 215
Doney, Willis 7, 82-3

esse is *percipi* 75, 83-6

God 75-7, 160-2 *passim*, 182, 186, 206-7, 212
Gotterbarn, Don 160-1, 162

Hume, David
  identity 204
  impressions/ideas distinction 73-4
  meaning 210n22
  possibility 59, 90n6
  relative ideas 134

identity 164-5
  generic and specific 129-30
  numerical and specific 203-6
innate ideas 162-3, 177-80, 188
intentionality 182-6
  descriptive and nondescriptive acts 183, 184-5
  meaning and 180-6
  ordinary objects and 200-8
introspection 30-2, 163-4

Kripke, Saul 131n7

laws of nature 70-3, 79, 161, 184, 202
Locke, John
  essences 16-18, 95, 110, 199-200, 202-3
  ideas 15
    abstract 5, 13, 14-18, 26, 29, 37, 41-4, 109-10
    relative 45-6, 134, 145-50, 215-16

inconceivability 33-4
substance 28-9
syncategorematic terms 8, 111-15

Mackie, J.L. 15
Malebranche, Nicholas 20, 21, 24, 210n27
mind 151-4, 166-7
    see also self; substance
minimum sensibles 50n50, 87-8, 91n18
Molyneux Problem 103-4

notions
    actions of the mind 155-7
    ad hoc 2, 169n8
    concepts 174-80
    describing model of relative notions 9, 137-42
    development of the doctrine 2, 215-20
    ideas and notions 192-208
    intentional acts 9-10, 180-92
    intuitive knowledge 152-4
    ordinary objects and notions 192-208
    positive notions 9, 134-7, 152-3, 154-6
    relations among ideas 159-60
    substance
        identical with substance 181
        immaterial 150-4
        material 142-50

objects
    ordinary 200-8
    real 69-74
Ockham's Razor 36

Park, Desiree 10-11n2, 171n30, 209n20
perception 10, 85, 150, 152-3, 154-5, 211n39
    passivity thesis 69, 193-9, 211n41
Pitcher, George 53n85, 169-70n10

possibility, criteria of 55-68
primary and secondary qualities 29, 86-8, 144-5
psychological uniformity 162-7

Quine, W.V. 131n10

Reid, Thomas
    abstraction 47n3
    conceivability criterion of possibility 34, 51n69
    conception 8, 134-6
    properties 135, 152
    relations 125-6, 147-50, 157-67
    representationalism 143-4
Russell, Bertrand 1, 9, 133, 141, 154, 170n14, 213

sameness *see* identity
scholastics 18-19, 23, 26, 217, 219
self
    immediate knowledge of 152-4
Sergeant, John
    abstraction 19, 23
    notions 9, 174-7, 178-80, 192
signification 38-9, 103-6, 119-20
spirit *see* mind
substance
    notions of 142-54
    substratum theory 27-8
    and abstraction 34-6

Tipton, I.C. 171n30, 209n20

understanding 197-200
Urmson, J.O. 15

Watts, Isaac 142
Weinberg, Julius R. 51n63
Winkler, Kenneth 2, 51n63
Wittgenstein, Ludwig 219
Woozley, A.D. 2

Yolton, John W. 52n80, 210n27